OXFORDSHIRE

John Steane was educated at Dulwich College and
Magdalen College, Oxford, where he read Modern History. He is a consultant archaeologist and
part-time tutor at Kellogg College, Oxford University's Department of Continuing Education. He
is a Fellow of the Society of Antiquaries and a
Member of the Institute of Field Archaeologists.
Previously, he was Headmaster of Kettering
Grammar School (1964–76), and County Archaeologist for Oxfordshire (1976–1990).

He has undertaken research into many aspects
of the historic landscape, including fishponds,
palaces and parks. He is the author of *The
Northamptonshire Landscape* (1974), *Peopling
Past Landscapes* (with B. F. Dix, 1978), *The
Archaeology of Medieval England and Wales*
(1984), and *The Archaeology of the Medieval
English Monarchy* (1993). He is currently work-
ing on aspects of the history of Magdalen College,
Oxford.

Pimlico County History Guides
(General editor: Christopher Hibbert)

Already published:

Bedfordshire by Simon Houfe
Cambridgeshire by Ross Clark
Dorset by Richard Ollard
Lincolnshire by Henry Thorold
Norfolk by Tom Pocock
Somerset (with Bath and Bristol) by Shirley Toulson
Suffolk by Miles Jebb
Sussex by Desmond Seward

Forthcoming:

Cumbria by Alan Hankinson

OXFORDSHIRE

JOHN STEANE
with a Foreword by Christopher Hibbert

A PIMLICO COUNTY HISTORY GUIDE

PIMLICO

An imprint of Random House
20 Vauxhall Bridge Road, London SW1V 2SA

Random House Australia (Pty) Ltd
20 Alfred Street, Milsons Point, Sydney
New South Wales 2061, Australia

Random House New Zealand Ltd
18 Poland Road, Glenfield
Auckland 10, New Zealand

Random House South Africa (Pty) Ltd
PO Box 337, Bergvlei, South Africa

Random House UK Ltd Reg. No. 954009

First published by Pimlico 1996

1 3 5 7 9 10 8 6 4 2

© John Steane 1996

Papers used by Random House UK Limited are natural,
recyclable products made from wood grown in
sustainable forests. The manufacturing processes conform
to the environmental regulations of the country of origin

Typeset by Deltatype Ltd, Birkenhead, Merseyside
Printed and bound in Great Britain by
Mackays of Chatham plc, Chatham, Kent

ISBN 0-7126-6199-9

Contents

To Elaine

Foreword

In *The Scholar-Gipsy* and *Thyrsis*, Matthew Arnold's elegiac verses on the beauties of the Oxfordshire countryside are pervaded by a sense of impending loss. The 'boys who in lone wheatfields scare the rooks' will age and die, while the 'purple fritillaries, the grassy harvest of the river-fields' will fade away like the cuckoo's parting cry. This same sense of loss is experienced by George Bowling, the hero of George Orwell's novel, *Coming up for Air*, when he returns to his childhood home in an Oxfordshire village and discovers that it has vanished:

> I don't mean that it had been demolished. It had merely been swallowed ... All I could see was an enormous river of brand-new houses which flowed along the valley in both directions ... Queer! You can't imagine how queer! All the way down the hill I was seeing ghosts, chiefly the ghosts of hedges and trees and cows. It was as if I was looking at two worlds at once.

This sense of a vanished world is vividly conveyed also in *Lark Rise to Candleford*, an account of life in the final years of the last century in a hamlet on the borders of Oxfordshire and Northamptonshire by Flora Thompson, the daughter of a builder's labourer. Pasted on the walls of her little cottage were pictures cut from newspapers which were changed each time the walls were whitewashed; and she remembered one picture in particular, a print with two rows of portraits of 'Our Political Leaders', men – for all she knew of the outside world – who might have inhabited a different planet. She had no idea even of what Oxford looked like, though it was no more than nineteen miles away, as she knew from having seen the figure on the milestone beside the turnpike. She and her sisters often wondered about Oxford and asked questions about it.

> One answer was that it was a 'gert big town' where a man might earn as much as five and twenty shillings a week; but as he would have to pay pretty near half of it in house rent and have nowhere to keep a pig or to grow many vegetables, he'd be a fool to go there ... To imagine a place without pigsties and vegetable gardens was difficult. With no bacon or cabbage what could people have to eat?

John Steane shares Arnold's and George Bowling's regret for this lost Oxfordshire world, lamenting the 'devastating effects' of modern farming methods on the countryside, the 'grubbing up of hundreds of miles of hedges with a consequent loss of wild life habitats', the elimination of wild flowers, insects, butterflies, the creation of 'a silent spring'. And it is the great strength of his absorbing, discursive and original book that by identifying the fragments from the past remaining in the county today, and by understanding them intelligently, he will help, as he hopes to do, to 'persuade society, public opinion and the planners to preserve them in the future'.

As befits a writer who was for fourteen years Oxfordshire's County Archaeologist, he is particularly interested in the evolution of the landscape from prehistoric times and its development by primitive man. He brings those early ages to life as he considers the mysteries presented by Oxfordshire's prehistoric ritual sites and imagines the Uffington White Horse standing in a landscape

> peppered with barrows, graves, cremations. This bleak high place must have reverberated with the cries of mourners, the crackling of sacrificial fires and the thud of earth piled over corpses. The horse figure, freshly cleaned at intervals, must in its heyday have been only one shining white feature among a group of chalk mounds, visible from afar.

He imagines also funerary processions wending their way across the tremendously broad Ridgeway beside the shining white chalk mounds of newly made barrows; and Roman engineers and surveyors laying out the courses of their roads with the help of wooden staffs with cross-bars from which hung bronze plummets suspended on plumb-lines; and along these roads, when constructed, legions marching, messengers galloping and bearers of the imperial post travelling fifty miles a day.

Beside these prehistoric tracks and Roman roads Steane traces the gradual development of settlements and field patterns, explaining how towns developed in the way they did and how they came to be given their names; how, for instance, the University of Oxford was able to benefit from the city's decline and why, for example, Wallingford, having been a prosperous early medieval market town, decayed and shrank while Abingdon prospered.

The prosperity that evaded Wallingford came to those large villages further north in the county whose comparative wealth was derived from sheep farming, as their names testify. Shipton-under-Wychwood and Shipton on Cherwell, as John Steane says, are obvious reminders of this. Shiplake was the stream where sheep were washed; Shifford was a sheep ford. Both Bicester and Burford had Sheep Streets. Ship Street in Oxford seems to have taken its name from the nearby sheep market. The Market Place in Banbury was formerly one of the county's leading wool markets; and by the end of the eighteenth century there were five hundred hand-looms in the town, operated by some thousand workers, many of them turning out the fabric with a cut pile known as plush which was later used to provide furnishings for the Palace of Westminster and to decorate the walls of Windsor Castle, as well as numerous restaurants and exotic houses of ill fame. Even more than in Banbury the cloth industry dominated life in Witney where, so an early seventeenth-century historian estimated, almost three thousand people, 'from children of eight years old to decrepit old age', were employed in the manufacture of blankets and where the houses of the well-to-do clothiers, several of which still contain seventeenth-century work, flanked the large triangular space known as Church Green. The handsome central thirteenth-century tower and spire of the nearby church of St Mary is, after that of Christ Church in Oxford, the most impressive tower of its date in the county and well reflects the prosperity enjoyed by Witney's medieval wool-men with their rattling looms and their fulling mills beside the clear, soft waters of the Windrush.

The craft of making cloth is but one of Oxfordshire's industries described in the book. The author explains the manner in which bark was stripped from trees for the tanneries of the county, the process of glovemaking in Woodstock and of the copying of manuscripts in Oxford, the mysteries of brewing at a time when every Oxfordshire town had at least one brewery. By 1860 there were two in Eynsham, Wallingford, Watlington and Henley, three in Witney, four in Deddington, five in Abingdon, seven in Bicester, ten in Banbury and fourteen in Oxford where, in addition, most colleges brewed their own beer. The Queen's College still produced its celebrated 'Chancellor Beer' in the 1870s and continued brewing until the outbreak of the Second World War. Its timber-framed brewhouse, rebuilt in the sixteenth century, still stands at the west end of the Fellows' Garden.

Both in the course of his work and by inclination, John Steane has travelled all over Oxfordshire, examining sites and buildings and asking himself and others questions in the manner advocated by that great historian of the landscape, W. G. Hoskins, whose teaching and example have inspired generations of younger historians, geographers and archaeol-ogists in their interpretation of the palimpsest of the English countryside. Steane shares Hoskins's curiosity and sharp eye. In 1981, in company with a friend, he took a punt to examine the underside of Folly Bridge which takes the Abingdon Road across the Thames into St Aldate's in Oxford. The original bridge here, so *The Encyclopaedia of Oxford* has it, 'was pronounced irreparable in 1815 and an Act was obtained for its replacement. The new bridge was completed in 1827'. Steane, however, noticed that in the middle of the underside was a series of semi-circular arches which appeared Roman-esque in character. Subsequent work established that these were indeed parts of the Norman bridge.

Folly Bridge is but one of several bridges which he

describes, Oxfordshire, so he says, being particularly fortunate in its high survival rate of medieval bridges, as indeed it is in its surviving eighteenth-century bridges such as the one across the Thames at Henley where two twelfth-century arches have been discovered, one in a cellar of the Angel public house on the Oxfordshire side of the river, the other preserved beneath Terry Farrell's Regatta Headquarters on the Berkshire side.

Interested as he is in the structure of such buildings, in, for instance, that 'veritable museum of brickwork' which has gone into the fifteen phases of construction at Stonor Park, in the disposition of the service rooms in the basement at Chastleton, and in the intriguing amalgam of architectural styles at Cogges Manor Farm, Steane is equally interested in the people who lived and worked in such houses, in William Morris's household at Kelmscott Manor and in the host of servants at Blenheim Palace – eighteen of them living in the Palace in 1891, including twelve maids, a butler, a footman, a housekeeper and a French chef.

He introduces us to the various people he has come across during the course of his career: old Mr Lee of Taynton who showed him over the now abandoned quarries which supplied the stone for Christ Church; John Buchan's widow, Lady Tweedsmuir, who, at Elsfield Manor, showed him the neat manuscript of her husband's book on Oliver Cromwell; Canon Jenkins, Regius Professor of Ecclesiastical History, who, his bookshelves being crammed, stuffed the overflow of volumes between the balusters of his staircase; and dear, fat, untidy Billy Pantin, Fellow of Oriel and Keeper of the University Archives, whose rooms were equally littered with books – one of which was once found to contain a sandwich used as a bookmark – and whose encyclopaedic knowledge of the medieval world encompassed the buildings of his beloved Oxford which John Steane here describes so well.

CHRISTOPHER HIBBERT

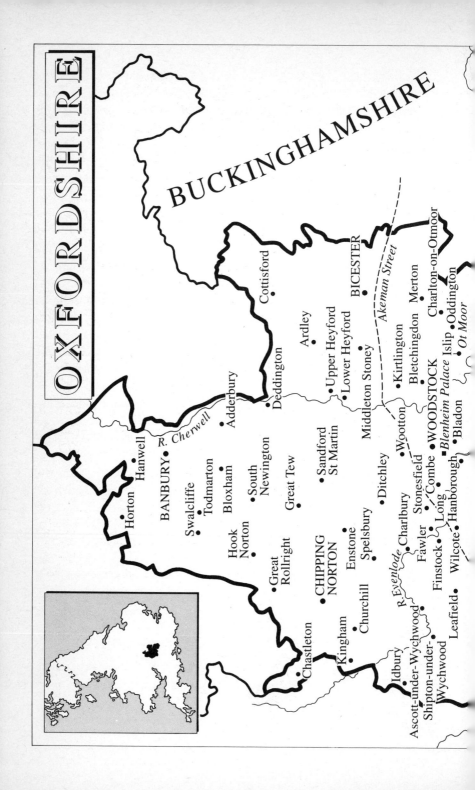

Introduction and Acknowledgements

Picture an ill-lit seminar room in the echoing halls of the Examination Schools at Oxford in January 1952. About a dozen undergraduates are seated round a teacher, their notebooks at the ready. A quiet figure sits there, hunched in an overcoat, shrouded in his doctoral gown. His head is massive, bespectacled, his face rubicund and weatherbeaten. He looks and sounds like a West Country farmer. He begins to speak in a soft Devon burr, slowly, courteously, insistently. The message is a revolutionary one: 'Put on your boots, go into the fields, leave the libraries.' The seminar is 'The Making of the English Landscape', led by William G. Hoskins. Attending this seminar (there were only six meetings in the short Oxford eight-week term) had an indelible effect on some of my contemporaries. It changed the course of my life. Up till that point of time I had studied the past through documents; Hoskins now directed my mind out of doors to the physical remains of successive generations, the landscape and structures. This book, forty years later, is the fruit of Hoskins' approach. Its themes would never have been pursued without Hoskins' inspiration.

Frank Emery's book *The Oxfordshire Landscape* (London, 1974) broke fresh ground in its comprehensive application of Hoskins' principle of using the landscape itself to construct a convincing story of how the county evolved over ten millennia. His approach was broadly chronological. In writing my book, twenty-two years later, I have abandoned the story approach and decided to look at the historical landscape thematically. I have broken up the county into what seem to me to be the main topographical components: rocks and soils, settlement, fields, woodland, roads and rivers, towns, industries and religion. My justification in

I

doing this is that if we can identify the fragments from the past remaining in the county today, and understand them intelligently, perhaps we may be able to persuade society, public opinion and the planners to preserve them for the future. The problem is that once the historical environment is comprehended it is generally recognized to be in dire peril from four directions. Agricultural interests operating on an industrial scale are inimical to fragile earthworks and the remains of former field systems. Secondly, urban developers, whether involved in building supermarkets, service stations, housing estates or factories, are keen to scoop maximum profit with minimum input into mitigating the disastrous effects of their proposals on the historic/archaeological environment. Next, and most devastating from Oxfordshire's point of view, are the mineral extractors who remove whole slices of the richly historic landscape. Finally, the road builders constitute a double threat: they destroy great swathes of the county and ensure that its remote fastnesses are easily penetrable by the car-abusing public.

To temper this pessimism, it has to be admitted that the twenty-two years from 1974 to 1996 have seen some moves that are beneficial to the historic environment. Central government has carried out a nationwide re-survey of the built heritage, thus multiplying the number of Listed Buildings of Architectural and Historical Interest by a factor of five in some parts. Oxfordshire now has between 12 and 15,000 buildings protected under the terms of the Town and Country Planning Acts. There has also been a rapid and wholesome spread of Conservation Areas. More painfully slow has been the progress of English Heritage's Monument Protection Programme aimed at identifying sites and ruins of national significance during the updating of the lists of Scheduled Ancient Monuments. All this legislation puts a great strain on District Councils and County Councils to enforce effectively and fairly. It isn't enough. The heritage cannot be saved by laws and local government officers alone.

The archaeological profession has come of age during this period. In this county, Trevor Rowley of the Oxford

University Department for Continuing Education and Jean Cook (formerly the first Director of the Oxfordshire County Museum Service) played visionary and key roles in the late 1960s and early 1970s. Surveys were initiated and grants procured. Bodies to meet the threats of central town redevelopment in Oxford and Abingdon were created. The M40 committee and the Upper Thames Archaeological Committee produced a flexible and effective response to road engineering and gravel extraction. These were united in the formation of the Oxfordshire (later Oxford) Archaeological Committee in 1974. Under three chairmen over twenty years – Trevor Rowley, Professor Frere and Professor Salway – the Unit has borne the burden of the digging and recording of Oxfordshire's archaeology. Many of its achievements are recorded in this book. Professionally speaking, the OAU is second to none in reputation throughout England.

But this would be to ignore the voluntary and amateur input who are among the most effective, altruistic and dedicated defenders of the future of Oxfordshire's past. In my view it is arguably the groups of men and women up and down the county who meet during the evenings or weekends after work, under the auspices of the Oxford University Department for Continuing Education and the Workers' Educational Association who make a major and unpaid contribution. They congregate in societies, in tutor groups and out in the field. They observe, draw and photograph, listen to lectures, publish news sheets and journals, research their families or their village's history. They frequent the County Record Office, the Centre for Oxfordshire Studies, the County Sites and Monuments Record. This book owes much to the groups of students from Newbury, Wantage, Faringdon, Witney, Woodstock, Oxford, Bicester, Henley-on-Thames, Wallingford and Hook Norton whom I have associated with, taught and learned alongside, over the period 1976–96. We all acknowledge the driving power of Trevor Rowley behind this remarkable programme, which has spread the teaching of archaeology and local history over three counties. It corrects the fleeting and fatuously nostalgic view of the past generated by the mass media.

The book is also enriched by my experience of working with colleagues at the Oxfordshire County Museum Service, including Richard Foster, James Bateman, Christine Bloxham, Martyn Brown, John Rhodes, James Bond, Sarah Gosling, Nancy Hood, David Smith, Ival Hornbrook, Elizabeth Leggatt, Ahmed Shishtawi and David Eddershaw. I also acknowledge the amiability and co-operation of the Conservation Officers of the five district councils, the late Daphne Ailwyn, Robert Parkinson, Grant Audley Miller, Tony Ives, Malcolm Airs, Nicholas Doggett, Sally Stradling, John Ashdown and Edith Gollnast. I have been helped in my understanding of quaternary problems by Derek Roe, Kate Scott, Philip Powell and my brother Christopher Steane. John Blair and Professor Martin Biddle have helped me with the Anglo-Saxons. Robert Peberdy, Graham Soffe and Max Satchell have contributed fresh ideas to the medieval period, James Ayres to historic houses, and Mavis Batey and Michael Pirie to historic gardens. I owe much over the last six years to the friendship and stimulus of members of the lunch club which meets on Wednesdays in the Old Schoolhouse and other venues: John Ashdown, Malcolm Graham, Malcolm Airs, Roger Ainslie, Brian Durham, Edith Gollnast, Julian Munby, Martin Henig and others. The book was much improved by the kind but often critical comments of Philip Powell (chapter I), George Lambrick (chapters II & III), Arthur Macgregor (chapters VIII & IX), Julian Munby (chapter IX) and Martin Henig (chapter X). I owe a great deal to the patience and efficiency of the staffs of the County Record Office and the Ashmolean, the History Faculty and Bodleian libraries at the University of Oxford; also to the enthusiasm of Janie Cottis, archivist of Magdalen College. Help also came from David Wilson of the Cambridge University Committee for Aerial Photography and from Bernard Nurse of the Society of Antiquaries, London. Although the names of the principal excavators in Oxfordshire will frequently appear in this book, I owe a special debt to Professors Sheppard Frere and Peter Salway, Chairmen of the Archaeological Unit, to Tom Hassall and David Miles, Directors during the period in which the book was in gestation, to County Councillor Geoffrey Fowler, a member of the Council, to David Jennings and to Louise Armstrong, its secretary. Anyone trying to say something new about Oxfordshire's history will acknowledge the painstaking erudition of Alan Crossley, Christopher Day and Simon Townley on the staff of the *Victoria County History*. I can only hope that the county will realize the immense contribution made by this gathering of scholars and continue to support their fruitful endeavours. It will be apparent that the officers of English Heritage and the National Trust have done doughty work for the conservation of the county's heritage. In particular, I acknowledge the assistance of Tony Fleming, David Sherlock, Stephen Trowe and Roger Thomas. Finally, my thanks go to Georgina Stonor for suggesting this book might be written, to Melanie Fyson for deciphering numerous handwritten drafts and turning them into legible typescript, and to Will Sulkin and Euan Cameron for seeing the book through the press promptly, courteously and efficiently.

I
Geology

One of the most electrifying exhibits to appear in recent years in the hall of the University Museum, Park Road, Oxford was the fossil skeleton of a 150 million-year-old pliosaur. This sixteen-foot (five metres) long marine reptile looked like a very large crocodile and swam as a turtle does, propelled by paddles in the warm seas which teemed with life. Its body, together with ammonites, belemnites, bivalves and worms, sank into the ooze, which ultimately became the grey Oxford clay, and was left undisturbed until attacked by the mechanical shovels of the gravel extractors in 1994. A sixteen-day excavation recovered the three-foot long, complete and well preserved skull, containing two-inch long pointed and enamelled teeth. The vertebrae, looking like a pile of toppled-over cotton reels, were mostly intact with one complete paddle and the remains of two more. The fossils were wrapped in bandages dipped in plaster of Paris, and in this secure jacket were conveyed to the Museum laboratory. Here, the hard limestone coating is gradually being dissolved away in acid. By Christmas 1995 the whole of the pliosaur should be on show.

The University Museum is perhaps the most startlingly original building of nineteenth-century Oxford. From the outside, it resembles a Venetian palace with a steep Northern European or Flemish roof. Inside, it is a gothic cathedral in iron and glass housing the University's collections of mineralogy, geology, zoology, comparative anatomy and entomology. At its inception in the 1860s, it was designed as a power house of science in Oxford. Here were deposited the scientific books; around the great courts were lecture rooms, studies and laboratories. The professors have now gone elsewhere into the science area which surrounds this historic edifice, but their titles are still inscribed over the doors. The structure itself is a museum of geology: the polished columns of the galleries are drawn from quarries throughout the British Isles. The sculptured decoration was derived directly from specimens sent up daily from the Botanic Gardens to be carried out by the ebullient and rebellious O'Shea brothers.

As the cases proclaim, three Oxford men made important contribution to the geology of the Oxford Region: William Smith, William Buckland and John Phillips. They all played a key part in the development of British geology in general and Oxford geology in particular. William Smith (1769–1839) was born in the north Oxfordshire village of Churchill, the son of a village blacksmith. His work as a canal surveyor led to several fundamental discoveries. The law of superposition of strata, whereby in three layers of rock the middle one is younger than the top one but older than the bottom, was significant enough. He also realized that beds of sedimentary rock could be dated by the fossils they contain. Beds of the same age need not be lithologically similar. As he recorded in his memoirs, he saw that 'each stratum (around Bath) had been in succession the bed of the sea' and that several of these strata contained an abundance of the remains of marine animals. He concluded that these animals had lived and died during the period of time which elapsed between the formation of the stratum below and the stratum above. He realized, moreover, that the fossil remains characterizing each period could be recognized as being peculiar to that era and that 'different strata could be identified in distant localities and otherwise doubtful cases by peculiar imbedded organic remains'.

From formulating these principles of stratigraphy, William Smith proceeded to demonstrate them by publishing a series of geological maps, the first to show by different colours the different beds he recognized as outcropping in Southern England. He was employed during the last years of his life in touring the principal quarries of England and Scotland to choose suitable building stone for the Houses of Parliament, renewed after their combustion in 1834. He was called the 'Father of British Geology' in his own lifetime.

The second of these Oxford-based colossi of geology was William Buckland (1784–1856), a man of extraordinary energies, an indefatigable collector, an inspiring teacher and a lovable eccentric. His father was a clergyman and he took holy orders himself after entry to Corpus Christi College. He was appointed Reader of Geology in 1818 and a canon of Christ Church in 1825. His rocks and fossils became the core of the University's collections and the basis for the new science of geology. He was a cheery, humorous and bustling man with an insatiable curiosity and a boundless enthusiasm for his subject. He examined coprolites (fossilized faeces) to reconstruct the diet of the saurians; he recognized that snails were responsible for boring holes found in limestones; he extracted gelatine from the bones of mammoths. In his canon's garden at Christ Church he enclosed toads in cavities to determine their tenacity for life, and he engaged in experimental archaeology by making living hyenas crush ox bones in order to furnish an explanation for the gnawing marks on bones found in cavern deposits. But it was his teaching technique that most commended itself to me. He took students up to Shotover Hill to inspect the outcrop of the Corallian limestone. He announced that his next lecture would meet at the Great Western Railway station at Oxford and that it would take the form of an extended and animated discussion of the geological strata newly exposed by the railway cutting between Didcot and Bristol. He was also highly adventurous in tasting everything that came to hand. This involved serving up crocodile to his guests in the canonry and swallowing (accidentally) an object claimed to be the dessicated heart of Louis XIV! Although criticized as a buffoon, Buckland attracted packed audiences to his lectures and made important discoveries in geology. He explored evidence for catastrophic transformations of the British landscape in the geologically recent past. His *Reliquiae Diluvianae* (1823) was seized on by those who wanted the biblical accounts of the Flood to be supported by scientific investigation. But by 1840 Buckland began to change his mind and to identify the smoothing and scratching of the rocks as the work of glacier ice. Moreover, his works included the discovery of the first human prehistoric skeleton, the so-called Red Lady of Paviland, and his account of *Megalosaurus* from Stonesfield is the first published description of a dinosaur. Buckland ended up as Dean of Westminster, but unlike Dean Stanley he did not allow his ecclesiastical preferment to deaden his intellectual interests. To sum up, Buckland laid the foundations of Oxford-based Geology. It was now (from 1850) possible to take an Honours degree in Natural Science which could include Geology.

Buckland's successor was John Phillips (1800–74) who again helped to push forward the frontiers of the subject and to consolidate geological knowledge. An orphan, Phillips had been brought up by his uncle, William Smith. He had helped him in cataloguing his collection, in preparing lithographs to illustrate his books and in mapping large areas of the country. After experience in academic posts in Yorkshire and Ireland, he came to Oxford in 1852, seven years before Buckland's death. He took up where the older man left off, producing a valuable synthesis, the *Geology of Oxford and the Thames Valley* in 1871, in which he describes the fossils in the region. Phillips is also remembered for having introduced the term Mezozoic to identify the era 250–65 million years ago, between the Palaeozoic and the Caenozoic. His interests extended into the geology of the planetary system; he studied the moon and produced lithographs of the moon's surface. In the wake of Buckland's enthusiasm, Phillips added academic respectability to Oxford's geological school.

It is on the foundations laid firmly by these three men that our understanding of the bare bones of the geology of the Oxford region still rests. Oxfordshire's structure can best be grasped if it is imagined that the rocks are disposed like a giant, layered cake tilting slightly ($\frac{1}{2}$–1°) towards the southeast. These layers of rock have been subject to erosion over millions of years so that progressively younger rocks, ranging from the Lower Jurassic (the oldest) to the Upper Cretaceous (youngest), are crossed as one travels in a south-easterly direction. The bands of rocks outcropping at the surface thus lie across the county in a diagonal direction from north-east to south-west. They consist of limestones, clays and sands. As in a layer cake again, there are contrasting hard and soft textures in the rocks of Oxfordshire. The three bands of high ground are built of rocks which resist erosion, the harder limestones and sandstones. The eastern Cotswolds are largely composed of the Great Oolite limestone; Corallian limestone accounts for the hills of Headington, Wytham and Cumnor around Oxford, as well as the ridge which extends roughly parallel to the Thames in a westward direction. The Chilterns and the Berkshire (now Oxfordshire) Downs are composed of chalk, which again has proved more weather resistant than the intervening clay. Between these bands of harder rock are the Lias, Oxford, Kimmeridge and Gault clays forming flat and relatively poorly drained vales.

Complicating this straightforward picture further are even younger deposits (the so-called Tertiary sediments), which were laid down on the surface of some of the chalk, and largely eroded away. During the Pleistocene 'Ice Age' material derived from ice sheets was spread here and there and, finally, the river Thames and its tributaries reworked the earlier Pleistocene deposits to form sands and gravels and distributed them in patches along the valleys. The most recent deposit is a band of alluvium, a silty mud which is annually added to when the rivers are in flood. Each rock series has created a unique landscape, the product of the underlying strata, the surface soil, the climate, aspect, vegetation and subsequent man-management.

The Cotswolds are part of a much larger and longer range of hills which stretch diagonally across Midland England from Lincolnshire down to Bath and Bristol. They were formed between 190 and 115 million years ago when the land was mostly under the sea. Banbury Ironstone (Middle Lias) is a highly ferruginous limestone deposited in a shallow, warm sea. When it comes to the surface in north Oxfordshire it produces the rich red loam which, in Arthur Young's words, 'may be considered the glory of the county. It is deep, sound, friable, yet capable of tenacity; and adapted to every plant that can be trusted to it by the industry of the cultivators.' (*General View of the Agriculture of Oxfordshire*, London, 1813, p. 5) The Middle Lias ironstone when weathered is a deep rust colour; when unweathered it is made up of a myriad of green chamosite ooliths and calcite shell debris. It provided local builders until the end of the nineteenth century with a hard gingery stone which delights the eye in dozens of north Oxfordshire villages. It is still used today. Quarries at Edgehill produce ashlar, fireplaces and flags. At Hornton Grounds rubble is quarried which has recently been used for houses at Deddington. It was also formerly worked as a low grade iron ore by the British Steel Corporation. These old workings are a distinctive feature of the area north westwards from Wroxton on both sides of the A422. Where the land has been restored after removal of the ironstone, there is a curiously slumped and depressed field surface with cliff-like exposures along the edges. If you wish to see these rocks in section, there are still quarries open near Hornton and just over the county boundary at Edgehill.

Above the Lias, the Jurassic rocks continue with Inferior and Great Oolite formations. These sediments were laid down in similarly shallow, tropical, warm seas swarming with swimming animals. In places, the size and luxuriance of the corals indicate equable climatic conditions similar to those prevailing in the Western Pacific today. When there were strong currents the ooliths and shell fragments were deposited in bands which have become cemented into solid but workable stone. As we shall see, Oxfordshire men have quarried these limestones at such places as Taynton and Burford for hard durable building materials for hundreds of years. At Stonesfield, sediments originating from lime-rich sand in the bottom of a tropical sea lagoon have been mined for roofing slates since the sixteenth century. These Stonesfield and other Cotswold slates are in reality thin slabs of sandy, oolitic limestones rich in brachiopods, bivalves and ammonites; they are also famous for fish, large reptiles including Buckland's *Megalosaurus* whose bones are popular attractions in the University Museum, and early scientifically important mammals. Robert Plot in his *Natural History of Oxfordshire* (1676), recorded that the slate stone was quarried from shafts, forty feet deep, taken to the surface and exposed to the winter frosts. It split along the planes of lamination providing a tough, weatherproof roofing material, still valued for its lichen-growing propensity. Nowadays the slate coverings of field barns are frequently cannibalized to provide roofs for commuters' conversions. The only sign of the slating industry at Stonesfield are the old tip heaps near the former shafts. A small village museum records the now defunct craft. Quarries making new 'slates' from the Forest Marble have been opened in 1981 at Filkins. The material is costly and most 'slate' used in West Oxfordshire is artificial.

Overlying the Great Oolite limestone are deposits of clay, the so-called Oxford and Kimmeridge clays which represent silt from river deltas carried out far into a profound, calm, tropical sea. These deep water conditions favoured the deposition of great thicknesses of the grey Oxford clay. As it continued south-eastwards, the deposit reached 110 metres (300 feet) thick and grew thicker still to the south-west and north-east. It is full of the skeletal debris of crocodile-like creatures such as the *Pliosaur* mentioned earlier, and the dolphin-like *Ichthyosaurs*. It has been extensively quarried all round Oxford (at Wolvercote, Summertown, Cowley, St Clements), in the nineteenth century to make bricks. Flooded brick pits lie half a mile north of Oxford station by the Oxford to Birmingham railway line.

At the end of the Jurassic period, Oxfordshire was uplifted and the rocks which have just been mentioned were subject to erosion. Since it was above the sea level of the time, no deposition took place and there is a great blank in the geological record. The invasion of the Cretaceous seas approximately 115–65 million years ago led to further sediments being laid down which are still visible in the south-eastern third of the Oxfordshire landscape. The Lower Greensand series were formed from coarse desert sands from a river delta near land. They can be seen as a series of rusty sandstones capping Boars Hill and the Cumnor Hills to the west of the city of Oxford. Further west, at Faringdon, is a series of quarries which have produced the famous sponge fossils. I recall scrambling over the gingery working face of the sandy quarry at Faringdon with Nancy Hood, the curator of the Wantage museum in the late 1970s, picking up the calcareous sponges, small cup-shaped fossils and bryozoans. They accumulated, 110 million years ago, in the base of submarine channels in shallow sea water. One of these old sand quarries which can be seen from the Faringdon by-pass is now filled with the impedimenta of a builder's yard. On the south side, at Wicklesham, there is one still open and producing sand.

The Gault Clay extends in a broad north-east, south-west ribbon and forms most of the floor of the Vale of the White Horse. It was a deep marine deposit in origin, and consists of silt carried from the land via river deltas far out into a warm, calm sea. The impermeability of this underlying rock has resulted in the poor drainage of the Vale of the White Horse. Even today the soil is a sticky clay. In the nineteenth century it made good pasture for dairy cattle providing milk, butter and cheese for the London market which was reached by Brunel's railway. With more effective drainage techniques the Vale is now largely ploughed up. Running parallel and above the Gault Clay is the Upper Greensand formed in slightly shallower seas.

To obtain an impressive view of the Upper Chalk, which forms the scarp and dip slope of the Chiltern Hills, you only need to watch from your car window as you shoot along the M40 motorway from Oxford to London. One of the largest exposures of Chalk in midland England is to be seen in the notch the motorway makes in Aston Rowant parish. This white rock with its very distinctive bands of flint is formed of the calcareous plates of minute algae, uncounted numbers of which fell to the bottom of warm seas 100–300 metres deep while the land was under semi-desert or desert conditions. It was the rocky result of a great warming event in world history. What then are the extraordinarily contoured shapes of the blue glassy flints seen in bands at regular intervals in the Chalk massif? The material derives from the silica deposited within the Chalk during its formation, following the hollows which may have originated as lobster burrows. This silica derives from sponge spicules and was concentrated in bands and ultimately changed into the exceptionally hard and horny shapes of the flints. While chalk is generally too soft to use as a building material; when burned as lime it is one of the components of the cement making process. The Chinnor Cement Works (by application) provides an opportunity for a more leisurely examination of the strata. The flint has been used by local builders throughout south and south-east Oxfordshire; often combined with brick, farm houses and barns have blueish flint walls with quoins, door jambs, window dressings in orange brick.

At the end of Cretaceous times the seas retreated and there was a long period of erosion and uplift. It is thought that about 150 metres of chalk was denuded in this way. This part of Oxfordshire was drained by rivers flowing eastwards, spreading their gravels towards the south-east. The sands, so moved, formed into weathering crusts under near tropical conditions. The water evaporates from the surface, more water is drawn up, evaporated in turn, depositing its dissolved silica. Thus the crust builds up. The result is that the indurated remnants of these sandy strata known as sarsens are scattered on the surface of the Chalk, particularly in the dry valleys round Ashdown House. They were a formidable obstacle to early agriculture and had to be dragged to the field edge or used in the foundations of houses and barns. Because they were so heavy and intractable, sarsen stones provided good markers; they are found lurking in many hedgerows, signs of ancient boundaries. At Stonor they were put round ponds. Lord Camoys has erected a ring of them in a modern folly 300 metres from the house.

Snaking across Oxfordshire from west to east is the river Thames. For most of the last thousand years it was a boundary between Oxfordshire and Berkshire. It is evident that it has drained large parts of central and southern England for a much longer period, in fact up to two million years. For most of this protracted period of time Britain was afflicted by periodic cold periods which meant that glaciers advanced and periodically retreated, planing, disturbing and contorting many of the surface rocks. The ancestral Thames was much larger and more braided than at present and it flowed east along different channels. For a time, it made its way out to the North Sea through the Vale of St Albans until blocked by ice. The pent up waters then forced their way through a narrow gap in the Chilterns and formed a gorge which has now broadened out to become the Goring Gap. The modern railway line from London to Oxford (and Bristol) passes through eight miles west of Reading.

During the tundra-like conditions of the cold periods and the more temperate intermediate periods the river waters were swollen and brought down immense quantities of broken rock, as well as soil in solution, in suspension and in grains. Some of this material was taken beyond the county by the river and ultimately made its way to the North Sea, but much was distributed along the banks where it formed spreads of sand and gravel. With each successive cold period, sea levels dropped as more water was locked up in enlarged ice caps, and down-cutting of river beds occurred; this meant that the river valley became ever narrower and deeper and sliced down through earlier spreads leaving the remains as terraces. By studying the provenance of the rocks represented in the gravel we can tell the extent of the drainage basin of the Thames at any one period. By looking at the fossil bones, plant remains, and snail shells (excellent indicators of changing habitats) we can reconstruct past fauna and flora.

There is, however, much debate among geologists and palaeontologists about the timing and numbers of the different sequences of warm and cold conditions. A broadly acceptable picture is emerging that the really rapid aggradation of terrace deposits took place during cold periglacial conditions. The river Thames is now seen as braided and gravelly bedded, flowing across a sparsely vegetated and treeless landscape. How is this to be reconciled with the fact that some of the gravels contain the bones of large mammals that preferred warm climates, animals such as the elephant and the hippopotamus? The answer lies curiously enough in the small shells of snails which are found associated with these bones. These creatures tolerate very cold conditions. The skeletal debris of the tropical animals are the result of the re-working of the earlier gravels. The river has washed them out of horizons laid down during the warm interglacial periods.

A visit to one of the numerous gravel pits which are splattered across the upper Thames Valley is likely to be an affront to environmental susceptibilities. It is hard to view with equanimity the systematic destruction of large stretches and the creation of unwanted linear lakes, much less the water parks as they are unsuitably named. It can, however, be a rewarding experience since examination of the exposures on the edge of the pits will illustrate the complexities of the Ice Age history of Oxfordshire just mentioned. Earlier channels of the Thames and its tributaries are seen cutting into the Oxford Clay at Stanton Harcourt, as they did formerly at Wolvercote and elsewhere at Sugworth and Highlands Farm, Henley-on-Thames. The form of the gravel itself affords vivid clues as to the conditions prevailing when it was laid down: ice wedge casts, where the ground has contracted to be filled with ice which has then melted, the void being filled with clay and silts; festooning where the frozen ground has been contorted; polygonal-patterned ground effects on horizontal surfaces – these can be seen on aerial photographs; the ferruginous cementation of gravels forming lumps. These lumps were used by the Neolithic builders of the Devils Quoits thousands of years after. All these features may be seen on the sides of gravel pits at Hardwick, Stanton Harcourt and Yarnton. Permission will need to be sought from the gravel companies, in particular ARC who have proved good friends to archaeologists in the past. Not only have they contributed relatively large sums to pay for archaeological investigation, but they have also, on occasion, been prepared to re-programme their operations to allow time for such detailed work.

The upper Thames gravel pits have produced the evidence for the earliest human presence in Oxfordshire. I remember visiting Dix's pit near Stanton Harcourt in the early 1980s in the company of enthusiastic local archaeologist, R. J. Macrae. In his professional life Mr Macrae laid flooring, and it was clear that he was equally at home on the floor of a gravel pit. He cultivated the friendly co-operation of gravel digging drivers who, under his tutelage, became expert at homing in on the prehistoric stone tools, moving with the gravel on a shifting serpentine band of the conveyor belt to the sorter and grader. I have vivid memories of 'Mac', pipe in mouth, breathing heavily as he attacked with his trowel the implement-bearing surfaces in the ancient river channel at Highlands Farm, Henley-on-Thames. He pulled out worked flakes, the debris of tool making, by the dozen. Macrae has demonstrated that Palaeolithic man in Oxfordshire used flint when he could get it to make his massive, ovate hand axes. He supposes that the axes were brought ready-made into the region because they are found in many sites without the tell-tale chippings which indicate a working floor. These early tool workers supplemented both the blue and the orange-iron stained flint with white quartzite, another hard material which could be sharpened to provide a fine cutting edge for butchering carcasses. The tools of Palaeolithic Oxonians which Macrae has collected over the years with such tenacity of purpose now reside in cardboard boxes in the Baden-Powell Quaternary Unit of the Pitt-Rivers Museum at Oxford. They await the next generation of scholars to rework the evidence.

The important thing to note about these Palaeolithic tools is that they tell us that during the Middle Pleistocene, humans had penetrated to the upper Thames Valley, an area which in the palaeontologist Derek Roe's words 'lay close to the north-westerly limit of human colonisation at this time' (c. 200,000 BC). He adds that these few families of nomadic hunters are unlikely to have occupied the area for any length of time. What brought them here? The answer is of course that they were following the herds of meat-providing wild animals. At present the Stanton Harcourt site has not demonstrated that the carcasses of the animals found, such as mammoth, bison, horse and straight-tusked elephant were exploited by humans. They died naturally and their bones were washed into the channel. Dr Kate Scott of the Oxford University Department of Geography has found that an interesting point emerges about the mammoth; far from being a hairy animal rampaging in the tundra it flourished in a landscape full of lush foliage. Since it could only survive by eating its own bodyweight of vegetation daily this is not really surprising.

In one place, however, a clear link has been established between tools and prey. In 1991 at Gatehampton Farm, in a buried channel close to the Goring Gap, Tim Allen of the Oxford Archaeological Unit and his team of field walkers found a scatter of artefacts and flint manufacturing debris. When a small area was excavated, it was seen that the late-Palaeolithic hunters who had made these tools had positioned themselves in a tactically strong position from which they could ambush their prey. These were probably herds of horses and reindeer using the shallow river as a crossing place.

Since we have learned so many new insights into the Pleistocene of Oxfordshire, it has to be confessed that from a heritage point of view all has not been lost in the insensate search for sand and gravel. As will be seen throughout this book, the heritage lobby in Oxfordshire has responded well to the threats of destruction of the environment. Policies are now in place at both County and District level to minimize the damage. Institutions such as the Oxford Archaeological Unit and the County Museum Service are sworn to implement these policies. The past, it is increasingly realized, is a scarce and rapidly reducing resource. It is up to the people of Oxfordshire to husband it carefully like any other non-renewable legacy.

II
Settlement

The Oxford region has been settled by farming groups since the fourth millennium BC. To begin with, the early herding communities and first farmers left sparse traces of their presence on the ground because they were largely nomadic. In February 1995 I recall seeing the site of a Bedouin encampment in Jordan where the transient occupants had moved on a week or so before. All that was left on the surface of the desert were lines of stones which had pinned down the edges of their tents for the duration of their stay. The ash from their fires had also left burned patches in the dust. No bones (all consumed by dogs), no rubbish (all recycled as is common with poverty stricken communities), no post holes, no ditches dug. The odd scattered Neolithic pits and post holes that we do find dug into the gravels and clays of the upper Thames Valley are consistent with this impermanent sort of existence and not with prolonged settlement.

These nomadic farmers, as will be seen in a later chapter, were capable of clubbing together to erect considerable earthen, wooden and stone ceremonial and funerary monuments. They also dug the five so-called causewayed enclosures found distributed along the Oxfordshire part of the Thames Valley at approximately ten-mile intervals. None of these is noticeable at ground level but they were discovered by aerial photography which can pick out the presence of long filled-in multiple ditches and flattened banks. The only one of the five to have been excavated is at Abingdon, and it now lies, destroyed, under a housing estate. It was sited on a promontory, cutting off a spur of gravel at the confluence of two streams, and some interesting calculations have been made about the size of the labour force that constructed it. Digging the inner enclosure would have involved some 1,400 man-hours and the outer one about 9,600. A group of about twelve able-bodied adults could have coped with this in one season. The function of the causewayed (i.e. interrupted) enclosure would presumably have been storage and herding. It is assumed that it would not have been occupied all the time by all the group. They would have been dispersed over the surrounding area and led a semi-nomadic existence, but would meet one another – and perhaps neighbouring tribes too—to engage in tribal rituals and exchange.

A search for the residential accommodation of Oxfordshire people in the Neolithic and Bronze Ages has continued over the last twenty-five years with increasing success. Between Yarnton and Wallingford there is now evidence for occupation during the Neolithic and Early Bronze Ages. Clusters of pits containing charred hazelnut shells, cattle and pig bones have been found. Large-scale gravel extraction in the early 1990s has enlarged our knowledge of the prehistory of seventy acres of Thames flood plain at Yarnton/Worton. Gill Hey, in charge of the archaeological team, has reported on two thousand years of human occupation. Attracted by the presence of a river channel (now filled in), successive groups of people had used a gravel island for their dwellings from the mid-Neolithic throughout the Bronze Age. In 3500 BC, settlement was sparse, scattered, constantly shifting and possibly seasonal in nature. A thousand years later things had become more stable. Traces of houses and associated activities such as cooking and wood-working could be seen. The Bronze Age farmers left worked wood, wood chips and bark, all preserved in the Thames side silts; even a small Bronze Age bridge had been driven across the channel. Enigmatic spreads of burnt stone and charcoal well away from the houses can possibly be explained as the remains of barbecues or even saunas. More prosaically, they may simply derive from a tree-clearing phase in the formerly wooded landscape.

All this early activity is separated by up to a mile from the modern (and medieval) village of Yarnton. One might well ask why the focus of settlement has so decisively shifted away from the flood plain into the terrace gravels? The answer may be related to climatic deterioration at the end of the Bronze Age with a general rise in the water table. The flood plain became too water-logged for settlement. People retreated to the higher ground around the later Saxon village of Yarnton, and the settlement gradually shifted along the edge of the gravel terrace. Another possible explanation is that the economy changed and the flood plain could offer excellent summer pasture.

Gravel extraction has thus increased our knowledge about Bronze Age habitation sites. Similarly, an opportunity arose when preparations were being made for the construction of the Wallingford bypass. Excavation next to the site of the new Thames bridge by George Lambrick revealed a late Bronze Age tool-making site and what had been a long cigar-shaped island; this included the remains of a bridge or jetty consisting of oak piles driven into the river bed in the edge of the buried river channel. A plausible explanation is that, like a better known and bigger site down river at Runnymede, the site at Wallingford may have functioned as an island port controlling river traffic and flourishing on the exchange of valuable commodities.

During the Early and Mid-Iron Ages (from 800 BC – 100 BC), hamlets and farms grew up dotted over the upper Thames Valley. Aerial photographs again show a mesh of these farms with their double-ditched drove-ways, round houses and clusters of pits, with occasional evidence of paddocks clearly delineated in the gravelly soil. Three types of land were favoured: the floodable river plain yielding rich pasture in the summer season, the easily workable, free-draining and early warming gravel soils of the terraces, and the limestone dip slope, with some woodland still left, dissected by numerous streams and harbouring plentiful springs. A great deal has been learned about these comparatively low status sites at Mingies' Ditch, Hardwick; Watkin's Farm, Northmoor; Gravelly Guy, Stanton Harcourt; Ashville, Abingdon; Farmoor, near Cumnor; Mount Farm, Dorchester; and Worton Rectory Farm, Yarnton. They were undefended except for stock-proof ditches and fences, spaced at times as close as one and two kilometres and comprised groups of round houses, surrounded by clusters of pits and four-post structures. Trackways led to enclosed paddocks and out into the surrounding fields. A degree of specialization was apparent in the economy. Sometimes it was exclusively pastoral as at Mingies' Ditch; at others occupation was seasonal as at Farmoor with small groups of herdsmen moving on and out at winter time. Others such as at Gravelly Guy and Ashville had mixed economies in which cereal production was much more important, with grain being stored in underground pits and seed corn carefully husbanded in granaries supported on four posts.

The houses of all these types of settlement were circular, constructed with inner rings of posts bearing the weight of the conical thatched roofs and outer walls either of cob (clay with chopped straw), or wattle and daub panels. Shallow gulleys were dug to drain water from their flimsy foundations. Inside are occasionally found hearths, clay-lined pits and cobbled areas, but in most instances the floors have vanished, removed by the all-pervasive plough shares of modern farmers.

The most impressive visual expression of the Iron Age inhabitants of Oxfordshire are without doubt the sixteen hill forts. Their massive banks are now grass-grown and their ditches filled with rich resources of flora. Farmers have frequently increased the number of entrances to create access for their vehicles. Unlike the farms and hamlets down in the valleys, the forts have not been the subject of recent excavation on a large scale, so consequently we know much less about their interiors and almost nothing about their history. The defences themselves, when sectioned, show a variety of construction methods including simple mounding of the upcast from external ditch into ramparts; the stiffening of such ramparts with timber lacing and palisades as at Blewburton Hill; the revetting of banks using sarsen boulders dragged in clearance operations from the surface of the surrounding fields as at Uffington and Alfred's Castle. The entrances, as has been proved at Blewburton Hill, can involve massive timber posts and gates. Not all the hill forts were in use at any one time. Rams Hill (already in use in the Bronze Age), Uffington and Hardwell are far too close to one another for comfort. Nor, despite the location of many of them along the Ridgeway, are they the result of a grand strategic design. We can only guess at their functions; some, like Chastleton and Alfred's Castle, are so small that they would have been hard put to contain more than one extended family. Others, like Uffington, may have acted as marketing, storage, or ritual centres. If they resulted from some short-lived political crisis they are very unlikely to have been occupied continuously for water storage, despite clay-lined pits and barrels, would have been an incurable problem. They need to be understood as focal points in a landscape of downs and vales covered in a network of arable fields or intersected with ditches demarcating ranches. The people who built them probably lived outside them for most of the time, in farms and hamlets in the downs or the vale, similar to those we know so much about in the Thames Valley in the centre of the county.

Although industrial and urban developers are often blamed for destroying our historic built heritage, in the long run it is farmers who wreak a greater havoc. The Iron Age forts of Oxfordshire are much damaged by pitilessly ruthless plough-ing. At Madmarston Hill, the multivallate fortress has been reduced to a shadow of its former self over forty-five years and this despite its scheduled status. At Ilbury, near Dedding-ton, bulldozing has flattened the eastern side of the pear-shaped contour fort. Even at the celebrated fort at Witten-ham Clumps, thoughtless tree planting puts at risk archaeo-logical deposits in the centre. A further potent threat are the burrowing proclivities of furry animals; badgers and rabbits seem to regard the defensive banks of Cherbury and Dyke Hills as a challenge. Cows, too, with their turf-cutting hooves, cause massive erosion on steep slopes. Whole areas of bank have dropped away at Alfred's Castle. The trampling of visitors, guide books in hand, represents the final threat to fragile grass-grown earthworks. The only owners of an

Oxfordshire Iron Age fort who have shown a consistently conserving policy are the National Trust. At Uffington Castle they have covered ground with plastic netting to encourage turf regrowth; they have diverted visitors away from vulnerable areas; they have intelligently sited the major car park well away down slope of the monument. Visitors are thus induced to appreciate the fort in its physically demanding context. For one American tourist, used to perambulating the sanitized pavements of Miami, the exposure to sheep smell and spoor on her walk uphill to the fort, while shod in court shoes, was overwhelming!

In a number of places in the upper Thames Valley in Iron Age Oxfordshire there are signs of denser occupation. The 'Big Rings' of Cassington may have been one such. Here air photography by Major Allen in the 1930s had detected a massive sub-circular ditch system with signs of extensive settlement within. I vividly remember cycling out with the members of the Oxford University Archaeological Society in the misty November days of 1951, plying my trowel on the gravelly section and then seeking a warm refuge in the Cassington public house. Sherds and cider: it was my first introduction to prehistoric archaeology. Before obliteration by gravel extraction in 1951, we sectioned the ditch and it was dated to c.100 BC, with signs of a refurbishing, of the defences, perhaps in the second quarter of the first century AD. The early fortification may have been in response to the threat of the Catuvellani, Belgic invaders of the Oxford region in the first century BC, and the second a local response to the Claudian invasion of Rome.

More exciting and more recent have been the discoveries at the Vineyard, Abingdon. Here, in the late 1980s, at the junction of the rivers Ock and Thames, Tim Allen and his team found a thirty-three hectare site defended by three concentric ditches. This, of course, made it much larger than any of the surrounding Iron Age hamlets at Ashville, Thrupp or Gooseacre Farm. Moreover, as pits and cellars in the modern town of Abingdon have shown for years, there was a dense Roman settlement witnessed by hundredweights of

24

pottery, painted wall daub and bone. There seems little doubt that Abingdon was one of the fortified Celtic strongholds or proto-towns known in Julius Caesar's account of the Gallic wars as *oppida*. A third site, with unusually dense occupation, is at Dyke Hills, half a mile south of Dorchester at the confluence of the Thame and Thames. The huge earthen banks and ditches (from which it gets its name) have a warlike appearance. Interestingly there are two World War II pill-boxes, one at either end of the dykes, exhibiting a military re-use for the site. Inside the banks, the aerial photographs show a mass of intersecting circles which are likely house sites; some, as at Ashville, are in rows with their entrances facing eastward, presumably away from rain-laden winds; a further thought provoking parallel between the two sites. Abingdon seems to have attracted the native peoples, including the local aristocracy, into the town, lured by the delights of Roman urban living. Similarly, there was a shift of settlement focus from Dyke Hills to the newly founded Roman town of Dorchester, half a mile to the north. Here the inhabitants enjoyed the security of walls, paved streets, rectangular timber and later stone buildings and the trappings of Roman life.

The existence of these defended sites during the last four centuries before the Roman occupation is a reminder that inter-tribal warfare was endemic. The tribal societies of the day had at their disposal considerable resources of labour and sufficient surplus wealth in the form of grain and cattle to engage in large scale fortification. A dramatic example of this is that Oxfordshire possesses the largest sub-circular territorial enclosure in the British Isles. This is the North Oxfordshire Grim's Ditch, recently surveyed by Tim Copeland, a series of earthworks that were constructed, not necessarily all at once, in the last century BC, between the valleys of the Glyme, Evenlode and Windrush. It included lengths of bank and dyke which enclosed an area of twenty-two square miles, including most of the parishes of Wooton, Glympton, Kiddington, Charlbury, Spelsbury, Enstone, Woodstock, Hanborough, Freeland, North Leigh, Ramsden,

Finstock and Cornbury. A number of gaps in the Grim's Ditch seem deliberate. They probably coincide with areas of uncleared woodland which would have been considered impenetrable at the time. Opinions vary as to the interpretation and function of the North Oxfordshire Grim's Ditch. If it was a military work it could have presented a barrier to chariot warfare. A large scale enclosure would have demarcated a territory which in the Roman period had included no less than seven villas with their estates. The most plausible proposition is that it was an enclave of the aggressive Catuvellani in territory otherwise controlled by the Dobunni. The Anglo-Saxons, separated by half a millennium from its construction date, attributed it sweepingly like other enigmatic earthworks to the work of the devil – hence its name. For them, Grémr, the person who conceals his name, is a by-name of Woden (cf. Wansdyke) who likes to go round in disguise.

Many of the hill forts continued to be occupied in the Roman period. Field walking at Madmarston, for instance, has yielded quantities of Roman pottery, evidence for continued usage of the hill fort, and the most recent work at Uffington has suggested that there may have been a shrine or a periodic fair within the hill fort. The upper Thames Valley also continued to be intensively farmed during the four hundred years of the Roman occupation. The villa owners, on the other hand, showed a curious reluctance to site their large houses on the river plain. As Professor Salway has pointed out, 'once the slopes of the Cotswolds are reached, the valleys of the tributaries of the Thames, particularly the Windrush, Evenlode and Glyme are thick with villas'. Their likely estate boundaries have been reconstructed at Shakenoak, Ditchley and North Leigh. They must often have gathered together, rather like their successors, the country gentry, in the eighteenth century; each seeking the congenial company of their neighbours, with whom they shared the opportunities for hunting and travelling along Akeman Street to the cantonal capital of Cirencester or to the more rustic amenities of Alchester only ten miles or so to the east. Deer bones, found at Shakenoak, show that venison figured occasionally in their banquets.

At the top end of the social stratum, the Blenheim Palace of its day, was the villa at North Leigh, now the only visible and visitable Roman building in Oxfordshire. It is run by English Heritage and is well signposted from the Bladon-Woodstock road. The site is a choice one: a sunny slope enclosed within a meander of the river Evenlode. There was good arable on the lower limestone slopes of the Cotswolds, sheep pasture on the upper heights, hunting and fuel in the nearby margins of Wychwood. Beginning as a simple winged corridor type with separate bath house and barn, North Leigh developed by the fourth century AD into a palatial courtyard villa.

Over 300 years of occupation it acquired no less than five bath suites, a succession of rows of rooms linked along corridors floored with numerous fine mosaics of the Corinian school, hypocaust under-floor heating, plastered and painted walls and more than a suggestion of symmetrical overall planning for external display. One problem of understanding the building is the bewildering succession of structures superimposed on one another. Moreover, the economic base is imperfectly investigated. Many other buildings such as barns and workshops have been detected by aerial photographs to the south-west of the site but are buried beneath the turf. The occupants of a villa on this scale are unlikely to have been mere merchants, administrators or retired soldiers; more probably they were one of the noble families of the Dobunni, with seats on the tribal council and a town house in *Corinium* (Cirencester) twenty-five miles to the west.

'Villa' is a catch-all term which covers farms of all sizes and shapes laid out in a regular Roman way. At the bottom end of the scale was a small working farm down on the gravels near Abingdon, at Barton Court. In its first-century AD phase it consisted of a long, rectangular timber building 8.5m (28ft) × 28m (92ft), having an extended family and its animals under the same roof. It could only be distinguished from nearby Iron Age predecessors by its rectilinearity and its scale; it was five times the area of a round house. In the late third century it was replaced by a so-called 'cottage' villa with eight ground-floor rooms and a cellar. What is particularly significant about the Barton Court site (and contrasting favourably with the North Leigh villa) is that area excavation techniques have traced all manner of ancillary structures explaining how such a farm worked in its heyday in the late fourth century AD. These included a grid of paddocks and a field system, two wells, waterholes for animals, a corn drying oven and a cemetery for infants. The agricultural surplus from the establishment was doubtless marketed in the thriving Romano-British town of Abingdon.

Instead of being engulfed in a tide of blood and flame at the end of the Roman occupation, the Roman villas and towns in Oxfordshire seem to have declined slowly and fairly peacefully in the fifth century. The barbarian emigrants, the Anglo-Saxons, are found slowly infiltrating and in many instances living alongside their Romano-British predecessors in the landscape. At North Leigh, for instance, squatter occupation with makeshift partitions of dry-stone walling were built across the floors and fires lit against them even on tessellated pavements. Such decorated floors evidently made a deep impression on the newcomers. Two places in Oxfordshire (Fawler and Floore) took their names from mosaic flooring. Otherwise, the great house at North Leigh had evidently fallen derelict and was stripped of its moveables. The fact that substantial wall footings were left intact is a signal of the proximity of alternative early worked resources of limestone. At Barton Court, on the other hand, where building materials were scarce and had to be brought in, the robber trenches outlining the villa show how total was the demolition. Here, seven *grubenhäuser* (sunken-floored buildings) and eight timber post buildings replaced the Roman farm layout. The Saxons avoided the site of the house itself, simply robbing out the walls and burying one or two of their people in it.

The last twenty years have increased our understanding of Saxon settlement sites in Oxfordshire by leaps and bounds. At Sutton Courtenay in the 1930s, E. Thurlow Leeds, an

Anglo-Saxon expert on the staff of the Ashmolean Museum, excavated a haphazard group of sunken-floored buildings now recognized as characteristic workshops and storage structures. He probably missed the less obvious traces of timber post hole structures. Gill Hey, digging at Yarnton/ Worton in the early 1990s, has found seventeen *gruben-häuser* and four timber halls. The former consist of rectangular pits approximately 4.5m (15ft) × 3.5m (11½ft) containing two or more posts which certainly supported gabled roofs with low side walls of timber, wattle and clay and may have contained suspended plank floors. The timber halls measured about 17m (56ft) × 6.5m (21ft) and were substantial dwellings probably for extended family groups. A similar mixture of sunken-floored buildings and timber hall-like structures was found at Barrow Hills, Radley in the 1980s. The tradition of building large multi-purpose house/barns has continued into the nineteenth century in northern Germany and in the German-colonized parts of Poland. The sunken-floored buildings were used as weaving sheds as the stone and lead loomweights suggest. The settlement at Yarnton also had a smithy with circular stone hearth, square stone working platform and deposits of hammer scale and slag. Fine sand and flux for welding was dug from nearby pits.

All four early-mid Saxon settlements at Sutton Courtenay, Barton Court, Yarnton, and Radley illustrate the phenomenon of settlement shift. In each of them the present village nucleus is some way from the early Saxon focus. Settlement studies elsewhere bear out the general thesis that the pattern was of dispersed farms from the fifth to the eighth century AD with a tendency towards nucleation (or 'balling' which is the fashionable but ungainly term) towards the end of the Saxon period. This obviously may have involved the abandonment of many individual or small groups of farms or resulted in the general drift of the settlement from one place to another. At Yarnton, the present village still seems to be on the move, being drawn inexorably towards the road system of the twentieth century. Its church of St Bartholomew with its twelfth-century nave and font is now at the far southernmost point of the straggling medieval settlement, but c.1100 was at the northernmost tip of the group of now vanished Saxon farmsteads.

What caused settlement in Oxfordshire and other areas of Midland England to favour nucleation and greater site stability? One reason is that the landscape was rapidly filling up. A recent attempt to map medieval settlement in the county shows that a high watermark was reached c.1300 AD when over 400 nucleated settlements were already in existence, disregarding the hamlets of two to three buildings and the single farmsteads. This meant that there was a tremendous pressure of population on land and a need to reorganize the land into the classic, communal two or three open-field system. Similarly, the evolution of the parochial system allied to the development of feudal authority meant that many settlements acquired planned elements imposed on them by rent-hungry lords. Most of these medieval settlement sites lie under the houses and gardens of their successors and cannot be made to yield information about their planning, houses, or way of life. About 150, however, have shifted, contracted or simply disappeared and their sites are available for archaeological investigation. This can take three forms: survey (of earthworks, hollow ways, ponds, toft and croft boundaries, house platforms), field walking (to record, but not necessarily remove, occupation material and stonework scatters on the surface of ploughed fields), and, much more rarely because of the considerable costs involved, archaeological area excavation. This latter is obviously the most informative, but we rely heavily on a very few sites.

The deserted village of Woodperry, Oxfordshire in the 1840s was one of the first occasions when Oxfordshire antiquarians turned their attention to medieval rural settlement. The church was recognized by reason of the carved stones and graves, 'while lower down in the field, the remains of buildings scattered thickly over part of it, and entering into a little close below'. Another important observation was the soil colour which, it was noted, was 'here naturally a cold clay' and had been turned 'into a rich black mould of some depth' which 'afforded convincing proof of long continued inhabitancy'.

The opportunity of finding more about roads, layout and house plans came when the Oxford Ring Road was under construction in the late 1950s. It ran right through and up the main street of the north part of the deserted village of Seacourt. Martin Biddle never found the original nucleus, nor was the church excavated; he did, however, demonstrate that the twelfth to fourteenth-century houses at the northern extension of the village were timber in construction to begin with, 3m (10ft) × 4m (12ft) internally with single unpartitioned rooms containing hearths. Ancillary buildings providing pig sties and barns, one was five bays in length (5m (15ft) × 10m (28ft)), were ranged round some of the houses. There were no long houses where the occupants share a building under the same roof with their animals. The timber buildings were replaced with those standing on dwarf stone walls or on stone walls up to eaves level in the middle of the thirteenth century. Both the early and later buildings were roofed in thatch. As the climate deteriorated in the fourteenth century, cobbled streets and stone yard surfaces were necessary to cope with the mud. A fragmented part of Seacourt remains unexcavated and can still be seen as humps and bumps between the foot of Wytham Hill and the river Thames. The reasons for its extinction are unclear.

Another of the 150 or so deserted village sites in the county at Hardwick, just a mile or two north of Banbury, was planned in detail by the Royal Commission on Historical Monuments in 1989. It developed from a specialized pastoral unit in the Pre-Conquest period into a small, fairly regularly arranged hamlet with a maximum of five holdings in the fourteenth century. The road running through the hamlet is no more than a grass-grown, hollow way. In the fifteenth century the houses were evidently derelict and the plough swallowed up the tofts (yards) and crofts leaving ridge and furrow over the former gardens. Only three holdings remained in 1509–10, and eight years later it was alleged that

William Cope, responsible for the depopulation of Wormleighton in neighbouring Warwickshire, had turned the hamlet into a single enclosed farm. The Copes rebuilt the farmhouse and gave it an ornamental setting with terraced gardens and a moat-like lake. The hamlet was dead; the gentry family very much alive.

A third example of a well-studied deserted site is Thomley, a hamlet on the borders of Oxfordshire and Buckinghamshire. Here, Bronac Holden has disentangled the reasons for the slow decline and eventual extinction of the community of about thirty homes. It was always in a marginal position between two flourishing villages and had no market, fair or mill. It was split between rival lordships including the monasteries of Oseney and St Frideswide's, Oxford. Its land was gradually bought up by outsiders which tended to undermine the sense of village community. By the sixteenth century, Thomley was reduced to one farm.

Readers may notice that so far I have not attributed the decline of rural settlements in the later Middle Ages to plague. The truth is that surprisingly few were rubbed off the map by the Black Death. Tusmore, in the north of the county, where in 1354 the manor was not taxed because of the severity of the Black Death, is an exception. Four years later, 'death from pestilence' of the bondsmen here implies the total desertion of the village. Tilgarsley, whose very site is still unknown, was in the thirteenth century larger than its fellow village, Eynsham. In 1327 there were twenty-eight taxpayers and twenty-seven in Eynsham. In 1359, it was claimed that Tilgarsley was abandoned because all its inhabitants had died in 1350. The trouble is that taxpayers often tried to pull the wool over the eyes of the royal tax officials, who were equally likely to record exaggeratedly low assessments in return for bribes, as happened regularly on the Merton College estates at Cuxham. One effect of the Black Death certainly led to a regrouping of settlement in places like Combe. Here, the village with a church on the banks of the Evenlode was abandoned in favour of a dry hilltop site and another church was built c.1380. Eynsham attracted the residue of the population of Tilgarsley, which was abandoned. Eynsham itself survived as a small market centre into the twentieth century.

Paradoxically, in the long run, the effects of the Black Death profited the peasant survivors. Their labour rocketed in value so they charged more in wages; they were able to move house into more desirable deserted holdings; they enjoyed the advantages of a more fluid land market and moved up in the world. Many of their families emerged as the yeomen of Tudor England.

The physical evidence for comparative manorial and peasant prosperity in the medieval landscape is to be found in the considerable number of houses and farm buildings which have survived the 400–500 years. Christopher Currie has reviewed and gazeteered the medieval buildings from the Vale of the White Horse. He reckons that a disproportionate number were built before 1350 and that there was a falling off of good quality houses in the later Middle Ages. Prosperous peasant homes, on the other hand, seem to increase in the century or so before 1500. Few manor houses in this part of the country were built completely of stone. Ashbury Manor (c.1480), a house of the Abbots of Glastonbury, and Charney Bassett (c.1300), built by Abingdon Abbey, are exceptions. The great majority were built of timber framing, sometimes on dwarf stone walls and cill beams, others resting with their sole plates directly on the earth. More pre-1350 wall framing has lasted here than in any comparable rural area of Europe. The houses are usually of single range plan with the hall in series with service rooms. Alternatives are with the chamber block at right angles to the hall forming an L or T plan. Also found is the H plan with projecting wings at each corner of the central range. The roof forms are extremely varied, showing great ingenuity and innovation on the part of the local carpenters. They start off in the thirteenth century with trussed rafter roofs held flimsily together by lap-jointed collars and braces. These were followed by crown post roofs, which went on being used into the sixteenth century, but were overtaken by the more long-lasting butt purlin type, where the horizontal members are tenoned into massive principal rafters at space intervals of eight to ten common rafters. Also found in comparatively large numbers, and again showing a long and persistent popularity, were roofs supported on crucks, either rising from the wall base or springing from the mid-wall in the stone regions of west Oxfordshire and the Cherwell basin. Medieval farm buildings are considerably rarer than medieval houses. This is probably because most of them were more flimsily built in the first place. Also, as agrarian practices changed, they were altered, added to, and in the end they collapsed and were cleared away. The only ones to have survived in anything like their original form in Oxfordshire were constructed carefully from costly materials such as good quality stone and well chosen great timbers by rich (usually ecclesiastical) landowners. Such is the majestic barn at Great Coxwell, one of the largest medieval agricultural buildings in Europe. William Morris, founder of the Society for the Protection of Ancient Buildings, regarded it as 'unapproachable in its dignity, as beautiful as a cathedral, yet with no ostentation of the builder's art'. The barn was built c.1305 by the Cistercian monks of Beaulieu, Hampshire, a monastery founded a century before by King John and richly endowed with estates in the north-west of the old county of Berkshire. Beaulieu administered its lands here from two granges, large estates with farms attached at Great Coxwell and at Wyke, half a mile north of Faringdon. Air photography has in the last four years located the Cistercian grange at Wyke, which originally was the centre of a farm of stupendous proportions (1800 acres). Graham Soffe has shown that it had a capacious courtyard surrounded by huge barn-like buildings similar in proportion to the barn at Great Coxwell. There was also a great house, a granary, a dairy for seven milkmaids, stables, a dovecote and a chapel. This grandiose establishment was considered important enough to house King Henry III and his family when they visited in 1269. Great Coxwell barn, now looked after by the National Trust, stands alone, below the medieval fields sloping up to Badbury hill fort. Its stone-slated roof is an intricate piece of carpentry, supported on alternate arcade posts and mid-wall crucks. These are tied together by double-braced tie beams. Above are four ranges of purlins. The limestone walls are punched through with putlog holes doubling up as air vents to cool down the damp crops of the deteriorating medieval summers five centuries ago. In one of the waggon porches are nesting boxes for doves. In the other is a flat for the granger, the monk or layman deputed to control the stacking of the harvested crops and the threshing process.

One other medieval barn can be visited. This is New College's Rectorial barn at Swalcliffe, built 1400–9 as a capital investment of the college of its estates in north Oxfordshire. It has been carefully restored by the Oxford-shire Buildings Trust and now houses a display of agricultural and industrial machinery, and vehicles for the Oxford-shire County Museum Service. Swalcliffe barn is, of course, a century younger than Great Coxwell. It is, by contrast, constructed of different materials: gingery ferruginous lime-stone from the marlstone beds of north Oxfordshire. Its great cruck trusses were chosen with deliberation from the forest of Bewdley by the warden of New College and his entourage. Smiths from Stratford made the ironwork to hang and secure the porch doors. The slates came from Upper Slaughter in Gloucestershire. Such a barn not only provided a safe lodging for precious and portable agricultural goods, it also contrib-uted with its blank, windowless, buttressed walls to a sense of enclosure and therefore security. Each bay could be used to store a separate crop, or house implements or lodge stock. Swalcliffe, Great Coxwell, Church Enstone (a barn built by Winchcombe Abbey in the 1380s) were also food processing plants. Here the sheaves were stacked until the time the college or the monks judged right for capitalizing on the resource. Sheaves were untied and the threshers were called in with their flails to begin their long, arduous and filthy task of separating the husked grain from the straw. Winnowing

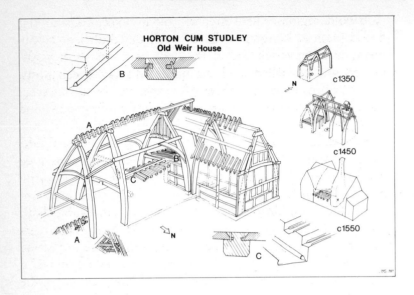

HORTON CUM STUDLEY
Old Weir House

c1350

c1450

c1550

Horton-cum-Studley. Cruck cottage at Old Weir House (*Steane*)

followed with a draught produced from the open opposed doors.

When barns are studied county-wide it is apparent that there are four clearly defined traditions of building in Oxfordshire over the period 1300 (the earliest) to the mid eighteenth century (the latest). The cruck tradition is found in the west and north-west of the county. It has two main variants. In the timber-framed areas of the upper Thames and the Vale of the White Horse the crucks are mainly of the base type. In the stone-built areas of the far west and north-west the crucks spring from the upper or middle parts of the walls. The third tradition, that of timber-framed barns with weatherboarding on brick and flint foundations, is in the south-east of the county, notably the Chilterns and extending into the east part of the Vale of the White Horse. The stone-walled tradition, with some form of roof involving principal rafters and tie beams, is found all over west Oxfordshire in the

Cotswold region. There are, of course, exceptions to this broad picture. Longworth Barn, a scheduled ancient monument, is a maverick. Here, the roof rests on short posts, braced and corbelled, and the trusses display queen posts, altogether a superior piece of carpentry of a different tradition to the vernacular in the surrounding vale and possibly late seventeenth-century in date.

The barns at Great Coxwell and Swalcliffe are easily the most celebrated, best documented and scientifically conserved in the county. Their restoration involved the powerful National Trust, English Heritage, and the locally based Oxfordshire Buildings Trust. Even more remarkable have been the efforts generated by one individual, Wantage's doctor, Dick Squires. After acquiring an expertise in putting up and taking down large timber structures, he developed a white-hot passion for saving sick buildings. He was the driving force behind a project to convert his old surgery in the centre of Wantage into a local museum and community centre. The rear of the site he filled with re-erected barns which otherwise would have ended up on a bonfire. This was done with volunteers from a local scout group, a JCB and a twenty-ton lorry. The museum is a great local amenity, offering lunches, teas, exhibitions and information. Squires's next 'do it yourself' coup was rescuing a derelict set of farm buildings at Lain's Barn, two miles east of Wantage. Again using young people, and this time depressed patients, he accomplished marvels of self help by restoring the barns to be used for harvest suppers, wedding receptions and dances, alternative uses which were immemorial in the case of rural barns. His third great venture was the re-erection of an elmwood barn, built in 1851 and now obsolete for farming purposes, together with four stables and cowsheds. Here on a site with spectacular views high above Wantage, is his Ridgeway Centre, used by hundreds of weary youth hostellers, archaeologists and nature lovers. Dick has saved, to date, eight barns and three houses. He has left a notably beneficent mark on the Oxfordshire landscape.

Both Great Coxwell and Swalcliffe barns are the lone

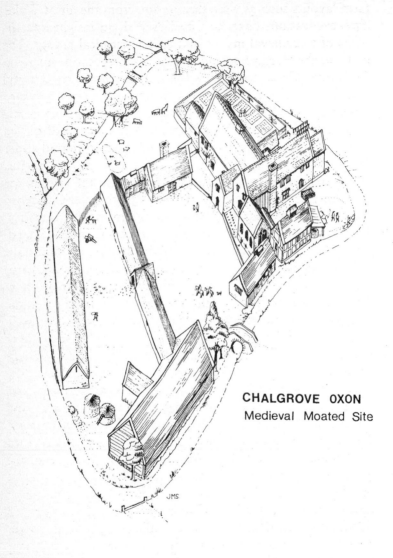

CHALGROVE OXON
Medieval Moated Site

Medieval moated site, Harding's Field, Chalgrove, Oxfordshire
(*after Beard 1983*)

surviving components of once much larger and complicated farm layouts such as were seen *in toto* from the air at Wyke. Two excavations have furnished us with an insight into the plans of a medieval manor and an ecclesiastical grange. The first was the Harding's Field manor of the Barentine family at Chalgrove. Here, in the early 1980s, James Bond (my deputy) and I surveyed two moats on the fringes of Chalgrove village threatened with a housing estate. Because of the nettle growth (which grows on phosphate-rich soil and disturbed land) we guessed that there were buildings to be found under the north end of the larger of the two moated areas. Subsequent excavation by Richard Chambers and Philip Page revealed a complicated story. The first buildings at Chalgrove were made of cob and dated to the early thirteenth century. The next phase c.1250–60 saw a stone-aisled hall added. This was associated with the Barentine family, an important knightly family who prospered with royal service and produced a sheriff, the chief royal officer in the shire in 1322–7. An indication of the growth in status of the family was the digging of the moat round their house. Moats were rarely serious fortifications; usually they were added to deter thieves, to drain wet sites and to raise fish. Local prestige could be enhanced by the addition of a moat. Next, the crosswing was added to the hall, and the manor was furnished with a detached kitchen (to reduce fire risk and obviate smells) and a bakehouse in the fourteenth century. The farm buildings were now arranged around a courtyard to the south. As yet there was no attempt to separate the economic aspects of the farmyard from the social niceties of the house. Two indications appeared of the continuing upward movement of the Barentine family. They now had themselves buried in some style in the neighbouring parish church; they also acquired a chapel, licensed in 1370. Long agricultural buildings were set round two courtyards in a final phase, dated c.1400. Chalgrove declined in the fifteenth century since the family moved its main centre elsewhere. By 1485 it had been abandoned, and in 1520 only one barn and a dovecote stood where the manor had been.

The medieval ecclesiastical grange at Dean Court, excavated by Tim Allen, was also discovered when a housing estate, part of Greater Oxford, crept up its green valley in the 1980s. Here, between two limestone outcrops, Wytham and Cumnor hills, the Abbey of Abingdon was encouraging assarting (clearance of forest and waste) in the twelfth century. By 1230 AD the monks had accumulated sufficient arable land to invest in an estate centre. To begin with, they put up a substantial, even prestigious stone range for their bailiff with two agricultural buildings, one a barn and the other a stable or ox house. The labourers were housed in flimsier dwellings in the valley below. At the end of the thirteenth century, further land acquisition was behind the redevelopment which led to the centre being shifted downslope. More elaborate domestic buildings, including a kitchen, store, fish tanks and a dovecote were now enclosed in a walled moat. A church, which has not been found, was part of the settlement. In the later Middle Ages the economic policy of Abingdon Abbey changed. They rented out Dean Court to farmers and moved their estate centre to the top of the hill in the centre of Cumnor village.

Among the reasons put forward for depopulation and, in some cases, the desertion of settlements in the rural landscape was the changeover from arable agriculture to sheep farming on a large scale. Certainly some monasteries such as Oseney Abbey were extremely interested in making money out of the sale of wool on the international market. Already in the thirteenth century, Oseney Abbey had flocks amounting to 3,000 sheep on their scattered estates of Forest Hill, Waterperry, Watlington and others in Gloucestershire. Each estate gradually began to specialize in one side of breeding sheep: some looked after the breeding ewes and produced the lambs (at Weston-on-the-Green, Cowley and Water Eaton), others were responsible for the bulk of the wool clip. The wool was gathered in a central collecting point (Water Eaton) and sent overland to Henley and thence downriver to the Italian merchants. This change of emphasis from arable to pastoral husbandry involved a marked reshaping of the landscape.

One of my favourite walks takes me out across the Cherwell meadows from Cutteslowe to Water Eaton where the gabled late Elizabethan house with flanking pavilions was built by Sir Edward Frere in 1586. The chapel, at the very end of the Gothic style, is dated 1610. There was uproar here in 1590 when it was alleged that 'Mr Fryer has destroyed the whole town'. The insurgents were proposing to meet at Enslow Bridge, attack the chief houses in the neighbourhood, murder the gentry, take the corn from the barns and 'cast downe the hedges and ditches'. 'It would never be merrye', one of the leaders is reported to have threatened, 'till some of ye gent were knocked down'. Certainly, Water Eaton is among the total desertions of Oxfordshire villages. Fragments of pottery from the twelfth to the sixteenth century can be picked up on a field edge to the north-west of the house, but otherwise all that is left are the corrugations of the field cultivation and the place-name.

I do not intend to duplicate the excellent guide to the *Buildings of England: Oxfordshire* by Sir Nikolaus Pevsner and Jennifer Sherwood (1990), but it is worth drawing attention to some of the more important houses accessible to the public.

There are three medieval manor houses of surpassing interest in the county. The most complete is Broughton Castle (Lord Saye and Sele). It lies low on an island ringed round by a very broad moat and is approached by a bridge through a castellated gate tower and a curtain wall, the results of a royal licence to crenellate in 1405. The Edwardian house so protected is a century earlier and consists of a block 160 feet long with a great hall amidships, linked one end (the west) with a kitchen and buttery and at the other with an undercroft with chapel and solar over. Sir John Broughton, a knight of Edward I (d. 1315), was the builder. The house was transformed to bring it up to Elizabethan standards of comfort and courtly splendour. In 1554–99 the plan was reversed: the kitchen end was converted into richly panelled and ornately plastered living accommodation; the dais end now led into the kitchen and offices while the front had two

two-storey bay windows added to produce a fashionably symmetrical façade. Within this restructured medieval house, William, 1st Viscount Saye and Sele (known as 'Old Subtlety' by his contemporaries) met other Parliamentary leaders in planning opposition to Charles I's government in the years leading up to the outbreak of Civil War.

Stanton Harcourt Manor House (The Hon. Mrs Gascoigne) survived in its medieval state almost intact until the middle of the eighteenth century when Earl Harcourt moved his family's power base to Nuneham Courtenay. Here he had built a Palladian house with a splendid view over the Thames Valley on the site of the village which he removed in its entirety out of the park, and re-erected as a row of small redbrick dwellings on the straightened Dorchester–Oxford road. The family has now returned to the old manor sited on the ditched, low-lying pastures of the upper Thames Valley. Fortunately Earl Harcourt's work of demolition had stopped short of destroying the chapel, Pope's Tower and the detached kitchen. This latter is one of the finest medieval survivors, with its wall fireplace, its bread and pastry ovens, adjustable louvres and octagonal roof with radiating beams, strengthened by Gothic-arched wind-braces. Alexander Pope, who made the tower at Stanton Harcourt his study in 1717–18 while translating the *Iliad*, compared it to the Forge of Vulcan, the Cave of Polyphemus and the Temple of Moloch. 'Once a year the Devil treats them with infernal venison, viz a toasted tiger stuffed with tenpenny nails.' Cream teas are now served here to thirsty tourists by village matrons.

A third less complete fortified manor house, Greys Court, stands on a slope above a wooded Chiltern valley (National Trust). In 1347 Sir John de Grey gained a licence to crenellate. It is a puzzling labyrinth of buildings, semi-ruinous in places and gardens. There was a rectangular enclosure of which the flint and early brick curtain wall, the 'keep' and towers at the south-east and south-west remain. Parch marks appeared on the lawn in the 1950s pinpointing the foundations of the medieval hall, porch, and service buildings.

Resistivity surveys carried out by Brendan Grimley of the University of Bradford in the 1980s have shown the position of the southern curtain wall under the grass. Other, more perceptible attractions are the donkey wheel driving the water buckets in the sixteenth-century wheel-house and the Jacobean mansion rebuilt by the Knollys family and upgraded in the 1740s by the Stapletons. Greys Court today has a mosaic of small gardens, some ingeniously incorporating old buildings. It is more a horticultural than an architectural experience.

In the south-eastern corner of Oxfordshire, with the suburbs of Reading lapping its park boundaries, is Mapledurham House. Sir Richard Blount began this, the largest Elizabethan house in the county in c.1585, using fashionable diapered red brick. The main front, with short wings and gabled façade is an interesting Georgian pastiche, imitating Elizabethan design of a century and a half earlier. The highly wrought interiors and irregular rear of the house are mainly Elizabethan and Jacobean.

Ashdown House (National Trust with limited opening times) stands solitary, high and remote on chalk downland near the Wiltshire border. Its builder was the chivalrous and endearingly eccentric little Lord William, 1st Earl of Craven. Craven, after a lifetime of mainly unsuccessful soldiering in which he got captured and had to be ransomed, poured out the residue of his landed wealth to support the wavering fortunes of the 'Winter Queen', Anne of Bohemia. *The Dictionary of National Biography* is circumspect: 'as to the precise nature of their private relationship even in this period, we are, naturally enough, without evidence'. It does seem that the house was built as a possible refuge for the Queen. It has been called by Pevsner 'the perfect doll's house, proof of a longing for neatness and all-round order typical of the years after the Civil War'. Built of chalk blocks and Bath stone, it looks like an Amsterdam town house: three storeys, hipped roof, a balustraded belvedere cupola; ideal, one imagines, for entertaining hunting parties and viewing the sport along the straight lime avenues converging on the house from all four points of the compass.

The designer of Ashdown House eludes us. Blenheim and Ditchley were the products of the genius of two of the finest architects of the age. Sir John ·Vanbrugh's Blenheim is so famed, advertised, written about and experienced by thousands of visitors that one might be forgiven for declining to add further to its outsize reputation. I do, however, deplore the decision of Sarah, Duchess of Marlborough, who insisted on pulling down the medieval royal palace at Woodstock. Sir John defended its continuance not 'for magnificence or curious workmanship' but 'because they were more lively and pleasing reflections (than history without their aid can do) on the persons who have inhabited them'. The Duchess was implacable; only a monolith on a swelling grassy mound reminds the visitor of the site of the Plantagenets' palace.

Ditchley Park, the house built by the 2nd Earl of Litchfied was designed in outline (he only charged ten guineas for the job) by James Gibbs. The site was that of a house belonging to Sir Henry Lee, the self-proclaimed champion of Elizabeth I and Ranger of Woodstock. The Queen visited him at Ditchley in 1592 and her portrait (now in the National Portrait Gallery) shows a stiff-ruffed and crinolined view of the monarch, standing on a map of England, her foot pointing to Ditchley.

James Gibbs had a clear idea of what he was about. He condemned Vanbrugh's 'heaps of stone' 'for it is not the Bulk of a Fabrick, the Richness and Quantity of the Materials, the Multiplicity of Lines, nor the Grandness of the Finishing that give the Grace or Beauty and Grandeur to a building, but the Proportion of the parts to one another and to the whole, whether entirely plain, or enriched with a few ornaments properly disposed'. (From *A Book of Architecture containing Designs of Buildings and Ornaments*, London 1728.)

Ditchley Park is the antithesis of Blenheim. Where Blenheim is ornate and vainglorious, Ditchley is sedate and restrained. Where Blenheim piles up the trophies of war, Ditchley is redolent with the gifts of peace. Blenheim sits

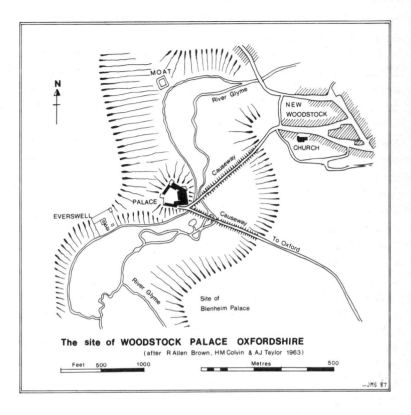

The site of WOODSTOCK PALACE OXFORDSHIRE
(after R Allen Brown, HM Colvin & AJ Taylor 1963)

Site of Woodstock Palace, Oxfordshire. The valley of the river Glyme was flooded by Capability Brown in the eighteenth century and the southern of the two causeways converted into an island. The site of the palace was levelled by order of Sarah, Duchess of Marlborough (*after Brown, Colvin and Taylor*)

crushingly surrounded by the most spectacular of English parks. Ditchley hides deep among the trees of Wychwood Forest: Winston Churchill, born at Bleinheim, sought out Ditchley Park for secret talks with his military advisers during World War II. The Ditchley foundation which now runs the house is a centre for international studies and debate.

The interior decoration of Ditchley Park employed several

supreme craftsmen and designers, including the Italian plasterers Artari, Vassalli and Serena, the carpenter Flitcroft, the
sculptor Cheere and the painter, designer and architect
William Kent. Kent's masterpiece in Oxfordshire, however, is
a few miles away in the Cherwell valley at the Cottrill
Dormers' house and garden at Rousham. Here, between
1738 and 1740, he created one of the most significant
gardens. He rejected geometric layouts and deliberately set
out to make a naturalistic landscape, complete with temples,
shaggy ruins, grottoes, cascades, twisting paths, rococo
sculptures and highly contrived vistas of the river and the
countryside punctuated by 'eye catchers' such as fake
'church' towers. All was in keeping with Addison's ideas of
throwing 'a whole estate into a kind of garden'.

Among houses lesser in scale, but equally important
architecturally and historically, is Chastleton. It was begun c.
1603 by Walter Jones, whose father was a wool merchant
and clothier, and who plied his own trade at Witney. This
has an extremely compact plan and has four storeys and
basement around a diminutive central court. The disposition
of the service rooms in the basement, although innovatory at
the time, was taken up in Sir Roger Pratt's notes in 1660: 'the
kitchen and all its offices to lie together, and the buttery and
cellar with theirs etc. and all these to be disposed of in a half
ground storey, with their back courts, convenient to them; in
that no dirty servants may be seen passing to and fro by those
who are above, no noises heard, nor ill scents smelt'.

At Chastleton the kitchen, pantry, larder, dairy, buttery,
beer and wine cellar are all half underground and connected
to the great hall and the other chambers by a majestic
wooden staircase. Pratt advised that the kitchen should not
yet be 'so far off as that your meat will be cold in bringing
from it, or your servants not presently at hand upon the least
ringing or call'. It takes forty-five seconds to take a dish from
the hatch in the servants' lobby next to the kitchen, climb the
stairs, through the screen, and to plonk it down on the table
at the dais end of the great hall. Walter Jones and his family
certainly had hot meals.

The Jones family also lived in rooms of considerable display and splendour. These the National Trust, the current owners, are restoring sensitively and gradually as this book is being written. They include a remarkable series of rooms with opulent Flemish decoration, a Great Chamber with lavish overall ornament, a long gallery with rich plasterwork; a carved screen in the hall. What is remarkable and rare is that Chastleton has come down to us in the twentieth century with minimum alteration. The explanation is that over four centuries the family's fortunes decayed gently but inevitably. Compounding an unfortunate tendency to support the losing side in the Civil War, a consequent flirtation with Jacobitism meant that the Joneses were never given the chance to profit from high office. Nor were they adept at estate management, and by the mid eighteenth century the head of the family spent time in Oxford gaol for debt. Fortunes revived in the time of John Jones (c.1780–1820). He at least managed to pay the bills and keep the house in good repair. But luckily for us the family never had sufficient resources to rebuild or bring the house up to date. It is a time capsule of the early seventeenth century. The National Trust will have grave difficulties in restricting visitor numbers in order to preserve some of the remoteness and the air of gentle decay which those of us who have known the house in the past value so much.

Stonor Park, seat of the Stonor family since the twelfth century, is in a most beautiful setting on the Buckinghamshire –Oxfordshire border and stands in a remote valley in the dip slope of the heavily wooded Chilterns. In c.1280 the chapel and the core of the medieval hall house were built. Sir John Stonor, Chief Justice of Common Pleas and adviser to the young Edward III, and whose tomb may be seen in Dorchester Abbey, enlarged the house and rebuilt the chapel c.1349. The house was re-shaped and added to, mostly in flint, brick and tile over the next 700 years. It is a veritable museum of brickwork with some fifteen phases of construction using the warm coloured material. There are splendid medieval timber roofs. Its Catholic owners in the sixteenth century took a leading part, short of treason, to oppose the Protestantizing policies of the Tudor governments. Stonor was visited by the Jesuits, Edmund Campion and Robert Parsons, and it was here that a private press was set up which printed Campion's famous pamphlet the *Decem Rationes*. During the period 1580 well into the eighteenth century the Stonors were stalwart recusants and suffered grievously in fines and imprisonments. The estates inevitably contracted as land was let or sold off, but the penalties encouraged prudent husbandry of woodland resources if the family was to keep its head above water. Stonor has emerged into the twentieth century with the great house largely intact. Its deer park, which suffered from hurricane damage in 1988 and 1990, has now been restocked and replanted. If I had to suggest to a visitor who had only one day to sample the beauties of Oxfordshire I would suggest a visit to Stonor and a walk through its delectable park.

A contrast with Chastleton and Stonor Park in some ways, because it was occupied in the post-medieval period by people somewhat lower in the social scale than the Joneses and the Stonors, farmers rather than gentry, is Cogges Manor Farm. Down a side road called Church Lane, surrounded by orchards and meadows, in a classic juxtaposition of church and manor house, Cogges has become known and loved by some 40–50,000 visitors a year. This group of farm buildings with their greystone walls and lichen-spattered slate roofs was chosen by the Oxfordshire County Council in 1972 to serve as an open-air museum. The barns, granary, ox byre, pigsties, shelter sheds, stable and rect yards were bought from a local farmer whose family had farmed here for 100 years. With the help of English Heritage and local sponsors the buildings have been restored systematically, season by season. The project opened in 1978 and culminated with the restoration of the manor house itself in 1995.

At first glance, the L-shaped house seems a typical example of a steep-gabled seventeenth-century house, characteristic of the Cotswold vernacular building tradition. On closer inspection it is seen to be an intriguing amalgam of architectural styles from the thirteenth to the nineteenth century. Each alteration, addition or subtraction over a period of 750 years reflects the activities, ambitions and family needs of a succession of medieval ecclesiastics and barons, Tudor farmers, seventeenth-century gentry, eighteenth-century schoolmasters, bailiffs and nineteenth-century farmers who have occupied it.

The standing building offers a mass of contradictory clues to unravel the complicated story. Excavations undertaken from 1988 to 1991 by the museum, the University of Oxford and the Oxford Archaeological Unit have revealed further missing pieces of the jigsaw. To the north of the present house, under the Victorian driveway, were found the remains of a good quality thirteenth-century building (known as the 'north range') accessed by an external staircase. This block was used as a service wing in its later phases and fitted out with fireplace and ovens. It was finally demolished in c.1790. Its discovery means that we now realize that the present house is only a truncated fragment, two sides in fact of a larger and more rambling group of medieval buildings, planned round a courtyard and plausibly entered from the south. The so-called 'dairy' to the north of the house has been proved to have been longer at each end. It may have started life as a detached kitchen, then a brew house and ended up in the late eighteenth century as a residence and work-place for dairymaids.

These external discoveries have been matched by exciting new information gained by a meticulous examination inside as the restoration of the building has progressed. A search was made for occupation material which had slipped through the floorboards of a number of the upper rooms and lodged between the joists and the ceilings below. Coins from the reigns of Elizabeth I and Charles II showed that the floors with their wide and irregular oak boards had bridged the room known as the hall kitchen for 350 years. The activities of the occupants were apparent. Several hundred bronze pins, dress-fastenings and buttons demonstrated that dressmaking and the repair of garments and bedding had gone on in this room, well lit as it was, by a four-light mid sixteenth-century window facing south. The cloth fragments – white cotton lawn, striped and sprigged lilac or pansies, typical cheap nineteenth-century printed textiles – suggest workaday garments run up by servants for servants. The presence of children was everywhere. Leather off-cuts showed that children's shoes were repaired there. Children's toys and beads were also retrieved in this dusty exploration. They included a painted and turned toy skittle, two slate pencils, clay marbles, a toy wheel and parts of a game consisting of squares of wood with printed pictures on their sides.

Children are among the most enthusiastic visitors to Cogges today. They enjoy seeing and touching the animals, they particularly enjoy participating in role play, dressing up and acting out the parts of kitchen-maid, parlour-maid, stable lad or groom. In so doing, they remind us of the key part, often unsung, of servants in the running of the greater and lesser houses of Oxfordshire. The census returns show that one of the main occupations after agricultural labouring was domestic service. At Stonor Park in 1871, Thomas, Lord Camoys had a family of ten; these were looked after by twenty-five servants consisting of a butler, an under-butler, two grooms, a housekeeper, three ladies' maids, four housemaids, a dairymaid, a kitchen-maid, a scullery maid, three laundry-maids, a nurse, three further ladies' maids, a valet and two assistant ladies' maids. Stonor drew its servants from far afield. Only two came from Oxfordshire, three each from Essex and Shropshire, four from Warwickshire and Cornwall and one each from Yorkshire, Durham, Cheshire, Norfolk, Sussex and Dorset. Even Stonor pales beside the glittering magnificence of the Ducal household at Blenheim. In 1891, over 150 people were living on the Blenheim Estate, and in the palace itself there were eighteen resident servants including a housekeeper, two ladies' maids, five housemaids, two still room maids, three kitchen-maids, a butler, a chef (from France), a footman and two steward's room boys. Not a single one had been born in Oxfordshire. The two dairy-maids, sisters, came from the Bristol area. The laundry-maids living in West Lodge came from Staffordshire and Cumberland. The housekeeper came from London. By contrast, the attenuated household of the Jones family at Chastleton is a vivid pointer to their comparative poverty. William Jones in 1871 had a family of three looked after by two servants, Elizabeth Bartlett (aged 26) and Anne Lock (aged 16).

While we can gain a lively and informed picture of life in the upper echelons of Oxfordshire society because of the relatively high survival rate of houses like Blenheim, Stonor and Chastleton, one's knowledge of working-class housing is much more sparse. The houses of the poor are badly documented, ill studied, cheaply built and therefore not very durable, little valued and likely to have been swept away. Consider the worldly possessions of Richard Churchouse, labourer of Taston whose one-roomed hut in 1592 contained a bed covering, three pairs of sheets and a bolster, a tablecloth, two pots, two kettles, a frying pan, two candlesticks, two platters, a porringer and a saucer, a cover (for the fire probably), a load of wood and a brandiron. The total value of his goods was 18s 8d and compares with those of a Marston yeoman who died in the next year, valued at £386 10s 8d.

The urban poor were even more wretchedly housed than the rural labourers. Henry Acland, the medical superintendent who wrote *A memoir of the Cholera at Oxford in the year 1854* (London 1856) recorded a plan of the houses in which eleven cases of cholera occurred. There were six families all living under one roof. Two had two rooms each, and the remaining four families each had one room. Eight rooms were occupied by twenty-seven persons. There was an open street in front, a passage at the side, a yard thirty-five feet long behind and a privy with a pump removed twenty feet from it. The one condition was of too many people in too small space. Acland sums it up: 'Life in poisoned air'.

A fourth house of surpassing historical interest is Kelmscott Manor. This is in the far west of the county, in the remote flat river plain of the upper Thames, its surrounding fields lined with willows. Here, from 1871–96, William

Morris, socialist, free-thinker, consummate craftsman and the finest designer since the Middle Ages, made his home. Morris described the house in *News from Nowhere*: 'this many gabled old house built by the simple country-folk of the long-past times, regardless of all the turmoil that was going on in the cities and courts ... we wandered from room to room – from the rose-covered porch to the strange and quaint garrets amongst the great timbers of the roof, where of old time the tillers and herdsmen of the manor slept'. May Morris, William's daughter, left the house to Oxford University and it was passed on to the Society of Antiquaries who have restored it closely following Morris' precepts. 'Every change, whatever history it destroyed, left history in its gap and was alive with the spirit of the deeds done midst its fashioning.' The house is of two main phases: a T-shaped plan of *c.*1570 with a late seventeenth-century high north wing. The roofs are slated in diminishing courses, as Morris put it: 'sized down, the smaller towards the top, and the bigger towards the eaves, which gives one the same sort of pleasure in their orderly beauty as a fish's scales or a bird's feathers'. The garden is currently being replanted most imaginatively by the Antiquaries.

William Morris is of key significance in the history of the conservation movement in England. He turned his considerable powers to protest against the harsh and insensitive restoration of churches engendered by ambitious architects and ignorant clerics. 'What I wish for therefore is that an association should be set on foot to keep a watch on old monuments, to protest against all "restoration" that means more than keeping out wind and weather, and by all means, literary and other, to awaken a feeling that our ancient buildings are not mere ecclesiastical toys, but sacred monuments of the nation's growth and hope.' The result was the foundation of the Society for the Protection of Ancient Buildings on 22 March 1877, known familiarly and affectionately as 'Anti Scrape', with Morris as its first Secretary. Kelmscott is full of furnishings, tapestries, embroideries and pictures associated with Morris, his family and circle. It can be visited on Wednesday and Thursday afternoons or by arrangement.

Oxfordshire witnessed several interesting social experiments which tried to provide a civilized and humane standard of housing. Charterville was the first attempt to provide large scale housing with no profit motive. Feargus O'Connor founded the National Land Company in 1845 to establish families from the factory towns on smallholdings where they could support themselves and qualify for a vote. Anyone could subscribe for shares and these gave their holders the chance of acquiring a house and a two-, three- or four-acre plot of land. By the end of October 1847, forty-seven houses had been erected at Minster Lovell, twenty-three two-acre allotments, twelve three-acre and thirty-eight four-acre plots. The ballots attracted people from Newcastle, Huddersfield, Norwich, Birmingham, Brighton, London, Pershore and St Germans. The houses which have survived are of great interest. They were single-storeyed and resemble closely in elevation thousands of Irish farmhouses. The front range has three habitable interconnecting rooms and the rear an outshut with service rooms. Behind is a concrete yard with pigsties. The Chartist National Land Company, despite its Utopian beginnings, was soon entangled in difficulties and was dissolved in 1851. One problem was that the area suffered from an acute water shortage and the plots were too small to obtain a livelihood. Eventually, however, Charterville prospered. It is still worth a visit today. Most of the cottages have been modernized and enlarged. Fifteen have been demolished, infilling has occurred but seventeen of the original cottages have been listed largely through the efforts of Daphne Aylwin, the energetic conservation officer of west Oxfordshire in the 1970s and 1980s.

More recently, a second experiment also took place in west Oxfordshire. Carterton was founded in 1901 when Mr William Carter, heading a firm called Housesteads, purchased Rock Farm, near Brize Norton. This had been bought in 1894 by Mr Thomas Arkell from the Duke of Marlborough. The 140-acre farm was surveyed and divided into plots suitable for smallholdings. Many plots were taken up in these early years by people wishing to make a living off the land by keeping poultry, pigs and growing potatoes for the Oxford market. Its original purpose did not particularly prosper, but after 1901 the Carterton estate grew rapidly as new housing 'homes fit for heroes' was in demand. The construction of R.A.F. Brize Norton in 1937 and its consequential rapid increase in size after World War II boosted the growth of Carterton, which rocketed in population from 6,000 to 12,000 in ten years. Right under the flight path of the aerodrome, one or two of the original houses of Carterton can be found gently rusting away, their single-storeyed low-pitched, corrugated iron roofs reminding one of the Charterville cottages built one hundred years earlier a couple of miles to the east.

III
Fields

War speeds technology, and one of the unexpected benefits accruing from World War I was the use of air photography in archaeology. If photographs could be taken from the air of the western front, producing plans of trench systems and other fortifications, the technique could equally be switched to the mapping of ancient landscapes. R.A.F. vertical air cover was used by P. P. Rhodes in the late 1940s to map field systems on the Berkshire (now Oxfordshire) Downs. There were a number of shortcomings in this early study. Most of the photographs were taken in June. This was too early in the year to show crop marks at their optimum. Also the vegetation was likely to obscure features such as banks and ditches. The same areas under cultivation in the winter would show soil marks. Consequently, Rhodes's maps err on the side of caution as far as areas are concerned. Subsequent work by Julian Richards and Richard Bradley has extended the area known to be covered by the network of field systems. They appear in two ways: in pasture, on areas where arable cultivation has been recent and short-lived, the fields appear as lynchets and downhill banks; where, however, ploughing has been constant over a long period, the flattened banks appear as white marks. On the surface lines of flints and sarsens (hard, weather-resistant, siliceous sandstone blocks found on the surface of the chalk) may indicate clearance lines. A sectioned lynchet at Streatley Warren was found to have such a stony layer when it was excavated in 1949. These lynchets may have started simply as a line of stones picked by early farmers from the surface of the field and dumped at the edge. Gradually, soil washed down the slope would build up against such a line forming a horizontal lynchet. Downhill banks grew more slowly even if defined by some form of fencing or low clearance mounding. The small rectangular blocks of land would suit the use of cross ploughing with ploughs which would do little more than scratch the surface.

There are several largely unsolved problems connected with the prehistoric field systems of the Oxfordshire (formerly Berkshire) Downs. How old are they? What is the significance of their planning? What factors determined their distribution? How long did they remain in use? There is little evidence to shed light on their origin. Occasionally they relate to dated settlement or ritual sites and this is of some use to establish their contemporaneity with them. For instance, some appear to be aligned on round barrows and are thus later than them. Some have been found stratified under the Iron Age ramparts at Rams Hill. Those on the dip slope to the south of Segsbury hill fort can be dated to the first millennium BC. It has also been realized that pottery scatters found on the surface of field systems are connected with manuring. Briefly, the argument is that the broken and discarded shards are thrown from the household onto the nearby middens and then carried out with the manure to fertilize the fields. They show which fields were in use but are of little value in dating the origins of the layout. A shortcoming of the value of the technique is that pottery from different periods degrades at different rates. Bronze Age pottery is not only more likely to erode on the surface: it is more difficult to see than industrially made, virtually indestructible Romano-British pottery. Consequently, a field with masses of Roman pottery may yet have come into existence in the Bronze Age. What is very clear, especially from the Maddle Farm project, which has studied in detail the evidence for field systems, manuring and settlement in the Berkshire Downs just over the county boundary, is that there was extensive agricultural development of this area in the early Roman period c.AD 50–150. The demand for food surpluses must be linked to the rapid growth of population and the emergence of urban centres through the country. Places such as the local *civitas* capitals of Silchester and Cirencester increased the demand for grain. There are similar signs for the intensification of agriculture in the upper Thames Valley.

An analysis of the layout of the fields themselves indicates two distinct types which Bradley and Richards (1978) have described as 'cohesive' and 'aggregate'. By 'cohesive' they mean fields which show a marked gridded regularity. They are based on long straight axes of up to 2.5 km and are found in large blocks, subdivided by access routes, sometimes double-banked trackways, which run through the whole layout. 'Aggregate' systems tend to be smaller and have a piecemeal appearance, suggesting they may have been added one by one as the need arose. Patches of them are found added to large areas of cohesive systems.

When the question of distribution arises, mapping shows that there is a pronounced density on the light chalk soils of the dip slope in the south-west of the county extending into north-west Berkshire. These early farmers tended to avoid the stickier and heavier areas of clay with flints, and while fields are occasionally found on hill tops and at the hill foot, most of the fields are between 150 and 230 metres (450–700 feet) above sea level.

Intriguing blanks in the mapping indicate where no evidence exists for fields either in the form of pottery scatters or earthen banks. In particular, the Lambourn valley where there was a large barrow group (of at least forty-six barrows), was devoid of evidence for cultivation. Bradley and Ellison, the excavators of Rams Hill (a hill fort on the ridge above the Lambourn valley) suggested that prehistoric farmers deliberately avoided disturbing such a ritual landscape. An alternative explanation might be that the Lambourn valley was beyond the limits of intensive cultivation surrounding settlements. Arable farming, with its manuring scatters and lynchet build-up did not spread so far. The Seven Barrows valley may well have been left under grass, used for pasture, but this kind of farming has left no discernible archaeological trace.

One more element within the prehistoric landscape of the Downs needs consideration: the linear earthworks. These are of two kinds: the Grims Ditch and linear ditches. The Grims Ditch is a twelve-mile long bank and ditch which runs in an east-west direction below the ridge of the chalk. At times, it changes direction apparently to avoid pre-existing features such as field systems. Legend linked it with the Devil. When the Devil ran his ploughshare through the soil, to form his ditch within a few hundred yards of Cuckamsley, he found it necessary to clean it. The lump of earth which fell off was Cuckhamsley, a large barrow. The fact that Grims Ditch is only visible from the Vale suggests that it may have defined an upland territory. Since there are relatively few prehistoric fields within the vicinity, this is likely to have been ranching country. The multiple pony burials at Blewburton hill fort certainly suggest that the horse was of considerable importance in this society. The other linear ditches demarcate long strips of downland and run off to the south at right angles to the Ridgeway. They extend four and a half miles down the dip slope. Some appear to cut through pre-existing field boundaries and thus postulate a radical reshaping of the landscape perhaps to accommodate stock farming on a large scale. Both the Grims Ditch and these linear ditches approach, and at times incorporate, barrows in their systems. The use of barrows as alignment points is also found in Anglo-Saxon boundary charters. Breezy walks along these ancient landscape features should enable visitors to test out for themselves the validity of these speculations.

Up to forty years ago, it used to be thought that prehistoric man favoured the high chalk downs of southern and central England as places for settlement. Here were the obvious signs of his activities: the ridgeways where he travelled; the dry, well-drained settlement sites and field systems standing out as earthworks on the chalk hills; the barrows and temples such as Stonehenge and Avebury. It is now realized that this picture was mistaken. Air photography first revealed the rich mesh of sites on the gravels of the upper Thames and, to a lesser extent, the clay Vale of the White Horse. Large-scale archaeological excavation before gravel extraction has confirmed the dense occupation of these lowland areas during the prehistoric and Romano-British periods. The sites were not immediately obvious before owing to the flattening and at times obliterating effects of subsequent farming practice. Very recent work on the upper Thames has shown that alluviation, whereby the rivers bring down waterborne clay, has masked the late prehistoric and subsequent land surfaces on the river flood-plain. This has led archaeologists to misinterpret these as 'blank' areas and to underestimate the number of sites of earlier settlement. In fact they are often better preserved (particularly if they are waterlogged) than those exhibiting surface evidence such as pottery, bones and stones brought up by the plough, which are evidence for destruction.

It is possible to trace the point at which man began to clear the woodland from the landscape by studying the relative amounts of tree pollen from peat and sediments found in wetlands. Obviously when the first pollen from cereals and from weeds of cultivation appear, agriculture has started. It is often accompanied by charcoal, the evidence for clearance by fire. A more dramatic picture of tree clearance has emerged with Lambrick and Moore's excavations (1987) of the gravels around the Drayton Cursus, near Abingdon. Numerous tree-throw pits were discovered with finds from the Neolithic and Beaker periods suggesting that fallen trees had become the temporary focus for domestic activity. The elusive marks of early agricultural activity in the form of Bronze Age ploughmarks have been traced, buried deep under alluvium when the Hamel, Oxford, was excavated. Whole field systems in the Thames valley are also likely to extend back to this time. At Northfield Farm, Long Wittenham were a series of trackways and twelve enclosures ranging in size from c.55m (180ft) x 30m (98ft) to 125m (410ft) x 70m (230ft) and covering six hectares. Entrances gave access from one enclosure to another and several contained wells. Their size was comparable to the so-called 'Celtic' fields found on the Downs.

As one would expect, the evidence for ancient fields increases in volume in the subsequent periods, the Iron Age and the Roman. Lambrick found Iron-Age field boundaries on the northern edge of the county at Rollright, and the dense linear distribution of pits on the Thames gravels at Gravelly Guy is probably to be explained by its abutting a field boundary. Fence lines have also been found in these gravel sites such as at Beard Mill and Gravelly Guy. A number of mid Iron-Age sites like Mount Farm and Appleford have produced ditched field systems which then go on being used in the Roman period. Lambrick considers that there was a major period of land division between *c*.100 BC and AD 200 evident all over the upper Thames Valley when trackways, paddocks and arable fields were laid out in orderly fashion. To take just one example: at Farmoor a huge reservoir has been created in the twentieth century to supply Oxford's needs for water. In advance of its construction, an excavation was carried out which showed that the gravel terrace next to the Thames flood-plain was divided up into fields in the Roman period. They consisted of small rectangular enclosures lining a droveway and stopped short of the flood-plain. The droveway turned to run along the edge of the flood-plain. The small fields contained pits and wells and there appeared to be gateways between one or two of the small fields. The basic environment was grassland and the field boundaries were probably hedged. The evidence for thorny hedges was the presence of prickles and scales and leaf abscission pads together with beetles which attack living trees or shrubs. Altogether, the Farmoor fields seem to have been used for the careful control of pasture by moving the animals between them. This would allow for the rapid regrowth of grass when not in use. A dump of hay was found in one of the pits within these enclosures. A further use of these flood-plain fields could have been hay meadows. A scythe blade 1.40m (4½ft) long was found which was doubtless used for mowing hay. Some of the small ditched gardens and paddocks near the houses at Farmoor may well have been used for the cultivation of vegetables and fruit. The leaves and shoots of box (*buxus sempervirens*) were retrieved; box would have made a good hedging plant and Pliny describes its use for ornamental hedges.

At Drayton, further to the east and a mile south of Abingdon, stratified within the alluvium was what has been claimed to be the first fully intact physical evidence for Roman fields in the Thames Valley. The gravel surface was scored with cross-ploughed marks made by ards (a form of primitive wooden plough); over this was 0.1m of ploughsoil containing pottery from manure. The field system was delimited by Roman ditches acting as boundaries and there was a boundary running parallel to the flood-plain. The siting of the fields here is of great significance. It indicates that land was so scarce at this time that ploughing was not confined to the gravelly dry spots but extended out into the flood-plain where it must have suffered from flooding from time to time. Possible Roman field systems showing some of the signs of centuriation have been photographed from the air south of the Roman town of Alchester.

An indication of scarcity of land and the pressure of population, probably in the late Saxon period, is seen in the stepped lynchets still existing at Blewburton Hill and at other places along the scarp slope of the Downs as, for instance, at about a mile to the east of Uffington White Horse. Here the steepness of the slope of the chalkcombe was too testing for oxen to plough up and down and so instead, they ploughed along the contour, the mould-board plough biting deep into the slope on the upper side and building the soil up and out in the form of a step on the lower side. We don't know the date of these lynchets but such features (Old English *hlinc*) figure in Anglo-Saxon boundary charters such as those delimiting estates at Uffington and Coleshill. According to Rackham, who has mapped a concentration of Anglo-Saxon terms referring to open fields, the Uffington region may have been the seat of the open field system which spread out to central and southern England. Such terms were '*Gore*' (a triangle in an open field), '*furh*' (a boundary furrow), '*acre*' and '*heafod*' (headland). They make up fourteen per cent of the boundary terms mentioned in the charters of this area.

Most of the charters date from 930–85 but there are a few which come from the second half of the previous century.

One of the most familiar sights to be seen out of the window of a railway carriage crossing the Midland counties are the grass-grown corrugations of so called 'ridge and furrow'. Air photography has confirmed that much of Oxfordshire was and still is covered with these remains of earlier cultivation systems. The only areas virtually devoid of it are the areas of extensive woodland such as the Wychwood district, parts of the Oxford Heights, the Chiltern dip slope and the downland tracts of the Berkshire Downs. Despite the fact that the Cotswold region of Oxfordshire had the highest density of plough teams, ridge and furrow is practically absent on these limestone hills, but it does turn up in excavation in some unlikely places, such as the fields bordering the Thames between Godstow and Medley, and has been noticed in section where the river has eroded the flood bank.

When the ridge and furrow is examined in detail, as Sutton has done at Water Eaton, the ridges are found bunched together in furlongs which vary considerably in length; above 350 yards (330m) is unusual, 500 yards (460m) are exceptional in length and below 100 yards (90m) is considered short. Widths are normally between 7 (6m) and 13 (11m) yards. An acre, of course, is 22 (18m) x 220 (210m) yards. The ridges tend to be higher and wider on heavy low-lying land such as on the Oxford clay round Water Eaton and across the Cherwell at Islip and Hampton Poyle. It is not uncommon to find two adjacent ridges occurring in which each is only half the width of its neighbours which could be the result of a division of a tenement. Seen from the ground it has often been remarked that the ridges and furrows swing away in a reversed S shape; this has been explained by the speculation that an eight-ox team would need a wider turning and that the reversed S was precisely that. What is less uncertain is that the large banks at the foot of the furlong-blocks known as headlands were built up over the centuries by earth being dropped off scraped from the turning plough. It is interesting to note that the ridge and furrow bordering the Thames mentioned in the last paragraph has no headland. In this case flood water fell straight into the river.

The open fields are so radically different from earlier field systems that they pose a number of difficult questions; why and when did farmers start using them? How did they work? They must have had some advantages to survive nearly a thousand years. Why were they totally abandoned in most places after the middle of the nineteenth century? One thing seems certain: their effective cultivation required communal effort; clearance from waste or regenerated woodland would have been eased by men working together to fell and clear the stumps of trees. It would have been natural to divide up patches of land so cleared. Partible inheritance may also have accounted for the mosaics of separate strips which the furlong-blocks were divided into. The ploughing again demanded co-operation both in assembling the eight-ox plough teams and in providing the labour to direct them. The open field made the best use of scarce grazing and reduced the necessity to maintain fences. It went along with the 'balling' of settlements, the process whereby men left dispersed single farms and hamlets and came to live in nucleated villages. Here the complex regulations of open-field agriculture could more easily be applied. From the lord's point of view the whole set up was more controllable: with open fields came more powerful lordship; barons, knights and churchmen together gripped the land and its inhabitants.

Ridge and furrow is now well preserved and easily visible only in grassland which ceased to be ploughed as a result of population decline in the later Middle Ages, as described in the last chapter. With a changeover from arable to stock raising and in particular to large-scale sheep farming, sizeable chunks of arable, previously run by open field custom, went out of cultivation. Hedged enclosures known in the north of the county as 'Grounds' replaced the open fields in some areas. In others the multiplicity of small strips characteristic of the open fields, and with them the continued making of ridge and furrow, remained in a medieval state in Oxford-shire until the middle of the seventeenth century. Michael Havinden, who has studied the period 1580–1730, reckons that the landscape was still almost entirely unenclosed before the Civil War.

Most studies of Oxfordshire's medieval and post-medieval farming systems have concentrated on such matters as labour services, crop yields, the decline of demesne farming, the changeover from arable to stock raising, from corn to wool. I shall suggest a different approach to supplement these. During the last forty years, under the influence of local historians such as William Hoskins and tutors working for the Workers Educational Association and University depart-ments of Adult Education, there has been a great flowering of interest in field systems. They have been mapped *in extenso* by David Hall in neighbouring Northamptonshire, while the Oxfordshire Federation of Women's Institutes has produced a series of remarkable field name parish maps for Oxford-shire which can be studied in the Centre for Oxfordshire Studies.

This study of field names has proved a rich quarry for interpreting the landscape. Town dwellers may be surprised to know that every single piece of land under cultivation has been given a name or a succession of names of its own. These names are more frequently used in speech than in writing and consequently change more frequently than place names. Difficulties arise when it is attempted to attach an old field name to a piece of land. Boundary changes and major rearrangements following the enclosure of the open fields and the recent grubbing out of hedges to further the consolidation of holdings have complicated the matter. Again, with changes of ownership there have been random and inexplicable changes of name. Despite these problems field names provide a window into the appearance of past landscapes and a rare insight into the minds of those who came into contact with the fields on a daily basis. We know that Oxfordshire had many examples of two- and three-field systems. At Cuxham, for instance, the three-field system functioned during the period 1318–50 with roughly equal acreages of winter and spring-sown crops.

The open fields all over the county were divided into a series of smaller areas known as 'furlongs' or shots and these were subdivided into a multiplicity of strips or plots held by individual tenants. The furlong-blocks were each named. Their shape sometimes provided the reason. Lanket (Waterperry) means a long narrow block of land, similarly Mantle Acre strings (in Steeple Aston) refers to a long, narrow piece. The ridges or balks in a single furlong are referred to as the nine stitches (Denton). The shape of the land (and the state of mind of the farmer) is summed up by the use of the word 'Erseputtes' (Stratton Andley) which refers to a rounded hill. The twin hills above Dorchester-on-Thames are similarly and vulgarly called Mother Dunche's Buttocks. It is difficult to see where the rounded hill was at low-lying Weston-on-the-Green referred to as Broadarse Furlong, but here it may simply have been the breadth rather than the height.

The intimate knowledge of the farmer for every acre abounds. His none too friendly feeling for the land is similarly evoked. Hence Hungry Hill (Shirburn), Greedy Guts, Grub Hill (Pyrton), Spiteful Yards, Stoney Close, Sullen Lands (Ipsden). These expressions recall the difficulty of arable farming on the thin soils of the lower slopes below the Chilterns. Once out in the clay vale the names remind us of the sheer intractability of the land. Honeycut land (Wolvercote) is 'a sticky piece of land'. The frequent use of catsbrain (e.g. Catsbrain Hill, South Stoke) was a vivid reference to the appearance of a coarse soil consisting of rough clay mixed with stones (Shirburn and elsewhere). Clay is also involved in clete furlong (Thame) and Great Clink and Clingefurlonge (Pyrton) is used of sticky land. The colours of soil are noted. There are fourteen references to Blakeland in the county. This is of interest to archaeologists because it often indicates the organic soil of occupation material of some former human settlement. Red Lane in Chinnor means 'Red land'. Redsand and Blackesand (Stratton Andley) show contrasting soil colours. Clearance and cultivation techniques were daily tasks taken for granted, but oblique references are sometimes found in field names. The question of assarting or clearance from the forest and waste will be considered in more detail in the next chapter. Land newly taken into cultivation was called Little and Great Breach at Tiddington with Albury. Burnt Bake in Pyrton refers to the breaking in process. Bake means 'to chop up with a mattock the rough surface of land to be reclaimed afterwards burning the parings'. At the head of the furlong-block where the oxen turned we find Sideland (North Aston). Lob Farm in Great Haseley means 'a lump, a large amount, a wide extent or surface'. The mosaic of strips is recalled in Butts Furlong, a strip of ground abutting onto a boundary often at right angles to other ridges in the field. The land on the edge of arable or pasture was known as Freeboard (Nettlebed). Such a jigsaw of rights led to numerous disputes. Flitenlande in Hampton Gay and Poyle means contested land. Dispute Furlong, found c.1200, at Thomley means what it says. One of the likely causes for disputes arose out of stock sharing limited land for grazing. Lain land was periodically allowed to lie fallow by being sown in regular laines or divisions. It is found in South Navington and Waterstock and elsewhere. Lammas (1 August) was the common time when stock were allowed into the open field to feed on the stubble.

It might be thought from this matter-of-fact acceptance of the hardships of the Oxfordshire farmers' life, implied in field names referring to the soil, that they would be blind to the rich variety of plants and animals which shared their lives. In fact, the field names referring to crops are outnumbered by those referring to wild plants and trees of all kinds. Nevertheless, manorial accounts show the overwhelming importance of wheat (bread corn) and barley (drink corn). The statistics available from a comparative study of the manors of Adderbury (New College), Cuxham (Merton College) and Witney (Bishop of Winchester) show very high yield ratios for wheat at Cuxham. Witney, an area of new assarting, achieved lower yields than either Adderbury or Cuxham. Cereal crops appear but rarely in the field names: wheat in

Whatcombe (wheat valley), Watlington and Wheatley (the clearing where wheat is grown) are examples. Barley appears at Barley Hill (North Stoke) and Rye (in Ryecote Cottage, Great Haseley).

Leguminous crops were numerous; Piss Furlong (Peas furlong, Warborough), Peascroft (Goring), Pishill (hill where peas grow), Beanlands (Finmere), Beneland (Stoke Talmerge). They helped by their provision of vegetable protein to build up the population in the twelfth–thirteenth centuries. Other crops connected with textiles were grown in smaller plots; Linton (flax enclosure) is found at Eynsham. Flex Gardens is flax enclosure at Newington. Hakelying Croft at Headington means the combing of flax which must have required retting in ponds before this process was carried out. Among dyeing plants was woad; hence, Wadbreche, 'newly cultivated land where woad is grown' and Valle de Wadyne – Woad Valley (Clifton Hampden). Saffron, a crocus-like plant which provides a golden dye, is found as a field name at Ewelme and Hethe.

More numerous and more scattered were references to plants which were not primarily food plants but which may well have had a subsidiary use as herbs or simples. The wheat fields of Checkendon in spring/summer were bright with chess (an old name for a kind of grass *Bromus Secalinus*) which grows as a weed among wheat. Cockle furlong in Drayton St Leonard referred to the corn cockle, a poisonous weed. Other flowers were Balsam (Tetsworth), the yellow flowered *Impatiens Noli-tangere*, the Blewbottle (until the sixteenth century the dialect form of the cornflower) found at Rotherfield Greys, the Sweetingal (Fencot) refers to the bog myrtle, while Nepfield (Benson) is a dialect name for catmint (*Nepeta Cataria*). Dill Ground must have been infested with vetch or tares (Begbroke). There are several plants which have dialect names, but are not definitely identified, or where the name refers to more than one. Such is the Hen and Chickens (Clifton Hampden) and Applepie puddle (Nuffield) and the Rattles (Nuffield) which simply means a plant whose seeds rattle. Spiers Hill Warborough refers to coarse tall

plants but doesn't say which. Ivory furlong (Benson) probably refers to ivy. Manthorn is an unknown plant. A number
of field names refer to 'golds' or golden and this has been
interpreted as mangolds. Guldeforlong (Checkendon) Gold-
enham, the golden meadow (Souldern), Gilden or Gildon
(Henley-on-Thames) 'the golden valley', but I question
whether perhaps another golden flower such as buttercups or
dandelions is meant.

When trees are mentioned singly it seems that they are
events in the largely cleared landscape. Such is Eldern Hill
(Warborough) and Eldenstubbe (elder stub) valley. Fringford
had a Walnut Tree Close, Noke recorded a single oak tree,
Barkecrofte again was a singleton (in Cassington). Groups or
whole valleys of trees were found at Bix (Boxwood): also
Boxmoor Wood (Ipsden) and at Bokendene (Shirburn), the
valley where beech trees grow. Holly was found at Hulvere-
scroft (Shiplake), ozier beds at Godington, but the most
frequent trees mentioned as field names are the various
varieties of thorns, presumably because of the ease with
which they are transplanted to become hedges. There is a
Thornbury – thorn tree hill in Binsey, a Gatethorn – or goat
thorn in Bicester, at Souldern 'a thorn bush in a gulley' and a
Haggethorn – the hawthorn at Bicester. Another tree favour-
ing the more watery places in the county was the willow
found under the guise of a number of dialect names: Wyrgs
path is the name at Iffley, withy eyot means willow pool islet
at Checkendon. Odd dialect forms are found for the ash; 'kit
keys' is the version at Shiplake and the spindle tree is Prick
wood or Prick timber at Swyncombe.

Another group of field names reminds us that the care of
domesticated animals was one of the farmer's main concerns.
Sheep, cattle, pigs, goats, horses all provide subjects for field
names. Oxenemed was the meadow of the oxen (Combe),
Rotherfield was 'open land where cattle graze'. Diseased
cows were buried out in the fields; cowberryes (Watlington)
was one such site. Pigs must have been frequently seen in the
woods; Swyncomber means 'pig valley'. Swinhege is 'pig
hedge' (Ambrosden) and Swinford the fording place of the

river Thames crossed by pigs. Lusemore (Wretchwick) was a pigsty. Sheep needed to be washed and dipped to rid them of infestation. Hence, Shiplake, the stream where sheep are washed and the Dipping Place (Forest Hill). The tenants of Cuxham Manor in the fourteenth century ploughed wholly with horses, but it was customary in the demesne land and in other areas to have mixed teams of oxen and horses. Horses were kept separately as is recorded in Horsgarstone, horse paddock in Chinnor, Studley, pasture for horses in Horton-cum-Studley and Stadhampton; a river meadow where horses are kept. Goats also required shelter as Gatecote (Thomley) recalls. Rabbits were semi-domesticated in specially built warrens. Conygree (Cottisford) and Clapperwood Hill, Henley mean rabbit burrows.

It is now possible to walk a whole day in the Oxfordshire countryside and not notice a single wild animal. They were a good deal more evident in the early landscapes if the field names are anything to go by. Wildcats figure in Catwell Field (Temple Cowley). Frogs and toads were seen crossing tracks as in Padlane and Froglane in Denton, and several other places. Brookhole recorded a badger set in Combe. Foxley Farm (Eynsham) and Foxtoneshull, Kirtlington, and a single reference to a wolf in Hampton Gay, show that there was still a need for herdsmen prepared to defend their flocks from carnivores.

Turning to the skies, recent attempts have been made in the Chilterns to restore the red kite. They were certainly there in the Middle Ages. Gledmoreshull derives from Old English *gleda* – kite (Mapledurham). Other birds of prey were bustard (North Alton), bittern (Eye and Dunsden) and hawks (Hawkerslinche in South Stoke). Cranemeresterte was a strip of land by a pool frequented by cranes in Kirtlington. Herons were commemorated in Rayford Lane in Steeple Barton. Corble Farm was a clearing in the raven wood (Piddington). Crowmarsh speaks for itself: it was listed under the lands of Walter Gifford in Domesday Book – hence the additional feudal element. Some birds were recorded but not identified, hence Fowlthorn in Hampton Poyle, which comes from Old

English '*fugol*', a wild bird. Trumpets meadow in Eynsham takes its name from a Trumpeter, a local name for an unknown bird. The woodpecker flew about a pond at Finmere while sparrows (dialect Pynnock) fluttered round the mill at Bletchington. The dialect name of Chattopie for magpie is found at Combe, while Larkehill gave its name to this now unlovely suburb of Oxford. The pheasant was an imported alien, but it left its name in Fesantes halle (Henley-on-Thames).

Goosegirls occur frequently in fairy tales. Of the domesticated birds, geese figure prominently among field names. There was a goose common fair held every Michaelmas at Chalgrove. Gossway (Kirtlington) was a goose enclosure. The slightly higher land at Goosey was known as 'Goose Island'. Pigeons were housed near Culverhouse furlong (Middleton Stoney) and doubtless were a grain-eating pest at Culver buttes, Islip.

During the first sixty years of this period, 1580–1640, Oxfordshire's farmers enjoyed a remarkable period of prosperity. It was an era of high prices and their wealth increased by sixty-seven per cent. Judging from inventories and the physical evidence of the houses themselves, farmers were in a good financial position to enlarge their dwellings and to increase their comforts. The second half of the seventeenth century was not so prosperous as prices of wool and grain either diminished or remained level. These fluctuations are also reflected in the rise and fall of activity in the land market. Sales burgeoned in the prosperous years. There was a reduction in the 1620s, an almost total cessation in the Civil War years, followed by increased sales as the defeated Royalists struggled to pay their fines and Crown and Episcopal land was sold off. Much was returned to their original owners after the Restoration of Charles II.

The open field system in our county showed considerable powers of self-renewal. Among the improvements which prolonged it was the introduction of leguminous clovers, especially sainfoin, grown on specially fenced portions of the fields. Better hay was thus produced contributing to the fertility of the soil by means of the nitrogen-fixing nodules in the roots. This in turn encouraged a dramatic rise in the numbers of livestock with corresponding increase in manure production. As this was spread on the land it encouraged the growing of wheat which increased at the expense of barley. The Chiltern farmers were already feeling the pull of the London food market by the end of the sixteenth century. They sent their animals to be fattened in the fields round the metropolis. Smithfield market was stocked with Oxfordshire beef and mutton.

There were also a number of technical improvements which enabled open field farmers to ward off the drastic effects of enclosure for another century or so. Many farmers dug chalk from small pits and spread it on the land. There are a number of references to lime kilns on the Cotswolds and the Chilterns during the late seventeenth century. The four-wheeled wagon was also introduced in this period and gradually supplanted the two-wheeled cart which figures in so many medieval manuscripts. There seems to be a connection between the slow introduction of such wagons in the vales, where there was little stone to improve the roads, a necessary objective owing to their greater weight, and the slower introduction of enclosure.

Enclosure, however, did come to Oxfordshire and rapidly gained momentum in the period 1730–1850. It radically altered the landscape by diminishing the area of waste, heath and common, substituting a hedged pattern of neat, enclosed fields and encouraging the planting of hedgerow trees and copses in odd corners. A good idea of the landscape in process of enclosure can be gained from looking at the new Oxfordshire parts of Berkshire as depicted in Rocque's map of 1761. Its social effects were to break down the old communal ties which had bound peasant cultivators, yeoman farmers and gentry landlords together. It created a rural proletariat: the landless labourers who were to pose such a problem for Poor Law administrators in the nineteenth century and whose lives are so vividly documented in Flora Thompson's *Lark Rise to Candleford*.

One of the features of the modern English landscape most under stress or threat of destruction are the unimproved meadows. In Great Britain as a whole, the Nature Conservancy Council considers it likely that ninety-five per cent of all old meadows which still remained in 1949 have in the last forty-five years been 'improved'; that is to say been ploughed, drained, sprayed, fertilized and thus developed; only three per cent have remained completely undamaged. Traditionally, these old meadows were of two types: hay meadow where the grass (and other flowering herbs) was allowed to grow, seed and then be cut for hay and were then opened up for grazing after the hay was mown. The second type were grazing pastures where the grass was not necessarily of poorer quality but was floristically impoverished because it was thus made available for grazing throughout the year.

Oxfordshire still has a few examples of both kinds of grasslands bordering the river Thames. Motorists speeding along the Oxford by-pass to the north-west of the city in June or July can see stretching away into a misty distance meadowland dotted with yellow, white and purple flowers. These are the Yarnton Meads, a group of ancient Anglo-Saxon hay meadows, including Oxey mead (sixty-six acres), West mead (seventy-five acres), on the north bank of the river, and Pixey Mead, which lies between the main stream of the Thames and Wolvercote Mill. Some fifty acres in the east part was included in the Yarnton's lot meadows; the west part belonged to Wytham parish, and the northern part was owned by Godstow Abbey in the Middle Ages and subsequently came into the hands of the Dukes of Marlborough.

These lot meadows were shared by the riverside parishes of Yarnton, Begbroke and Wytham. Good quality hay was a fundamental necessity to the medieval farming economy. It was used to feed the eight-ox plough teams of oxen which needed to be well fed to have the stamina to plough the heavy clay land. Those fed only on straw or other fodder collected from commons, woods and wastes would not have sufficient nutrition to perform these heavy ploughing tasks.

Great care was taken to ensure an even distribution of the

good and not so good meadowland. At Yarnton up until 1978, on successive Mondays following the feast of St Peter and St Paul (29 June), a small group of farmers under the direction of the meadsmen could be seen walking the meadows of Oxey, West Mead and Pixey. The fields were divided into thirteen lots and these were represented by thirteen cherry wood balls each inscribed with the name of a lot. Nine belonged to Yarnton and four to Begbroke. The shots were divided into thirteen strips; the strips and the shots were marked at their ends by pegs or stones. The names on the balls go back to farmers who were there in the thirteenth century. The allotments were made (usually by a lady present) by drawing one of the balls out of a bag at the head of each strip. The owner would then carve his initials in the turf on the strip and so the process would go on until the whole shot was allotted. Some lots were divided into halves or quarters.

The methods used in the hay harvest were immemorial. An essential prerequisite was to level the surface of the hay meadow. Harrows including those made from bushes and rollers were used to level rutting by cattle, mole hills and even earthworm casts. The time chosen was crucial; it varied from mid June to early August when the saccharine juices of every species of grass, but especially the Poa (meadow grass) and Festuca (fescue), are in greatest abundance. Accomplished mowers could scythe an acre a day. The mowers were followed into the fields by other men, women and children who spread the swathes (rows of cut hay). In fine weather the drying grass would be shaken out or 'tedded' once or twice in the course of the day. Thus the grasses would be cured as speedily as possible to retain the greenness (the nutritional quality) as much as possible. The drying grasses were raked into long narrow rows (called wind rows) and afterwards pitchforked into small 'cocklets' or 'footcocks'. Care was taken not to open the cocks while the dew was about. Rakes were used to ensure that every scrap of hay was picked up and carried to the stack or rick. These were ideally square in shape with sides that sloped in towards the bottom to prevent water flowing down from the thatched roof. Sometimes stacks were built on beams supported by stone or iron staddles to keep them dry. Wet hay might always combust. At times, stacks were opened in the winter to find that the outside was a mere crust and inside was a fire blackened void.

The long block of land lying to the south of Yarnton Meads, in effect an island, is known as Port Meadow. This pasture, as George Lambrick and Mark Robinson have pointed out, has been grazed by the animals of successive societies since the middle Iron Age. It was also a perquisite of the Freemen of Oxford since the founding of the city in the late ninth century AD. In 1086 Domesday Book recorded that 'all the burgesses of Oxford have pasture in common outside the wall which renders 6s and 8d'. It has also been the subject of 'intercommoning' from the farmers of Wolvercote and Binsey. Port Meadow, however, bears the marks of continuous use by men since the Bronze Age. When seen from the air, particularly in a drought summer such as that of 1976, the surface was seen to be intersected by dark curving bands; these were the earlier channels of the braided Thames.

Also showing up vividly as green circles in the grass covered by yellow buttercups were the ditches and the flattened remains of Bronze-Age barrows. Further straight green lines were recognized as the ditched fields and paddocks of Iron-Age farmsteads. The lowest-lying areas between the former shelving gravel islands and shallows of Port Meadow have been covered with a thick belt of alluvium, fine particled clay originating on the uplands to the west. It has been brought down in solution by the river in flood and spread year by year, burying the old surface and masking features like barrows and ditches dug into it. It is the evidence for widespread forest clearance and consequent run-off during the extension of arable farming in the early Iron-Age and Roman period.

Port Meadow today during the summer season is an immensity of grass bounded by the smooth and shining Thames waters, only rippled by the oars of rowers. In the far distance as seen from the towpath are the towers and spires of the university town. Dotted over the herbage are cattle, horses, geese, ducks and water fowl. There are now signs of overgrazing, particularly in the winter, but formerly steps were taken to limit the amount of grazing by stinting according to a Freeman's rank and his ability to keep his animals off the pasture in winter. The Mayor of Oxford had the right to pasture eight beasts, the stint allotted to the Aldermen was six beasts and so on past the Councillors (two beasts) to the ordinary Freemen (one beast each). By 1680, however, this regulation seems to have been abandoned and has not been reintroduced. The result is that during the winter flooding areas became poached or cut up by animals' hooves and turned into grassless mud. Port Meadow has been used for purposes other than grazing. It was the scene of horse racing from the seventeenth to the eighteenth centuries. Zacharias Conrad von Uffenbach described the scene in 1710:

> we took a boat up the Thames which flows past the fields in which the races were held ... it is much more suited for a race course than the one at Epsom though it is somewhat marshy. Many booths had been set up where beer was sold, each of which had its sign, a hat, a glove and suchlike ... the horses which were to run were six in number and had to race twice round the whole course, five English miles which took inside ten minutes.

The Duke of Marlborough's course can still be traced together with the depressions in the gravel left by illicit gravel diggers. When the southern or lower end of Port Meadow floods and freezes skating is a popular winter diversion. The northern part of the meadow was an airfield during World War I. There is a memorial to two airmen killed in one of the first crashes of powered aircraft on Godstow bridge. In recent times, the City operated a rubbish dump on a strip of land to the east and the silence of the meadow was shattered by the noise of hundreds of lorries crossing the land every week to the tip.

Over sixty years of botanical research into Pixey Mead and Port Meadow, begun by H. Baker and comprehensively

revised by Alison McDonald, has established that the differential use of the two areas has resulted in remarkably
different plant cover. The old hay meadow has favoured the
growth of plants which flower and set their seed before the
hay is cut in June or which manage to reproduce themselves
vegetatively. These plants, which have been listed by Alison
McDonald, include herbs such as Yellow Rattle, Ragged
Robin, Cowslip and the Green Winged Orchid, which flower
before the surrounding vegetation overtops them, and herbs
such as Meadow Vetchling and Tufted Vetch. A number of
the plants put forth flowering stems which grow above the
mass of vegetation. Their names are significant: Meadow
Foxtail, Meadow Brome, Meadow Sweet, Meadow Rue; also
Oat Grass, Great Burnet, Devil's Bit Scabious. These plants
cannot survive heavy grazing and thus are absent from Port
Meadow and Wolvercote Common.

When Baker did his survey of alluvial meadows in 1937 he
found that of ninety-five species occurring only thirty were
common to both the hay meadows and Port Meadow.
Thirty-nine species occurred in the meads only and twenty-
six on Port Meadow only. Since then, the different regimes
such as drainage caused by the building of the footings for
the Oxford Western By-pass in 1958 and the filling up of
ditches following dumping of waste have caused changes in
the relative numbers of species. Over-grazing because of lack
of regulation has led to the increasing dominance of unpalat-
able but robust species such as thistles and ragwort. The
latter, which is toxic to cattle, has now been eliminated from
the southern end but is strongly resistant to attempts to
remove it.

The city is also surrounded to the south and east by further
meadows, two of which are in the possession of Christchurch
and Magdalen Colleges. Christchurch Meadow was partly
the gift of Elisabeth Montacute (whose tomb is in the
cathedral) to the canons of St Frideswide's Priory to maintain
a chantry. The meadow was handed on to Wolsey's college
and by the seventeenth century had been laid out in tree-lined
walks. These were removed in the Civil War to make room

for fortifications. There were 'several bulwarks upon it, and the Rivers Cherwell and Thames were by his Majesties souldiers turned in upon it and lay all over it'. Dean Fell's rebuilding programme provided stone and rubble to create an east-west causewayed walk over the floodable land. This was known as the White Walk, later corrupted to the Wide and then the Broad Walk. Great elms lined this and Dean Liddell, the father of the little girl for whom Lewis Carroll wrote *Alice in Wonderland*, planted a poplar avenue to connect with the Thames. Thomas Sharp, town planner in 1948, argued for an inner relief road to be called 'Merton Mall', which would have run across the meadow along the line of the Broad Walk. Vigorously conserving Oxford opinions dished this outrageous plan and the City Council first built the Donnington Bridge and finally opted for the ring road which now encircles the historic city at an acceptable distance.

Two of the meadows to the east of the city are on the flood-plain of the Cherwell. They were named after two of Oxford's most celebrated coaching inns, the Angel in the High Street (on the site of T. G. Jackson's Examination Schools) and the Greyhound on the corner of High Street and Longwall Street. They leased the meadows from Magdalen College to provide hay for horses and thus gave them their names.

Just as the cultivation of open field villages required co-operation between groups of farmers, so there is evidence for mutual self help between villages in 'intercommoning'. This was where two or more settlements shared the products of land not under cultivation. Steve Ford, looking at parts of the Warwickshire Avon, demonstrated a pattern of linked settlements which shared meadow, pasture and woodland. In 1984, Beryl Schumer found there were examples of the same kind of intercommoning working in and around Wychwood Forest. Eynsham, for instance, claimed common of pasture on Spelsbury at least until it was renounced in 1306. The Bloxham highlands were virtually treeless and their lack of woodland was compensated for by the connection to Bloxham Manor of two woodland areas in Wychwood Forest. Bloxham Wood is now represented by Kings Wood and Kings Wood Farm and is part of Woodstock Manor. The same principle links Charlbury to the hundred of Banbury despite their being fifteen miles apart. It again implies a shortage of woodland around Banbury as early as the seventh and eighth centuries. The farmers round Banbury had to walk to the nearest bounds of Wychwood Forest for their woodland swine pasture. Another area where woodland rights were shared was the Chilterns. Cuxham, a property of Merton College, sent its herds of pigs to another college farm at Ipsden; here they could graze on the mast of the Chiltern beechwoods while timber was also available to the Cuxham farmers. A third area where intercommoning is found is the Cherwell Valley. Here at North Aston the hay was shared between the men of Aston and Duns Tew. A lot system similar to that which operated at Yarnton is found; names such as Crown, Millbrand and Snipe were used to allocate strips of meadow. Strict regulation ensured that the agreed timing and the stock numbers were adhered to. The animals were allowed onto the fields only after Lammas; each yardland was limited to three cows per yardland and a similar number of horses on the horse common.

Such movements of beasts cannot have been easy in a regulated and well-filled landscape. Transhumance, if that is what it was, probably dates back to an earlier phase of agriculture when settlements were farther apart and when there was more room for movement. It has even been suggested that there was nomadism in the upper Thames Valley in the early Saxon period. Sturdy noticed that the ancient estates belonging to St Frideswide's, the mother church of Oxford, were widely scattered. Summer grazing for cattle and woodland feeding for pigs were found on the lowland estates of Binsey, Cowley and Cutteslowe whereas upland sheep pastures were found near Tackley. He postulates transhumant farmers moving from place to place with their flocks and herds. This is hard to believe given the density of known settlements in the preceding Romano-British period, but it is likely in the Early to Mid Saxon period that at this time arable was a comparatively minor and shifting element in a primarily pastoral landscape.

Another line of evidence leading to similar conclusions is parish boundaries. In many cases these followed the same lines as earlier pre-Christian estate bounds. Cumnor and Eaton each have long sinuous curves which snake out to enclose valuable pieces of meadow. Wootton, a 'land-locked' parish, had a meadow outlier by the Thames near the present site of Donnington Bridge and the road linking them was already known by the tenth century as the 'Hig Weg' or 'Hay-way'.

The traditional image of the English village is a huddle of houses grouped round the church, the public house and the village green. In fact the village green was not nearly so ubiquitous. The only general survey of greens (by Stamp and Hoskins in 1963) listed forty-two extant greens in Oxfordshire. To this number must be added a dozen from the part of Berkshire absorbed in 1972. If, however, we consult maps from the mid eighteenth century it is evident that a large number have been lost in the last 200 years. Jeffrey's map of 1768, the first of which is of large enough scale to display details of village topography, shows forty more greens which have disappeared, and there are another twenty or so which were then lying next to larger commons. A good example of a lost green is that at Weston-on-the-Green. Here, all the houses lie exclusively on the western side of the main Oxford-Brackley road, the old A43. Jeffrey's map shows a long wedge-shaped green running the entire length of the village on the east side. This had already been divided up into four closes by the time that Davis drew his map of the county in 1797.

To understand the functions of these greens the example of Marsh Baldon, a few miles south-east of Oxford, may be taken. Around the largely rectangular area of twenty-four acres, practically all the houses in the village bordering the green face onto it; only the church and manor house lie away from the green, possibly because they were both late-comers. Formerly, all the inhabitants of Marsh Baldon had the right to graze horses, cows and sheep upon the green. 'The custom was to inclose it for hay from Lady Day to Whitsun Eve and then throw it open for horses according to every tenant's yardlands ... from about Lammas cows without limit could be turned out to feed with the horses and at St Andrews tide it became common for sheep. When the hay crop was growing the green was inclosed with mounds ... it is still gated' (Victoria County History, *Oxfordshire* V, 30). A corner is still used for fairs and traditionally games are played on the green. This is where the maypole would be set.

This does not explain the origin of greens. The deliberate placing of houses around the green, as has happened at Marsh Baldon, certainly suggests that some advantage was in mind when the plan form was adopted. The central green could act as a stockade within which to drive animals in times of trouble. But there must have been other reasons since many greens show signs of having been added at a late stage and to the outer margins of villages. At times, greens were even created over the ridge and furrow furlongs of the open fields. Other villages had their house frontages set back far enough to permit a grass space where the village street moved when it thought fit. Even with greatly increased traffic these settlements have broad grass verges, useful rough grazing for tethered animals; such is Standlake, a long village with what amounts to a linear green along its street. Other, more dispersed villages have several 'ends' (or outlying hamlets), but here the houses lay scattered along the green rather than the green being situated among the houses.

Village greens were, and are the cause for disputes. Returning to Marsh Baldon once more, a local farmer by the name of Richard Clinkard sent fifty-five pigs down from Toot Baldon with a keeper in 1763 to Marsh Baldon and they were immediately impounded by the outraged villagers. The gentry also quarrelled over the green. Yateman, the impropriator of the parsonage, had a bridge made onto it to enable his carts to pass over it. The lady of the manor, Mrs

Lane, retaliated by stopping up the trackway with pales. When he drove his carriage through the green in front of his gates, she ordered a trench to be dug in the green before his gates. He then put planks over the trench, but she had elm trees planted in strategic positions. By the present century it seems that two farmers had virtually monopolized the grazing on Marsh Baldon green; their ninety pigs and thirty cows made the so-called beauty spot very dirty. However, the green survives.

The lanes leading to such greens also seem to have been regarded as part of the village common land and indeed in eighteenth-century maps they appear to funnel into the green at places like Stadhampton and Warborough. At Stadhampton it is recorded in 1799 that an agreement was made in the village between all persons present that 'Richard Hood is appointed ... to be hayward to pound all kind of cattle'. He was to levy fines of 2d for those beasts belonging to the inhabitants of Stadhampton and 4d from every person out of the parish. This rule included geese at the same price. The areas involved were the Green and Copson Lane.

Copson Lane is a long, curving, green lane with thick, overgrown hedges on either side. It comes out of Stadhampton and runs north-westwards. It is lined with allotments which run parallel with it for the first quarter of a mile. It is likely that the lane was formerly wider, offering an increased amount of herbage to the commoners, and that these allotments have been taken out at the southern end. That the lane belonged to the village seems undoubted because its fencing maintenance is mentioned in the village accounts now in the County Record Office:

> June the 6 (1798) for menden at
> Copson Lane Gate and reles (rails)   0–2–7
> [Sept] the 27 for menden of Copson
> Lane gate and reles   0–1–8
> 1799 Feb the 26 for menden the reles
> at Copson Lane and the pound past 0–1–10

Currently there is a dispute between the parish and a local

farmer who has stopped up a section of the end of the lane, claiming ownership.

The reasons why greens and commons so often sparked off hostile disputes are doubtless connected with the fact that they contributed materially to the livelihood of poor commoners. Six tenants of the Earl of Shrewsbury who claimed rights of common at Lew, near Bampton, were prepared to travel to London in c.1495 to pursue their rights. They were trying to prevent the sheep of the Dean and Chapter of Exeter Cathedral from grazing on the same common and had to be bought off with wine and fair words before they could be induced to return back home.

The inclosure landscapes, the creation of the parliamentary commissioners (1750–1850), lasted without serious change until the outbreak of World War II. English agriculture went through a long period of depression occasioned by the unimpeded influx of cheap American grain and chilled beef and mutton from Argentina and the Antipodes. Many Oxfordshire farmers went out of business. Some switched from arable to stock breeding and then to dairying. Capital investment dried up and farm buildings became ruinous. The break-up of great landed estates and the destruction of county houses was a national phenomenon in the first half of the twentieth century. Prosperity returned as the county was forced to feed itself during the years 1939–45. Revolutionary new techniques, increased reliance on fertilizers, genetic engineering and the development of ever larger machines have had devastating effects on the Oxfordshire countryside since that time.

It has led to the grubbing up of hundreds of miles of hedges with a consequent loss of wildlife habitats; monoculture has eliminated wild flowers, insects and butterflies producing 'a silent spring'. The soil structure has been altered for the worse by the introduction of toxic herbicides and the impaction of heavy machinery. Governments have veered crazily in their policies of paying subsidies to remove hedgerows and to plant new ones, but at least there now seems a general realization that more trees would be a good thing. The over-production of food with unsaleable surpluses has doubtless contributed to this thinking and trees are seen as combating global warming and offering a long-term investment. The part played by trees and woodland in the Oxfordshire landscape will now be considered.

IV
Woodland

A glance at the modern Land Ranger Ordnance Survey maps
of Oxfordshire shows only a few irregularly shaped scraps of
green indicating woodland. This largely unwooded landscape
is no modern phenomenon. Domesday Book, written over a
thousand years ago, records that only about fifteen per cent
of the English countryside was still wooded. Evidently man
began to remove the forests a long time before that.

How do we know? The technique successfully used in
reconstructing the post-glacial vegetational history of Britain
is pollen analysis. All trees and flowering plants produce
pollen in varying quantities during their life cycle. Pollen
grains from different sources are distinct and variegated.
During summer they float into the air and are blown by
winds eventually settling on the surface of the land. Where
this is water the pollen grains sink down and become
embedded on the silty floor of the lake or pond, layer upon
layer. The tough pollen is preserved in these anaerobic and
acid conditions. To extract pollen, cores are taken; the silts
are sorted; the pollen grains are separated by using a
centrifuge and are then identified, using a microscope, and
counted. Some plants such as hazel produce much more
pollen than others and this has to be taken into consideration
when constructing pollen diagrams. These have two axes:
time divided into various zones on the vertical axis; the
relative number of pollen grains found in each zone is shown
on the horizontal axis. In this way it is possible to show an
image of the relative dominance or decline of each species at
different times since the end of the fourth and last Ice Age.

Recent work by Petra Day of Wolfson College using pollen
analysis from two Oxfordshire sites at Cothill Fen and
Sidlings Copse has provided detailed information about

woodland development and human interference with it during this remote period. Cothill Fen is a calcareous valley about four miles south-west of Oxford in the parish of St Helen Without. The deposits examined consist of peat and marl. Here, between c.10,000 and 9,500 BP (before the present) there was a fen with swampy vegetation. The main tree species at the time were birch and pine, with some willow. During the next 700 years or so the birch reduced in numbers and was replaced in the pollen spectrum by elm. The fen was taken over for a time by a closed canopy woodland with a low frequency of herb pollen. This expansion of elm lasted about 300 years and then gradually began to be replaced by oak c.8,800 BP. Pine persisted after the initial expansion of hazel, oak and alder, but declined after c. 7,700 BP. Lime occurred occasionally. From the presence of charcoal in the cores at this point it seems that the climate may have been relatively dry, making forest fires more likely. It is possible, however, that these fires were man-made; mesolithic hunter gatherers burning vegetation for an unknown purpose. As the climate gradually changed again with more damp conditions the vegetation responded. Alder spread and moss peat accumulated. A series of openings in the woodland canopy is suggested by the presence of bracken and this again could have been caused by human activity. Between c.0850–0550 BP there was a greater depth of water on the site. The pollen of lime, alder and beech now became more frequent. The alder in particular was encouraged by the increased waterlogging. A single cereal type pollen grain (*Triticum*) occurred in this zone. It predates those found associated with the pre-elm decline but may have resulted from contamination. The Cothill Fen sequence unfortunately ceases here, being truncated by later disturbances including ploughing.

Sidlings Copse is a wooded valley in the parish of Stowood about two and a half miles north-east of Oxford. Here Day discovered a sequence of turfs, peats and muds which had embedded in them a sequence of pollen dating from c.9,500 BP to the present day. At the start, the valley bottom supported wetland vegetation containing willow with sedges. Around it was an open environment with grasses, patches of birch and hazel scrub. By about 8,800 BP, calcareous clays were being deposited on the valley bottom. Hazel woodland now began to cover the area. Oak was present, but elm was not yet recorded. A fluctuating water-flow led to tufa being deposited in the valley. High frequencies of hazel pollen indicated that hazel was now dominant with lower abundance of oak and elm. As the hazel increased there was a drop in the lime and elm – the so called 'elm decline' which occurred all over the county c.5,000 BP.

The 'elm decline' has been explained in a number of different ways. The leaves of both elm and lime are palatable to cattle. The collection of leaves and branches by Neolithic farmers may account for a reduction of pollen though not necessarily of the trees themselves. The lack of cereal pollen contemporary with the elm decline seems to rule out the effect of arable farming. The most likely reason is disease (perhaps a forerunner of Dutch Elm Disease) which could account for the synchronous decline of the trees over a wide area. This probably attacked the trees on the woodland edge leading to clearings. Men at this point may have moved into the woodland, damaging the trees by cutting off branches for leaf fodder. In this more open environment the trees would have been more vulnerable to disease.

As the elm and lime declined at Sidlings Copse so a thick tangle of hazel and alder developed. Major disruptions of the woodland occurred at c.3,800 BP in the late Neolithic/Early Bronze Age. Grazing animals inhibited regeneration of woodland; their activities probably led to a decline of lime and elm. Sheep like grazing on hazel and some of the clearances may have been caused by farmers cutting trees down for arable agriculture. The appearance of cereal pollen and pollen from weeds of cultivation strengthens this likelihood. The clearance began with the drier soils, but by the Roman period it had spread on to the damper levels. Alder and oak were reduced substantially probably to produce pasture and meadow. This relatively open environment, consistent with limestone grassland communities, persisted until c.1,000 BP. There seems to have been a regeneration of woodland in the early medieval period which is likely to have been associated with the traditional management system of oak standards and hazel coppice. In her latest thoughts on the subject (1993), Petra Day now considers that the royal forest may well have contributed to this late expansion of woodland. Her suggestion that much of the present woodland in the Oxfordshire landscape has not come down to us intact from the Middle Ages but is the result of regeneration at some point is certainly borne out in other parts. The woods within the circuit of the Abbot of Glastonbury's park at Ashdown in the Vale of the White Horse have a network of prehistoric fields running underneath them. Here, woods have once more returned to a bare and cultivated prehistoric landscape – probably as the result of planting since the seventeenth century AD.

Further insights into this problem of when the woodland cover began seriously to decline are obtained from studying the ground surfaces covered, and therefore sealed, by Neolithic long barrows. At the Hazleton North Cairn in the neighbouring Gloucestershire Cotswolds study by soil specialists indicated possible tillage of the buried soil c.3700 BC. At roughly the same time, the buried soil beneath the Ascott-under-Wychwood long barrow showed no such evidence. Here, the snail shells found in the soil were predominantly woodland-loving species. Again the buried soil beneath the Neolithic chambered tomb of Waylands Smithy, on the top of the chalk ridge in the far south of the county (as enlarged in 1972), demonstrated more evidence for ploughing. Two of these three sites then show that the woodland clearance in these areas was well under way in the fourth millennium BC.

The mention of snails may be puzzling, but in fact they are reliable indicators of the current state of the landscape. Some are shade loving and flourish in woodland; others find stagnant water a desirable habitat, others flowing. Still others prefer open grassland. When therefore their hardened and calcified shells are found in soils which have built up in ditch fills they give a good idea of what the vegetation was like at that particular time. The Devil's Quoits, near Stanton Harcourt, a mighty ceremonial stone circle with surrounding ditch and outer bank dating back to the third millennium BC, has produced interesting snail-shell evidence for the changes taking place in the upper Thames landscape at this remote period. The ditch must first have provided a standing water habitat at least during the winter months. Scrub soon developed because the ditch was speedily colonized by shade loving species. By the mid third millennium, the snail shells found indicate that the ground around the monument was dry and open, the result of a long period of over-grazing or ploughing in the vicinity. In the upper horizons no snail shells were found; the likely explanation is that there were long dry periods during the later Bronze, Iron and early Roman periods. Soil mixing caused by frequent ploughing will have prevented the calcification of the shells, thus destroying this particular piece of information.

The first county-wide survey of woodland is in Domesday Book. To the north of Oxford in the mid eleventh century was a broad belt of woodland from Wychwood in the west to Shotover and Bernwood to the east. The Chiltern ridge to the south-east with its patches of clay with flints was also well wooded. By contrast, the parts of the modern county which used to be in Berkshire were practically devoid of woodland, except for the northern corner bounded by the Thames and even now covered by woods around Wytham and Bagley. The chalk downland, in particular, had precious little and this bare landscape extended across most of the Vale of the White Horse and the upper Thames Valley.

The monarchy was deeply interested in this area of Oxfordshire and by the end of the eleventh century much of the Oxfordshire woodland was classified as royal forest. The king's demesne forests are described in Domesday Book as extending for nine leagues in length and nine leagues in breadth, forming a discontinuous band across the centre of the county. The word 'forest' was a legal term referring to a tract of land outside (Latin *foris*) the operation of the common law and within which the forest law operated. This had as its principal aim the preservation of the beasts of the forest for royal hunting: the so called '*ferae naturæ*' included red deer, fallow deer, roe deer and wild boar. An army of officials headed by the justices of the forest and backed up by verderers and woodwards enforced the forest law through a series of courts. Their aim was to exact fines rather than impose expensive imprisonment.

The lure of the royal forests in Oxfordshire to the Norman and Plantagenet kings was certainly attributable to their potential for hunting. Royal interest in the chase led to the establishment of a hunting lodge at Woodstock in the reign of Ethelred II (978–1016) when a witan was held 'at Woodstock in the land of the Mercians'. Henry I is said to have created the park and he made it the 'favourite seat of his retirement and privacy'. Chroniclers asserted that he built the first park wall *c.*1110. Within its seven-mile circuit was a menagerie for wild animals. According to Henry of Huntingdon, Woodstock was 'the celebrated place which Henry had made for the habitation of men and beasts'. William of Malmesbury elaborated on this, recording that Henry 'was extremely fond of the wonders of different countries, begging with great delight from foreign kings lions, leopards, lynxes and camels, animals which England does not produce. He had a park called Woodstock in which he used to foster his favourites of this kind. He had placed there also a creature called a porcupine sent to him by William of Montpellier.'

Clearly the house, manor or palace of Woodstock was an excellent base from which to hunt in the park and in the forest of Wychwood which adjoined it to the north-west. Henry I also ordered the construction of a house at Oxford. It was sufficiently advanced for him to come to stay for Easter 1133. His grandsons Richard Coeur de Lion and John were born here. Nothing remains except a street name, Beaumont, and a few architectural fragments. From here, the forests of Shotover and Stowood which reached the bounds of the city of Oxford on the east could be hunted. Another royal hunting lodge lay at Brill over the county boundaries in Buckinghamshire. This was convenient for making hunting forays into the forest of Bernwood.

Royal hunting influenced the lives of many of the local inhabitants. Tenants from Bladon had to make hay in Long Acre and mow Law Mead in Woodstock Park. In the winter they had to cut fodder for the king's deer. The villeins of Combe likewise had to perform mowing services within the park. Other duties included driving deer in Woodstock Park whenever a view to check the numbers was taken and carrying hay to the king's barn in the park from the royal meadows there. Further reminders of the practice of royal hunting are seen in field names, particularly in the Wychwood area. The field name Purrance or Purrence in Leafield, found as early as 1300, refers to Purveyance, the compulsory purchase of provisions for the royal household while in the area. This was unpopular because goods thus bought were well below the market price.

Kingstanding Farm (in Wychwood parish) refers to 'a hunter's station or stand from which to shoot game'. The fifteenth-century text of the Master of Game refers to this: 'then shulde ye maister of ye game ... meete ye kynge and brynge hym to his stondynge and telle hym what game is withinre ye sette'. A number of field names including the element 'plain' refer to the hunting term for open country unobstructed by trees, as opposed to woodland. Such are Newhill Plain and Stag's Plain (both in Wychwood parish), Leigh Hall Plain (in Asthall) and Hardley Plain (in Swinbrook). Buckleap Copse and Sore Leap denote a gate or low place in a fence or hedge where deer may leap over. Hartsole in Combe is probably 'hart's soil'.

The forests also provided kings with the means to reward their civil servants, favourites and relatives. This took three forms: lordly donations of timber for building (*maeremium*), more workaday gifts of essential firewood (*robora* – dead

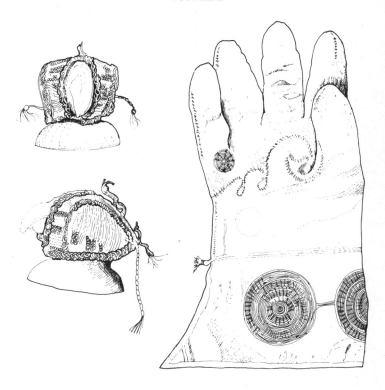

Hawks' Hood. Early sixteenth-century hawking glove traditionally attributed to Henry VIII (*Ashmolean Museum, Tradescant Collection*)

trees or *subboscus* – underwood), grants of deer to be hunted or to be caught live and transported. The Close Rolls (so-called because they were confidential royal letters copied onto a parchment roll before being sent out sealed to ensure authenticity) record hundreds of such gifts and some idea of the scale of this royal exploitation of the forest of Wychwood can be seen in these totals:

1227–31	gifts of trees 45: firewood 74: deer to be hunted 46: live deer 49
1237–51	gifts of trees 121: firewood 10: trees 2 cartloads: gifts of deer to be hunted 143 (including 100 for the king's own use) and gifts of live deer 58.

Many of the gifts of trees were tied to specific building projects. Ralph, son of Nicholas, for instance, was allowed three oaks to build his houses at Eaton while the Earl Ferrers was given fifteen oaks to help him build his manor at Framford. The King's interest in the Church and in charitable giving is reflected in his allowing the parson of Calverton five oaks for repairs to the chancel of his church. The brothers of the Hospital of St John at Lechlade were given five oaks towards the repair of their houses. Nearly all houses at this time were heated by open hearths situated in the centres of the halls. Dead trees were granted away as firewood. The friars preachers of Oxford were given thirteen *robora* as firewood. The Abbot of Bruern was allowed two cartloads of firewood for his hearth.

The King sometimes used the wood for his own purposes. Henry III authorized John of Hanborough to take timber with loppings from the park at Woodstock to build a bell tower (*clocherium*) at Woodstock manor. The royal household needed barrels for storage so William de Aleman, a servant of the King, was deputed to make them from a maple tree in the Forest of Woodstock. Other woodland crafts included the making of charcoal, pottery and treen. Thomas of Langley, the King's forester, was ordered to provide the Sheriff of Oxford with fifteen *robora* or dead oaks to make into charcoal for the use of the Friars Minor of Oxford. Michael Belet was given five *robora* to make a certain potter's oven. Leafield later became a notable centre for pottery making. It is interesting that as early as the second half of the thirteenth century, another potter, brother John, the King's almoner, was provided with two maple trees in the wood at Cornbury to make pots for the use of the King. In this case it is more likely that the vessels were made of wood – maple wood was favoured for ceremonial vessels known as mazers. All Souls College has a remarkable group of medieval mazers including a bowl and cover given to the college by Thomas Ballard in 1448, and three bowls with gold and gilt mounts. These oddly escaped Charles I's treasure-seeking forays during the Civil War.

Gifts of the royal deer were highly prized; they were given in the form of the right to hunt so many bucks and so many does. Nearly always the does exceeded the bucks by about three to one. Sometimes the royal huntsmen were ordered to hand over the venison to the beneficiary: Pontio de Ponte was granted two bucks in this manner. But more often the King was giving away a day's hunting as well as the meat itself. William, the Dean of St Martins, was granted the right to take a single buck and John de Bello Campo was permitted to take four bucks for the use of his mother, Eve de Gray.

Deer parks were prestigious accessories to lordly power. Royal permission to impark was eagerly sought for by ambitious barons and ecclesiastics. The King, with the vast reservoirs of game available in the royal forests, was in a position to help stock these new parks. Deer were given live (*damas or damos vivos*) for this purpose. Presumably they were netted, trussed and carted off across the country. Richard of Cornwall, the King's uncle, was given fifteen does and five bucks to stock his park at Hailes in Gloucestershire, where he founded an abbey. The park belonging to the Abbot of Westminster at Pershore was similarly stocked with the King's deer from Wychwood. During the vacancy of bishoprics, episcopal estates often were plundered. Henry III helped to restock the Bishop of Winchester's lands by providing him with deer from the royal forests, including Wychwood.

Deer and timber were not the only products to be exploited in royal forests and parks. Falcons, dogs and horses were bred there. The bailiff of Woodstock had the custody of an eyrie of falcons in the park. Falcons needed constant nourishment and one local tenant held his lands in return for the service of carrying feed to the King's falcon there. The King's hunting dogs were kept at Witney in 1210 for seventy-five days at a cost of 3s 3½d. Other dogs were there for more than three quarters of the year of 1211 at a cost of 7s 3d. The itinerary of King John shows that he was often at Witney, attracted no doubt by the proximity of rich areas of hunting. The Bishop of Winchester, who had a palace at Witney, paid

2s 10d for a pitcher and tub for a bath for the King. Recent excavations at Mount House, Witney, have exposed the remains of garderobes especially renewed for the royal visit.

The wood pasture available in Wychwood Forest made it highly favourable for the breeding of horses. The Abbot of Bittelden kept horses there and a stud (*horatulum*) in the forest. The King, too, reared horses at Woodstock. Stables are referred to in 1254 and 1325, while in 1334 straw, hay and litter are recorded as being brought for the King's stud. After 1361 the horses and mares in the royal stud at Woodstock were ordered to be sold. Another sport, tournaments involving horses, added the name Baynard's Green to the map of Oxfordshire. This is a large area of open rolling country between Brackley and Mixbury, partly in Northamptonshire. The site was licensed for tournaments by Richard I, along with four others, all stretches of open country on or near to a great main road. Here Richard I held a tournament in 1194 and Henry III another in 1249. Bayard is the stock name for a bay horse and is found in Bayswater brook and Bayards leap.

The royal forests were not continuous tracts of woodland. They contained ploughed lands, even open fields, many dispersed settlements and some nucleated villages. From the point of view of the peasant cultivators whose dwellings ringed the woodland or penetrated deep within it the forest represented land for expansion. The population over the whole country was growing in the twelfth and thirteenth centuries and there was pressure of people on the land. Despite the forest laws, the woods rang with the sound of felling axes as farmers cut down trees, grubbed out roots and made assarts. Particularly active were the tenants of the Bishop of Winchester who began to attack the woodland to the north-east of Witney. The results were a series of straggly forest-edge settlements named Delly End, Poffley End and Gigley Green. These woods were already familiar with the men who lived along the margins of the forests. The farmers of Stonesfield, Coombe and Hanborough had a customary right, recognized since the reign of King John, to graze their goats in Wychwood.

Assarting was also proceeding from the south of Wychwood. In 1080 Coombe was one of the most extensively wooded parishes with woodland said to measure $1\frac{1}{2}$ by $1\frac{1}{2}$ leagues. Assarting really got going here in the late thirteenth and fourteenth centuries, while the acreage under arable hardly changed between 1080 and 1279. Thereafter, woodland was cleared on a scale which suggests that royal policy was changing: one hundred and two acres of freshly assarted land were recorded in 1298; in 1303 another seventy-one and a half acres were cleared. By 1609 only one solitary wood of nineteen acres, known as Notoaks, was left by the manor house, a remnant of demesne woodland.

To the south of Wychwood and south of the Evenlode was Hanborough. The demesne woodland lay along the northern edge of the parish. Here again assarting was active in the late thirteenth century. Individual assarts were small, varying from five foot to a rod although there were eight of half an acre or more. In the east this new land was at the expense of the marsh or scrub along the Evenlode rather than from the wood. A place name, the Breach, which means 'land newly taken into cultivation' is given to the two furlongs and six acres which William of St Owen gave to Oseney Abbey between 1267 and 1284.

A wood in the middle of Hanborough parish has a number of the characteristics of medieval woodland. It is mentioned as Pinsley Wood in 1254. It appears virtually in its present state in the Langdon map in Corpus Christi library dating from 1608. It is oval in shape and retains the characteristic curving wood banks on the northern and western sides. Its indented outline on the south and east shows where it has been bitten into by assarts. There are also signs that it was once more extensive on the western side. The wood is likely to have been managed by coppices and standards in the Middle Ages and up to the eighteenth or even nineteenth centuries. It has recently been clear-felled in the centre and replanted with conifers, but a strip of the old coppice and standards is left on the fringes recalling the ancient management.

It will perhaps be useful to explain briefly these different techniques of woodland management because the parts of woodland such as the Chilterns, which were never part of the royal hunting forest, were worked on a crop producing basis. Some stocks like pines can be got rid of by cutting them down; their stumps rot and they do not regenerate. Others, however, grow again from the stump or root system. There are four ways in which this can happen. Maple and wych-elm can be cut at the base or stool. This sends up shoots and these become an indefinite succession of crops of poles which are cut at intervals of some years. Aspen and most elms sucker, and the root system sends up similar successive crops of poles. One problem is that the shoots while growing are vulnerable to the depredations of cattle, sheep and deer. Pollarding, whereby the tree was cut at between six and fifteen feet above the ground – well above the browse line of animals – produced again an indefinite succession of poles. A variant of pollarding, not very often done now, was shredding: cutting off the side boughs of trees leaving a tuft at the top. A picture attributed to Paolo Uccello in the Ashmolean Museum entitled *A Hunt by Night* shows a wood full of shredded trees.

Some form of coppicing must have been practised as early as the Roman period in order to supply the very large quantities of firewood to fuel the pottery kilns. These were built in large numbers in the second and third centuries on the high ground to the east of Oxford. A policy of simple clearance without regeneration would have resulted in the rapid exhaustion of woods within easy distance of the kilns. A controlled system of coppicing would have resulted in a steady supply of poles for fuel.

Much of the medieval woodlands of the Chilterns consisted of shaws, pieces of woodland left between areas of cultivated land and coppice with standards. The traces of this system of management are clear on the ground. The woods themselves were surrounded by massive banks with stock-proof fences on them and external ditches. Within, they were divided into coppices with lesser (and usually later) banks: three to four metres wide and one and a half metres high. While the coppices were growing up they needed protection from animals and fences made of hurdles were used for this purpose.

The main coppice wood during the Middle Ages was likely to have been beech. This was a favourite fuel for domestic or industrial use. In an Eynsham Abbey account in South Stoke, for instance, the woodward recorded sales of underwood called 'beckenwood' from Abbots' Wood for 60s 6d in one year in 1448. Nothing was wasted. The billet itself ideally would have been at least ten inches in diameter. The spray or bushy tops were made into faggots or bavins tied with withies. These were fed into domestic hearths or for heating bakeovens. They could also be tied into bundles and poles inserted to make besom brooms.

Hazel was a common form of underwood; it provided material for hurdles, thatching pins and wattle. Ash was also coppiced. Wroxhall Wood in Goring contained many ash stools possibly of medieval date. Oak coppice is rare in the Oxfordshire Chilterns, but oak pollards are frequently found in hedgerows and at the corners of fields; they are often used to mark boundaries, presumably because of their massive size and their longevity. Among the oldest living organisms in the county are the crevassed shells of ancient pollard oaks in Blenheim Park, which are still sprouting new shoots. They date back to the time when the park was royal and are at least 500 years old. Hornbeam is very rare in Oxfordshire, but the boundary bank between Goring and Woodcote has a line of very old coppiced hornbeams. It is a brittle wood but useful for making the cogs of water wheels as well as the beetles or wooden mallets. Other trees which coppice well are cherry, maple and wych-elm.

Coppice was usually grown interspersed among standards. These were timber trees grown from seed or suckers. Stands of tall trees such as oak, ash, beech were planted together to draw them up to the light, thereby producing straight long trunks. These 'great trees' were those used in the construction of houses, bridges and the roofs of churches. Spindly oaks of only sixteen years' growth were used as rafters in the thirteenth-century roof of Standlake Rectory. The number of trees used in any one building is considerable. Rackham has worked out that the construction of a timber-framed farm-house – Grundle House, Stanton, Suffolk c.1500 – used up 330 trees. Large trees would be felled and transported by horse and cart to nearby markets such as Watlington or to an entrepot such as Henley-on-Thames. Horses were preferred to oxen for pulling timber. The Oxfordshire Chilterns have a network of tracks, deeply hollowed in steep places, used by those involved in the timber trade. Wood was removed by many tenants as part of their customary duties. At Whit-church in 1279 tenants had to carry two cartloads and others had to carry wood for two days. Such heavy loads rapidly wore deep hollows and a number of roads bear traces of earlier abandoned routes below them as they climb the steep Chiltern slopes. Good examples are Pyrton and Rotherfield Peppard. Sawpits, now mere dimples in the leaf-mould, are found in the woods between Stonor and Bix and it is likely that timber for individual buildings was framed up in the woods themselves. Then the trusses were taken apart, marked and transported with a minimum of unnecessary loppings. Woodmen probably made hurdles, besoms, wattlework and faggots in the woods. They were still using temporary huts in the nineteenth century. The chief tool was the billhook, a broad single-bladed cutting edge with a small hook on the end.

While most of the coppice wood was used locally, the large timber and the fuel was likely to end up in London or in the Thameside towns. As we have seen, it was taken by cart to Henley-on-Thames where there were wharves. A record of fifteenth-century wood sales at Stonor mentions firewood being sent from Stonor to the Lord's household in London probably by barge from Henley. In 1299 a load of 2,500 beech faggots was sent to London from Henley. It is noteworthy that the Thames provided the transportation route for timber from the royal forest of Windsor. Barges containing timber travelled from Abingdon in the west, a distance of thirty-five miles, to Grays Thurrock in the east, a distance of forty-five miles. Some came westwards to Oxfordshire from the forest of Windsor. The bridge at Henley-on-Thames was repaired in 1233 and 1235 with eight *fusta* (trunks) for the posts and horizontal beams. We know from a Dutch painting in the seventeenth century (now in the Tate Gallery) that the bridge, while stone-arched at either end, was a trestle-timber construction in the centre.

The ownership of woodlands is a complex matter. Many people had the right to use woodland resources such as pannaging pigs or helping themselves to fuel without actually owning the wood. Pannage, the right to feed pigs on autumn falls of beech mast (or nuts) and acorns, was commonly granted to tenants in the Chilterns. This was sufficiently important in some areas for woodland to be measured as 'enough for so many swine'. In 1279 the tenants in Woodcote paid dues for rights of pannage 'when the wood carries it'. Beech mast is a rather unpredictable crop and sometimes occurs only every five to seven years. Tenants were also allowed 'heybote', or wood for fencing, 'housbote', timber for repair of houses, and 'ploughbote', to provide wood for repairing agricultural equipment. Charcoal burners also practised their craft in the Chiltern woods. In the Stonor district in 1482 'XXX qtrs cole' were sold. The woods between Stonor and Bix in addition provided fuel for the pot makers at Crockerend and the brick and tile makers of Nettlebed. One of the earliest bulk purchases of bricks was made in 1416–17 when 200,000 bricks were purchased from 'Les Flemynges' at Crockerend for £40. The Nettlebed brick and tile industry went on working into the eighteenth and nineteenth century. Early photographs show a wasteland of worked-out claypits and brick ovens. A bottle-shaped one has been preserved by the County Museum service at Nettlebed.

All these activities provided rents and were more or less

profitable to the owners of woodland. Donations of land from an earlier more devout period had endowed a number of ecclesiastical bodies with woodland in both the Wychwood area and the Chilterns. The Abbey of Eynsham, for instance, had woods in both. Abbotswood in Woodcote, comprising 348 acres, had been acquired in 1109. It was retained by the Abbey until the Dissolution when it was given to Christ Church. In other places, such as the slopes of Shotover, various colleges gave their names to their woods: Magdalen Wood and Brasenose Wood. Small landowners in the Chilterns also gave their names to woods. Chazey Wood derives from the Chausey family, who held the manor of Mapledurham Chazey. The Bardolfs, who are buried in Mapledurham Church, owned Bardolf's Wood. The wood belonging to Kidlington Manor was given to Osney Abbey in 1216; Osney Wood lies immediately to the north of Cogges Wood and is an interesting example of a manorial wood detached from its original parish centre.

A vivid insight into the management of college woodland is provided by the Progress Notes of Warden Michael Woodward, in charge of New College from 1658–79. The college had suffered from mismanagement during his predecessor's time which had coincided with the Civil War. Much damage had been done to the College woods. No less than 5,000 trees, principally at Stanton St John, were cut down during George Marshall's wardenship and farm buildings and property had been allowed to fall into disrepair everywhere. Woodward was no great scholar but proved to be an excellent manager. Consequently, when he set off annually with his outriders, his purpose was frankly financial: 'That the college was much behindhand and wanted money very much, that our fines did not fail as much as also our sales of timber.'

Warden Woodward inspected the woods belonging to the college and marked and priced the trees that were to be sold. He also considered claims by the tenants for trees to repair the buildings on their copyholds and for ploughboot, fireboot and so on. 'We assigned unto the tenant there, for cart-boote [an allowance of wood to a tenant for the making and repair of carts] and ploughboote to the value or quantity of 2 tunnes, or oake and ash for those purposes to be assigned in fit places and of fitt timber by the supervision of Mr Cox' (5 April 1660). The woods round Stanton were coppiced:

> On that day [2 May 1663] we rode to Stanton from thence we went into the woods to see for a tree that I am to buy for my parsonage at Brightwell, about 18 inches square and I hope a good one. The coppice is not all cutt downe, as it should bee, only some part of it, whereby the coll: cannot bee served with their whole wood and 2ly [secondly] the young standards of the 1st sale or ffelling are now by the buyer or buyers of the wood cutt downe soe that by this meanes wee shall have little or noe supplie of young timber in the coppice.

Constant requests were made of the warden to supply trees for different purposes. The miller, for instance, needed the wood of a wild service tree for renewing the cogs of the mill machinery. The young men of Stanton 'had cutt downe a tree for a maypole about one or two & 30ty feet log of a foot square, 3 of them came before us, I required a mulct of £5; others said 40s'. In the end they agreed to pay 30s. Many people applied for trees to repair their houses and barns.

> He desired in Mr Knowles his name some allowance of timber & promised to rebuild it, my selfe and Dr Deane allowed from off the premises 40 feet of timber for plates, side pieces and rafters by the oversight of Mr Cox but I condition with Mason that the end of the house eastward (x inches without the beam that yet remains) should bee made up with stone & the walls on both sides into the house ovessees, which hee promised soe to doe.

Thus a college was attempting to recoup its financial resources in the seventeenth century. An Oxfordshire Catholic family, the Stonors, which had suffered heavily from recusancy fines in the sixteenth and seventeenth centuries was engaged similarly in managing its Chiltern woodlands more strictly. Before leaving to live abroad in 1750, Thomas Stonor handed over the administration of his estates to his uncle, Talbot Stonor, with detailed instructions: 'The woodmen order the workmen what trees are fite to be felled and when a wood is felled sufficiently. They are to give notice to the steward that he or his Deputy take the tale (counting the individual trees) thereof and immediately pay the workmen for the same.' The woodmen, as the instructions continue

> in the first week of the month of February they bring in their accounts together with a general Tale of the wood fell'd which is to be compared with the Stewards Talebill delivered in the May before ... I also expect of them that during the felling time they attend the workmen particularly at night at their going off from work and that no shoulderstick be allow'd to be carry'd off by the workmen but that no more be allow'd them to take away than a Brush fagot or some such thing.

Other duties involved mending fences broken down during the processes of cutting and drawing out the timber; also to see that there is 'no trespass of cattle which does incredible damage'.

The main timber products of the Stonor woods were oak, beech, ash and some chestnut. One or two lime trees are mentioned but they were not at all common. There is a notable lack of conifers in the eighteenth century. Oak timber produced oak bark which was often bought while still on the trees. The workmen were allowed to enter the woods to strip the bark, dry, harvest and weigh it, and carry it away. An average tanner used the bark of three or four dozen mature trees a year or even more, so there was a great pressure on coppice trees to provide sufficient for their craft. 'Town billet' was firewood sent to Henley-on-Thames for transport by barge to London. Loads of 'water wood' also landed up on the wharf at Henley for use in piling and lining canals. Beechwood was especially favoured by the furniture makers of the Chilterns. The beech polls, the top cuttings from pollarded beeches, were sold at 10s 6d per load and went to local bodgers (as the makers of hand-lathed furniture legs were called). The legs ended up in High Wycombe as parts of chairs. Other firing products had specialized uses. Bavins, for instance, were bundles of brushwood of light underwood such as were used for bakers' ovens. They differed from faggots by being bound with only one withy or band instead of two.

A conservation-conscious generation such as our own will be interested to know that already in the Middle Ages some people were aware of the dangers of ruining the woodland environment by overfelling. Grants of timber were made provided that 'harm is not done to the forest', and in 1257 Henry III suspended such benefaction 'because of the destruction caused'. It was not until the end of the sixteenth century that systematic attempts were made to plant trees. Landowners such as the Spencers in neighbouring Northamptonshire marked plantations of trees in their park at Althorp with inscribed stones. John Evelyn's 'Sylva' of 1664 took up the theme since it was realized that a lack of timber would cause acute shortage of naval supplies. Warden Woodward was keen to encourage planting and many of his permissions to fell were accompanied by directions to plant.

Ornamental planting on a large scale came to Oxfordshire in the eighteenth century. The royal park of Woodstock, the favourite hunting place of medieval kings, was in a poor state in the seventeenth century. In the northern part most of the timber was said to be fit only for fuel, except for 2,500 trees marked for use by the navy. Although these trees were in fact saved, waste and felling were still causing concern in the 1670s. Some small-scale planting was already being carried out, however, including the creation of ash and walnut nurseries. Circular and triangular plantations, seen in the eighteenth-century maps of the park, are thought to date from this time. But the really large-scale plantations had to wait until the park had changed hands. In 1704 the crown decided to donate park and a new palace to the Marlboroughs to express the nation's gratitude to the victor of Blenheim.

Three years later some 1,600 elms had been established in two great avenues. One stretched north from the bridge in front of the palace to the Ditchley Gate. Such monumental planting, clearly in emulation of Louis XIV's work at Versailles and elsewhere, created a great avenue one and half miles in length, consisting of double ranks of four centred on a great ellipse. The persistent idea that its design represented the disposition of the opposing armies at the battle of Blenheim has no real basis of fact. The central elliptical feature halfway along its length may have been designed to have a monumental column but in the event this was placed on the high ground between the bridge and the ellipse. The avenue was in a poor condition in 1900 and was replanted from end to end in 1902 by the 9th Duke. Dutch elm disease began to damage the avenue in the 1970s and it was replanted for a third time, with limes. The Grand Avenue however was never widely used because it pointed in the wrong direction, away from London. A second avenue, the Mall, was designed from the eastern front of the house, connecting it with the Oxford road at the Hensington Gate. This double avenue survived into the nineteenth century. Its restoration began in the 1890s, but again Dutch elm disease destroyed it and it had to be replanted in 1976 by a mixture of planes and limes.

The chalk downland in the south of the county may well have been covered with light woodland some four thousand years ago. Much clearance took place in the Neolithic and Bronze Ages and it probably remained bare of trees until the eighteenth century. Beech clumps which were purely ornamental began to be planted by landowners such as the Earl of Craven at Ashbury. During the 1880s and 1890s many of the woods, copses and shelter belts were planted on the estates of Lord Wantage around Ardington and Lockinge. Lord Wantage had been a soldier in the earlier part of his life and had won the Victoria Cross in the Crimea at the battle of Alma in 1854. Just as at Blenheim belief grew up in the locality therefore that these trees were planted on a plan of the opposing armies before the battle of Alma. There is little evidence to support this, but Lord Wantage may have commented that the tree lines reminded him of the battlefield and thus started the story.

The nineteenth century took an increasingly pragmatic view about the landscape. It was expected to yield a profit and Lord Wantage's woods were an integral part of the estate economy, not a decorative appendage. They provided shelter for livestock on these bare chalk hills. The estate timber yard provided material for the construction and repair of farm buildings such as the stables in Ardington for the Lockinge Shire Horse Stud; cottages on the estate, fences, gates all required timber which the self-sufficient estate could produce.

In the western and central parts of the county the Crown was active in Victoria's reign in ensuring a bigger financial return on the royal forest of Wychwood. Already in 1792, the commissioners who had been appointed to report to parliament on the state and condition of the woods, forests and land revenues of the Crown had brought the lamentable state of Wychwood to public notice. From 1700–86 no timber had been supplied from the forest for the use of the navy. The deer were running riot among the trees and underwood, injuring the new young growth. Despite the fact that the herd of deer was said to number 1,000, only six does and six bucks made their way to the royal larder. 'The greater part of the timber has been cut at much waste and loss to the Crown and ... there is now little left.'

It was decided in 1853 to pass an act for the disafforesting of the forest of Wychwood 'that the said forest might be made much more valuable and productive if it were disafforested and the deer removed therefrom. The award put an end to ancient rights.' The office of ranger was abolished. The commoners who had pastured their sheep and swine were compensated. The morals of the forest dwellers had troubled the authorities. 'The vicinity is filled with poachers, deer stealers, thieves and pilferers of every kind.' The benefits of civilization were brought to deepest Wychwood. It was made into a separate parish and a church at Leafield was soon built. Some ten miles of new roads were set out and all other existing roads and ways were shut up and discontinued.

The biggest change in the landscape took place on the 2,000 acres of the Crown allotment. Here, the timber trees were felled and sold for £34,000, the ground cleared and the stumps removed. Seven new farmsteads were created. King's Standing Farm is a typical example, with its walls built of local stone, marked with the initials of the monarch and the insignia of the Crown. The land was divided up into straight-edge fields; on the northern edge of Wychwood these can easily be identified, cut with mathematical regularity on a north-east/south-west axis along the edge of the surviving woodland.

V

Roads

The Prehistoric Period

Man has always been a mobile animal. During the hunter-gatherer periods of the Palaeolithic, when the climate favoured it, groups of men moved round the Oxfordshire landscape in search of prey. They were uninhibited by territorial divisions but constrained by the physical barriers of a landscape, very different from the present, which had large stretches of marsh, broad rivers running in different channels from those of today, and much as yet unpenetrated woodland. The stone artefacts left behind by these early hunters are often rolled and damaged as though they have travelled a distance, being moved by glacial flood waters before their final resting place in the gravels. Hand-axes, cleavers and choppers of flint and quartz make up these Palaeolithic finds, usually picked up singly and occasionally found in numbers, as at Wolvercote and Highlands Farm, Henley, on the second gravel terrace of the Thames. In 1991 an important discovery was made, close to the narrowest part of the Goring gap at Gatehampton. Here, judging from the scatter of flint work found, the upper Palaeolithic hunters had stationed themselves at a point where they could ambush animal herds crossing a shallow river. Their knives and choppers would have enabled them to butcher the carcasses of their quarry, probably of reindeer or horse.

These movements of men and herds of wild animals probably produced the earliest pattern of communication in Oxfordshire. With a more settled landscape of the Neolithic the first tracks appear in the archaeological record. Prehistoric trackways have generated a mythology of their own. They are linked in the popular mind with ridgeways, partly because there is a belief that prehistoric man kept to the high ground in his travels and avoided the allegedly impenetrable forests of the valleys. The argument is flawed. The forests had begun to be cleared even in the Mesolithic, that is to say from c.10,000 BC, and the process was well under way when shifting agriculture was adopted in the early Neolithic. The presence of imported products demonstrates lively trade across long distances, and if not trade at least gift giving of exotic articles. Windmill Hill and other sites in Wiltshire used oolitic limestone which can only have been brought down from the Cotswolds. The Bronze Age settlers of the Cotswolds used chalk-derived flint which must have originated from the Berkshire (now Oxfordshire Downs). Rams Hill, a Bronze Age defended enclosure near Uffington, when excavated by Professor Bradley in 1975, yielded evidence for trade across the Vale of the White Horse. Stone objects were brought from the Corallian outcrops several miles to the north, and others from the sandstone deposits in the Coles pit area near Faringdon. All this implies traffic across the grain of the county, not along the high ground. Furthermore Humphrey Case has built up a powerful argument for early routes linking the ritual and cemetery sites round the Devil's Quoits, near Stanton Harcourt, with the barrows found in the Vale of the White Horse and then on to Rams Hill on the chalk ridge. Barrows in the Thames valley gravel region have produced plenty of evidence for long distance trade whether it was by land or river. At Cassington, for instance, shale or jet objects were brought in. Gold earrings and knives of copper from Ireland were imported to Dorchester and Sutton Courtenay respectively.

So why were the ridgeways thought to be the sole routes used by these traders, priests, farmers and warriors? The answer is in the subsequent agricultural history of the region. Intensive farming techniques, particularly in the vales and river valleys of Oxfordshire, have eliminated the physical evidence for prehistoric activity generally, not just tracks, but also barrows, field systems, settlements. They have been reduced to crop-marks, soil marks and scatters of artifacts. Roads are particularly vulnerable to total removal from the landscape. Even the celebrated ridgeways themselves have been subject to extensive re-shaping over the centuries.

Take the Berkshire (now since 1972 the Oxfordshire) Ridgeway, perhaps the most celebrated of prehistoric routes, now followed with delight by thousands of walkers, whose activities conflict with motorcyclists, the drivers of farm vehicles and yuppies with four-wheel drives, complete with lethal and totally unnecessary roo bars. Sir Richard Colt Hoare, the notable antiquary of Wiltshire, recommended riding along it in 1815. 'This ridgeway is a curious fragment of British antiquity and its whole course is most singularly preserved to the present day ...'. In fact, the date of the Ridgeway is disputed and its course in prehistoric times is uncertain.

To begin with, the travel writer John Anderson's statement that 'it has a fair claim to be considered the oldest road in Europe, for men and women of the old Stone Age walked it long before Britain was an island, before the onset of the last ice age' is unsupported by any shred of evidence. Not a single old Stone Age implement has been found along or near its route in Oxfordshire or Berkshire. There is little to be said for its existence in the Neolithic because while it is true that near its course are one or two long barrows, including Wayland's Smithy and one on Churn Knob, there are few other Neolithic finds, not even at the supposed crossing point of the Thames at the Goring-Streatley gap. Here only a single axe of Neolithic manufacture has been found.

There is certainly more to be said in favour of a Bronze Age origin for traffic along the Berkshire Downs. Stone and other artefacts are thought to have been moved easily along the chalk ridge during the period that Rams Hill was being occupied. There is also evidence for movement of goods north–south from the Vale of the White Horse and from the Downs. Leslie Grinsell, who in his lifetime has visited all the barrows of Southern England not just once but on a number of occasions, noticed the linear distribution of Bronze Age barrows across the chalk downland of Berkshire and regarded the Ridgeway as being 'almost certainly a recognised highway in the Bronze Age'. The Ridgeway at this time may have been a religious as well as a commercial route. One is reminded of the theory propounded by Sophus Müller in Jutland, where the long winding lines of Bronze Age round barrows are most easily explained as marking the course of ancient lines of communications: 'coffin ways' they might be called. We can imagine funerary processions wending their way along the Ridgeway. The newly made barrows would have stood out, shining white mounds of chalk, along this high route.

When thinking of the Ridgeway in modern terms it is difficult to rid ourselves of the view that here was an early road. Recent research, however, indicates that the present course of the Ridgeway is comparatively recent in date. Air photographs show that there is a big difference in the nature of the western and eastern parts of the Ridgeway. The eastern course, all the way from Hendred to Streatley, is a multiplicity of braided tracks which cause confusion as to which is the precise course of the Ridgeway. Here, we are looking at a broad band of country used, among other things, for communication, rather than a road. The reason is that in prehistoric times and indeed later this area was largely pastoral in use. Flocks and herds roamed freely over these downs and there was no point in hemming in the road with fences or hedges. The western course, on the other hand, is a well defined, narrow, curving, single course running between long linear mounds topped by hedgerows. This present route is largely the work of the inclosure commissioners of the eighteenth century who deliberately altered the course and narrowed the width of the Ridgeway in a number of places to suit their surveyed allotments. This can be seen when comparing the course of the road in Rocque's map of 1761 and the Tithe Award maps of Aston Tirrold and Upthorpe in the 1840s. It is also likely that the Ridgeway, even in prehistoric times, may have been less spread out in this area owing to the fact that it had to make its way through a network of small fields.

The Ridgeway then is likely to have been a wide zone of communication in the prehistoric period. Its tremendous width was graphically demonstrated in the 1980s. A farmer at Aston Tirrold who owned lands adjacent to the Fairmile, one of the routes of the Ridgeway, decided to plough up part of it. He claimed that the highway was at the most thirty feet wide and so he put the rest under cultivation. Despite the combined attempts of the District and County Councils, he continued to prevent highway access to a broad swathe of the Fairmile for a number of years. It was not until proof was forthcoming that traffic used the full width of 120 feet that he was led to desist. This was done by cutting a series of archaeological trenches across the old highway; these clearly showed up rutting in the sections which could only have been caused by centuries of trotting animals and wheel ruts cutting into the road surface. The Fairmile has now been restored to its former width. A threat of action in the High Court backed by irrefutable archaeological evidence seems to have done the trick.

One other ridgeway, this time on the northern edge of the county has some claim to be prehistoric. In a recent study (1983) of the Rollright stones, a late Neolithic and Bronze Age circle on the limestone hills, George Lambrick points out that it is on or near a trackway which crossed Midland England from the north-east diagonally in the direction of Crickley Hill (and so towards Gloucester). The course of this track may even have traversed the circle of the stones themselves until it was narrowed by walls determined by the inclosure commissioners of the late eighteenth century. It provided travellers with another broad zone of communication. We shall see that the packhorses of the salt retailers used it in their journeying westward to Rollright in the eleventh century. Such trackways were brought about by long usage and were quite different in character from those which were imposed on the landscape by the Romans as an act of government.

The limestone Cotswolds then are likely to have been traversed by at least one well defined prehistoric ridgeway.

The chalk hills to the south by another. The Corallian ridge overlooking the Thames in the centre invites the possibility of a third. All this is seen to be hedged round with qualifications. Let us turn to waterways. What seems to me undoubted is that the river Thames was the principal highway in the prehistoric periods. Men were attracted not just by the possibilities of an easy passage, but because the route passes through the most fertile and easiest worked soils attractive to arable farmers, and with its annual floods the river ensured rich pastures on the flood-plain. The linear distribution of Bronze Age weapons and tools is a good indicator of the importance of this major line of communication at this early period. About half of the finds of weapons made in bronze coming from Oxfordshire were fished out of the Thames, mainly as the result of modern dredging operations. It is unconvincing to explain these through the actions of incompetent boatmen or forgetful smiths. Nor is it at all likely that they were washed out of the sides of riverside settlement. The objects themselves show little trace of use. They are superior in technique from the workaday scraps found in settlements. The one well accredited Bronze Age settlement, on an island south of Wallingford, is in fact below the place where many of the finds have been made. Other explanations are that these finds locate the sites of battles, or that they were perhaps deliberate deposits, the sacrifices to water deities. Professor Bradley of Reading University has recently suggested that the deposition of weapons in the rivers may have been partly the result of a new type of burial ritual. A shield from the river at Long Wittenham was pierced with a spear before it was dropped in the water; a complete cauldron, a high status find probably used in feasting ceremonies, was placed in the river at Shipton-upon-Cherwell. This deliberate destruction of wealth, Bradley maintains, was meant to control its circulation. From the ruling élite's point of view, the families who could command the production of this expensive gear, its gift value would be reduced if there was too much of it around. So it was disposed of and dropped in the river. The gods would be appeased and the prestige of the person making the sacrifice would be enhanced. The difficulties of recovering such material would mean that no rival could pick it out and continue to pass it round to social peer groups in the constant round of gift giving which is likely to have characterized Bronze Age societies. I think that if one accepts this argument it emphasizes that goods were not traded simply to supply economic needs but to fulfil social and religious functions. Similarly, roads and rivers were not simply modes of travel for the distribution of goods. They were there to link communities and to provide a theatre for social action. At times they were processional paths, at other times funeral ways.

Roman Roads

The Oxford region was linked to the national communications network by the Romans during the first century AD. The two walled Roman towns within the county were preceded by military bases. A fort is thought to have been built at Dorchester at the confluence of the rivers Thame and Thames. A military origin has also been postulated for Alchester where soldiers' equipment has been found. Military occupation was followed by road building. Two roads linking these centres quartered the county area. Alchester is situated at the junction of the north–south route which runs from Towcester on Watling Street to Silchester, while Akeman Street runs east–west from Verulamium (St Albans) crossing the later county of Oxfordshire to Corinium (Cirencester). Both these roads are thought to have been established within a few years of the conquest. A third major road has been traced going in a south-westerly direction from the Oxford area, via Frilford in the Vale of the White Horse towards Wantage.

Ian Margary in his classic survey *Roman Roads in Britain* has tracked down in detail the courses of these roads using aerial photography, place name evidence, and meticulous fieldwork. It is worthwhile following one of them to gain some impression of the magnitude of the Roman road-builders' achievement as well as an insight into their construction techniques.

Akeman Street (the name is thought to relate to an earlier form of the place name of Bath. Akeman is probably an Anglo-Saxon personal name, perhaps an early ruler of the Bath region, so the road which eventually terminates at Bath took on the name) was an important east–west thoroughfare which ran through the south Midlands. It comes through Buckinghamshire keeping to the low, flat ground and, according to Margary, where it meets the river Ray it makes a change of direction to the south. Thence, aiming at Graven Hill, it makes an angled turn to the south-west, near Chesterton, and heads off on a fresh alignment westwards.

How did the Romans plan their roads with such skill? The corps of surveyors (called the *agrimensores* or *gromatici*) laid out their course in long straight alignments with the help of the *groma*, a wooden staff with cross bars from which hung bronze plummets suspended on plumb lines. This contrivance was used in conjunction with ranging rods and smoke or fire signals. The roads could be made straight because they had little to avoid except natural obstacles. Air photographs remind us of this. The fact that all field and other boundaries came up to the road but do not cross it indicates that the road was there first.

Akeman Street meets the north–south road a quarter of a mile north of Alchester, by Chesterton Lane. Here a section was examined in 1937 and it is possible to reconstruct the methods used. Although different parts of the road were built in slightly different ways, the main techniques of road building were as follows. Along the surveyed course a swathe of trees was cut down. This would produce raw materials and would improve security. A plough was employed to mark out the road zone and sometimes small ditches were dug on either side of the road to improve drainage. Where the ground was boggy brushwood and tree branches were spread. The road was built up by using layers of locally won material. Borrow pits are frequently found alongside. In this case the metalled road was twenty-nine feet wide, composed of large slabs of limestone laid horizontally but in no apparent order, twelve to fourteen inches thick. Other sections cut through Akeman Street, near Asthall, show that repairs consisting of further layers of clay and small pieces of limestones, topped with gravel, were piled on top. The road sections nearly all show a pronounced camber which must have aided drainage. The net effect of these works was to produce a low but distinct bank, the so-called *agger*. On occasions this was heightened to produce an impressive and doubtless prestigious display of Roman might. There were in fact political as well as economic reasons for this great expenditure of central government effort.

Pursuing its way westwards the *agger* of Akeman Street is visible at the point where the old road enters the grounds of Chesterton Lodge. There the modern road follows the course of the Roman road all the way to Kirtlington. A fine straight stretch of three miles or so, marked by hedgerows, leads the road to cross the steep valley of the river Cherwell. The *agger* is plainly visible, as Margary noted, as the road nears the canal bank. Hedgerows continue the line up the further slope to Tackley Park. The *agger* is thirty feet wide and three feet high along the park boundary and continues as a field track for a mile followed by a lane crossing the river Glyme at Stratford bridge (the place name is significant. Old English *strat* meaning a prepared road). It then crosses the main Oxford–Chipping Norton road, the A44, and enters Blenheim Park. Here a less destructive agricultural regime has resulted in a well preserved stretch. The Roman origin has been recognized since the seventeenth century when Gibson related that 'through this park runs the Consular Way, called Akeman Street, in a raised bank meeting it at Wootton Gate and going out of it at Mapleton Lodge'.

We have now entered the villa-rich zone of north Oxfordshire where there are as many as thirteen villa sites as well as other lesser Romano-British settlements. They include the palatial villa of North Leigh and the excavated site at Ditchley. It has been suggested that these villas, each the centre of a large estate run by slave labour, would have produced a substantial agricultural surplus which would have found its way by means of Akeman Street to the markets of Cirencester, Alchester and even Verulamium. Judging by the mass of pottery finds made by archaeology in these midland sites, the roads would also have been used to transport bulky goods such as pottery from the east Oxford kilns. Nearly every Roman site around here yields oyster shell, another indicator that the roads were efficient and speedy enough to transport this perishable commodity from the East coast.

The rest of the course of Akeman Street continues on a largely straight alignment through the southern part of Wychwood Forest. There is an interesting crossing at Wisdom's Copse and Standridge Copse (the latter place name means stony ridge and may refer to the road). The road approaches the valley edge in a shallow cutting, then it slants down the hillside as a terraceway to an embanked bridgehead that protrudes into the little valley. No doubt there was a timber bridge here which will in its turn have replaced a ford. A similar feature leads the road up another slanting terrace to resume the original alignment at the top of the slope.

The second major Roman road runs north–south from Towcester (Northamptonshire) to Silchester (Hampshire) through Oxfordshire and was very completely described by the Revd Robert Hussey in 1840. At Alchester it is plain to see, as an *agger* can be traced right to the stream which forms the southern boundary of the Roman town. It ran across marshes and the yet ill-drained Otmoor and crossed the river Ray just north of a slight rise named, significantly, Street Hill. Here, wooden piles for a bridge were discovered by R.A. (Charlie) Chambers of the Oxford Archaeological Unit in 1981 during dredging to enlarge the channel of the river Ray. Two large timbers 1.3 metres long and approximately 0.4 metres square, with pointed ends, were picked out of the river. When the water level dropped during dry weather the stumps of more oaken timbers were revealed *in situ*. It seems that the bridge was supported by two lines of timbers possibly designed to revet the bridge abutments. Dendrochronological sampling established a felling date for the oaks of soon after AD 95. If this is so, the timber bridge built at the end of the first century AD replaced a ford in use for the previous half century.

The route of the Alchester–Dorchester road is clear to the south of Otmoor. It leaves the flat land and climbs the high ground in the middle of Beckley ridge. Before the village it can be seen as a somewhat damaged *agger* and I noticed it in one of the cottage gardens. The limestone rubble metalling was obvious in section.

The course can be picked up again as a deeply sunken lane and footpath which mark its line on to Stow Wood. Margary suggests that this may be a cutting through the highest part of the ridge but nearly two thousand years of usage may have produced the effect without the necessity of engineering. Along the edge of Stow Wood is an *agger* twenty-four feet wide and one foot high. South of Stow Wood it is followed by the modern road down to the Bayswater Brook. At this point modern Oxford's development obliterates every trace. It is fortunate indeed that the Revd Hussey recorded it in detail 150 years ago. It runs for several miles through the Roman industrial region with dozens of pottery kilns.

The Roman road appears again at the south end of Bullingdon Green where a former lane bordering the back of the motor works marks the line. Beyond the railway the lane still runs south. It is known as Blackberry Lane north of Toot Baldon and south of the village where it becomes a sunken lane it is known as the Roman road. Past Pebble Hill, past the east side of Marsh Baldon Green, the *agger* is yet again to be seen about 20 feet wide and 1–2 feet high as it follows the straight line unwaveringly on to Dorchester.

These roads performed political and administrative, as well as economic, functions. They were designed for 'the rapid conveyance of people and messages' (Peter Salway's phrase). Troops moved along them and were supplied by them. They also carried imperial messengers and authorized officials. Along them sped the imperial post which could average a rate of travel of fifty miles a day. Governors were responsible for seeing that the main highways were maintained, hence the evidence for repair and maintenance. There was also a system of stations for changing horses (*mutationes*) and posting houses or inns (*mansiones*) but nothing of this kind has been so far located in the county.

A third major Roman road runs out in a south-westerly direction from Oxford towards Wantage. Margary suggested that this road may have crossed the river Thames from Osney to North Hinksey to the west of the city. From North Hinksey village a remarkably straight track leads up through a low col between Hurst Hill and Henwood towards Besselsleigh. Here the main alignment is seen in the park as a low ridge planted with old fir trees. At this point the modern road (A338) takes up the line through Frilford and Garford to Grove. Just to the north of the crossing of the river Ock was a small Roman urban settlement consisting of a cemetery, a temple, an amphitheatre and associated buildings. The straight alignment runs over the flat land of the Vale of the White Horse for about four and a half miles; it is slightly raised on a bank about two feet high. Recent Roman remains have been found at Wantage, but the further course of the road is unknown unless it links up with the Romanized Port Way running roughly parallel along the foot of the downs.

Apart from these through routes there are two stretches of minor road which display a number of puzzling features. Another Port Way, so called, leads off from Akeman Street at the north-west corner of Kirtlington Park. The modern road follows its course to a point a quarter of a mile to the east of Upper Heyford. The airfield has obliterated it here for a couple of miles but it appears again as a footpath, green lanes and a raised lane.

About half a mile north from the Port Way's junction with

Akeman Street another major archaeological feature known as Ash Bank, Wattle Bank or Aves Ditch branches off to the north-east. Since it runs in approximately the same direction as the Port Way it appears to duplicate its function if that was primarily to serve as a road. It is a very considerable earthwork in its own right, consisting of an *agger* in one place thirty feet wide and two feet high. It has even been claimed as a defensive work and not a road, but this seems untenable. It provided a clearly demarcated boundary for several Saxon settlement boundaries including Somerton, Fritwell and Ardley. (Here in an Anglo-Saxon charter it is called the Great Dyke.) As with the Port Way, no definite destination of Aves Bank has yet been determined unless it serves to connect a Roman settlement at Croughton with Akeman Street. Recent field work has shown that both these roads exhibit multiple slight changes of alignment round Fritwell which seem to be aimed at keeping the road on a higher level. (*Council for British Archaeology Group* 9 Newsletter 1974; 10–11 1975 16)

Anglo-Saxon Roads

If there are many unanswered questions about the Roman road system the picture is still relatively clear compared with the fogs which obscure the communications of Anglo-Saxon England. Virtually nothing is known until we reach the period in the ninth and tenth centuries from which the oldest English land books (or charters as they are commonly called) date. These contain innumerable references to short lengths of roads and tracks bordering properties, the boundaries of which they describe. Unfortunately, since they never indicate the farms or villages between which these roads run, it is a matter of great difficulty to construct a map. However, it is clear that there is already a hierarchy of roads in existence. There was the *portstraet*, a road leading to a town or market, a *cyngesferd straet* along which the local militia would move, a *herestraet* or *herepath* suitable for the passage of an army, a *hryegweg* was a ridgeway, or a road which follows the comb of a ridge.

John Blair has attempted to reconstruct the evidence for trade and communications in the Mercian period and he postulates several north–south routeways crossing the upper Thames well above Oxford. In particular, he sees a road coming south from Burford, crossing the Thames at Radcot, and continuing on to Stanford and Wantage. Another from Bampton, an important place in the eleventh century in his estimation, but thereafter declining, goes south and crosses the Thames, so connecting with the main road running from London via Faringdon westwards and marked on the Gough map.

His detailed field work, combined with a close study of the maps, has convincingly resurrected a lost crossing of the braided course of the Thames at Binsey. Before the construction of the Botley causeway in the sixteenth century there were bridges across the Seacourt stream between Seacourt and Binsey and a ford across the Thames at Medley known as Binsey ford. Anthony à Wood, the seventeenth-century Oxford antiquary, believed that the now deserted village of Seacourt had been 'a thorough fare towne from Einsham and the westerne parts to Oxon (long before the other way by Botley was thought upon) with a bridge at the crossing of the Seacourt stream indicated by stones lying in great abundance in the river'.

One of the most important roads in Anglo-Saxon England was the north–south route which bisected the Midlands and joined Northampton to Southampton via Brackley, Oxford, Newbury and Winchester. Along its course, as we shall see, grew up the Anglo-Saxon town of Oxford whose early commercial connection with Lincolnshire and Cambridge-shire is demonstrated by the presence of Stamford and St Neots wares, both distinctive pottery types found in profusion in late Anglo-Saxon and Norman levels in Oxford city. This road, the modern course of which goes north out of the city as Banbury Road, is called *portstraet* in the Cutteslow charter, *straet* in the charter of Shipton-on-Cherwell and *portstraet* in the charter of Whitehill in Tackley.

Going south from St Giles, the course is taken up by Cornmarket, past Carfax, down St Aldates, and then downhill and out of the walled city by the south gate and across the river Thames by Folly Bridge. At Oxford, the river Thames has been forded or crossed by a succession of paved, hard surfaces, causeways and bridges since the eighth century AD. It has been suggested that the first modification of the river crossing may have been undertaken during the reign of the Mercian King Offa. Oxford, after all, may have started life as a frontier town, with the river Thames forming the boundary between Mercia and Wessex. A Saxon ford which preceded the construction of a clay banked causeway went out of use. Archaeologists still dispute as to whether the clay covering it is the result of human agency or alluvial deposition. What is certain is that Robert d'Oilly, the first Norman Constable of Oxford Castle, decided to replace the late Saxon crossing at this point with a *grand pont*. I remember investigating the underside of the arches in 1981 in a punt with Cynthia Bradford. We noticed that the present structure of Folly Bridge, to the south of the three navigation arches of the eighteenth century, was the result of a number of masonry builds, separated by straight joints. Embedded in the middle, and between 3.9 metres and 4 metres wide, were a series of semi-circular arches which appeared Romanesque in character. Subsequent work by Brian Durham and the Oxford Archaeological Unit has established that these are indeed parts of the Norman bridge. Furthermore, the Grand Pont was seen to be a great causeway extending for one and a half miles across the braided course of the river Thames with as many as forty-two multiple flood arches. The present Abingdon Road runs south of the city along the top of this causeway. The bridge itself has been claimed to be one of the earliest stone bridges to have survived from medieval Europe.

A second road existing in Anglo-Saxon times ran eastwards along the High Street, through the east gate of the city and over the Cherwell where there was a bridge from at least

1004, later known as Pettypont East Bridge, and finally Magdalen Bridge. The recovery of Viking stirrups from the river bed nearby may indicate that before these bridges there was a fording point. The old road ran towards London by ascending Headington Hill as far as Cheney Lane where it divided. One route went up over Shotover, the other passed by way of Cheney Lane and Old Road. The road over Shotover (now in the Country Park) is a broad green track and, according to Grundy, was used by drovers taking cattle to London right up to the railway age. The drovers of the eighteenth and nineteenth centuries were jealous of attempted encroachment on the breadth of these drove or driftways. Their cattle fed on the grassy borders beside the track. They were broad so that when a track became rutted and miry it could be bypassed by another. The track converts to a road before Wheatley is reached and traverses the village by the main street before descending by a long hill to the river Thame. It is called *straet* in the Cuddesdon charter and the ford by which it crosses the Thames is called *Herepath Ford*, ford of the army path.

Major changes in the road pattern have taken place in the roads coming into Oxford from the east and west. The main road from London to St Davids approached Oxford by three stages: Uxbridge, High Wycombe and Tetsworth, along the course still taken by the A40 until Forest Hill. The Gloucester road at this point went through Forest Hill and Islip and so westwards without going through Oxford. The climb to Oxford over Shotover had always been difficult and in winter almost impassable. It was turnpiked in 1718, and in 1770 the trustees constructed a new route over the lower ground to the north. This became the modern A40. The Shotover route along the top of the ridge has remained unmetalled and is now no longer part of the through route.

To the west of Oxford, the Witney road, before the building of the A40 in the twentieth century, began its circuitous route by climbing up Wytham Hill from Botley Lodge. A track now runs west-north-west through a belt of woodland, past stands of beech and filled in gravel pits onto the top of Wytham Hill. It drops down the slope of Beacon Hill and crosses the Thames at Swinford Bridge, constructed by the Earl of Abingdon in the mid eighteenth century to replace the pig ford. It then makes its way via Eynsham to Witney and so over the Cotswolds to Burford, Cheltenham and Gloucester.

Wallingford, Abingdon and Oxford

The diversion of a road or the building of a bridge could have a crucial effect on the fortunes of a town. There are three examples of this in Oxfordshire. The Saxon burh at Wallingford acquired its great rectilinear earthen rampart in the late ninth century as part of King Alfred's system of defence against the Danes. The grid of its street pattern was laid out at the same time. The Normans confirmed the importance of Wallingford by building a great castle there and constructing a long, multi-arched bridge part of which contains structure dating back to the twelfth century. Wallingford, it would seem, was all set to become a prosperous medieval market town with a guild hall and separate corn and fish markets. In fact, it decayed from the mid thirteenth century and the town began to shrink in size and population. In Henry II's reign it is said to have had eleven churches; these had declined by the fifteenth century to four. An outbreak of plague in 1343 severely damaged the town, but the *coup de grâce* was given by the diversion through Abingdon of the main road from London to Gloucester and South Wales in 1416. By the nineteenth century, great gaps had opened up between the houses, shops and market places. Wallingford has large grassy areas behind its walls because it has never recovered the prosperity promised in the early Middle Ages.

Wallingford's downfall was Abingdon's opportunity. By the early fifteenth century, silting of the Thames, the dangerous passage of the ford and the frequent floodings of the intermediate road threatened to cut off the town from the metropolis and the arterial waterway of the river. A group of Abingdon businessmen decided to help themselves and the town by building two bridges, one at Culham and one at Abingdon, the so called 'Burford' bridge, and link them with a causeway. This work was largely financed by Geoffrey Barbour, an Abingdon merchant who gave 1000 marks towards the works. In 1453 William Hales, and Maud, his wife, added three arches to one of the bridges, the road still being subject to inundations. The result was that goods could then be unloaded at Culham onto wagons and taken, by means of the causeway, across the Burford bridge to Abingdon. Even more important, road traffic heading west towards Gloucester had previously gone by means of a circuitous route via Wallingford. It was now moved directly through Abingdon and contributed to its prosperity.

Oxford's fortunes were also closely linked with the river Thames. The building of Robert d'Oilly's causeway at the Grand Pont would have led to the deepening and canalization of the river. Weirs and mills also began to be constructed in large numbers, with the result that the river became both deeper and slower and therefore more suitable for navigation. By the thirteenth century, however, the number of weirs had so increased that navigation began to be severely disrupted. Despite legislation attempting to restrict the number and the height of weirs, complaints continued, and we read of them throughout the thirteenth and fourteenth centuries. The wealth and population were shrinking during this period, and as urban rents diminished, houses were pulled down. With rent and accommodation so cheap the poor scholars of the University benefited. As the urban fortunes of the city declined so the University grew. Newly founded colleges were able to buy up sites in the eastern part of the city cheaply. The result is the amazing compactness and density of the collegiate buildings which make Oxford unique in the way it has spread over more than half the medieval city. The difficulties of river navigation thus account for the University's early growth.

Medieval Bridges

The medieval communications system has been shown by modern research to have been a good deal more efficient than used to be thought. Already, by the end of the Middle Ages, the Thames and other principal rivers in England had been bridged by about 200 stone and timber structures, supplemented by ferries. Oxfordshire is particularly fortunate in the high survival rate of its medieval bridges. The Thames is still crossed by bridges constructed by medieval engineers at Radcot, Newbridge, Abingdon (Burford), Oxford (Folly), Culham and Wallingford. There is another long bridge at Abingdon crossing the Ock. The Thames tributaries are similarly served. An early sixteenth-century bridge crosses the Evenlode at Burford. The Thame has three; at Chiselhampton (the upstream side is medieval), Ickford and Wheatley (a single arch in an otherwise eighteenth-century rebuild). A number of important bridge discoveries have been made in recent years. Folly Bridge, as we have seen, is now recognized as having Norman stonework embedded in its widened road way. Two twelfth-century arches have been discovered at Henley-on-Thames a little to the south of the eighteenth-century replacement. One is in the cellar of a public house on the Oxfordshire side of the river; the other has been preserved under the headquarters of the Henley Regatta building on the Berkshire side. Furthermore, the county bridge engineer, John Andrew, recognized that under the Woodstock–Chipping Norton road, where it crosses the Glyme at Old Woodstock, there was a Gothic arch. He took great delight in persuading me to crawl along a dark, wet, muddy culvert to inspect it in the early 1980s. Finally, the Cherwell was crossed by a Gothic arched bridge with a long causeway and flood arches at Heyford; and Banbury has two thirteenth-century arches with ribbing where the road to Brackley crosses the Cherwell by the station.

There were no doubt a myriad of smaller timber bridges across minor streams which have now disappeared. Sometimes the streams themselves have been diverted or culverted beneath towns. The river Stert at Abingdon still flows as such an underground stream below the church of St Nicholas. At Abingdon, too, Tim Allen of the Oxford Archaeological Unit found such a wooden bridge dated by tree rings (dendrochronology) to c.1510. It consisted of trestles of elm laid on the bed of a wet ditch, with uprights and braces still in place. It has been lifted and conserved, but at present languishes undisplayed in the County Museum Store at Standlake. Other Thames bridges had a timber component. The seventeenth-century paintings of Henley-on-Thames bridge show a timber trestle upperwork; the bridge at Caversham seen in the eighteenth-century engraving was partly of timber construction.

The ancient bridges of Oxfordshire are fortunate to have been the subjects of a series of watercolour sketches by Mrs Davenport, who accompanied her husband, the County Surveyor, as he went on his rounds of inspection in the 1870s. Her sketchbook, in the County Record Office, gives valuable details about the condition of bridges before the radical repairs of the motor-car age.

The physical characteristics of medieval stone bridges can be easily summarized. Often, as at Heyford, Folly Bridge Oxford and the Ock Bridge Abingdon they were approached by long 'causeways over dirt'. These causeways were pierced with minor arches designed to take floodwater and remind us of the very different circumstances prevailing in these valleys in the upper Thames basin in the Middle Ages. They were all braided streams, shallow and shoaly, and during each winter flooded broadly over the neighbouring meadows. Heyford Bridge has carefully cut Gothic floodwater arches. The Grand Pont at Oxford, as we have seen, has no less than forty-two arches over a one and a half mile causewayed length. The arches over the navigation streams were often humped in profile, with the central arch higher and wider than the rest, as at Newbridge, Burford and Radcot. On the upstream side were cutwaters, which were triangular in shape, designed to divert the pressure of the stream away from the bases of the bridge through the arches. These cutwaters were continued to parapet level, providing pedestrian refuges. The Romanesque arches at Oxford and Wallingford were semi-circular in shape; all the rest are pointed Gothic, strengthened with projecting ribs similar in construction to Gothic vaults. Sometimes the ribs are cut away, as at Newbridge, to widen the arch for larger barge traffic. Medieval bridges in the main were built to take only one cart width. They were very frequently widened from the seventeenth to the twentieth centuries. This was done without taking the whole bridge down – traffic must not be interrupted. Further additions were usually made on the downstream side, but sometimes the medieval bridge was embedded in widenings of a different period on both sides as at Wallingford. The only way to sort this out is to inspect the underside of the bridge when the straight joints between the different masonry builds can be detected. Wallingford is particularly interesting in this respect because it was enlarged in the sixteenth century with moulded stones taken from one of the twelfth-century churches in the town.

How were these long-lasting bridges paid for? Medieval English society was agrarian based and very poor by modern standards. Its economy approximated in many ways to modern 'third world' countries. Late Saxon government laid down the so called '*trinoda necessitas*', the obligation of local communities to contribute towards bridge building. They sought the permission to levy pontage grants in the thirteenth and fourteenth centuries, royal licenses authorizing the levying of tolls on goods crossing the bridge in order to pay for construction or repairs. Pontage was granted for Radcot Bridge in 1312 for five years. Subsequent grants gave the lords whose lands adjoined the bridge the right to exact tolls. Here, the responsibility was shared equally by the Oxfordshire lord of Radcot and by the Berkshire lord of Faringdon. The bridge was damaged in the Battle of Radcot Bridge in 1387 and so there was a further pontage grant to John Symond and John Fissher of Radcot for two years.

Taxation for specified purposes such as bridge maintenance was supplemented by endowment for devotional and pious reasons. The Guild of the Holy Cross was set up at Abingdon to maintain the Burford Bridge built across the Thames in 1416. It also had the task of maintaining thirteen poor old men and women and supporting two chaplains. When guilds were abolished in Edward VI's reign, the functions of the Abingdon Guild were discharged by Christ's Hospital. Chapels were founded on or near bridges. At Oxford, the town appointed bridge hermits in the thirteenth century, entrusted with alms for carrying out repairs. The Hermitage or Bridgewrights' place stood opposite the way-side chapel of St Nicholas, where alms were collected for the upkeep of the bridge. Its position within Berkshire, and yet also at least half inside the boundaries of the city, led to confusion over the responsibility for repairs. The Mileways Acts of 1570 and 1593 provided for the maintenance of roads and bridges within a mile of the city by the inhabitants who lived within five miles. Even this failed to provide enough funds and the bridge continued to cause problems until it was completely rebuilt in 1827. A toll house, which is still there (acting as a kiosk), was added, but by 1850, the trustees having recouped their investment, the bridge was freed of tolls.

In Henley-on-Thames the maintenance of the bridge during the later Middle Ages was undertaken by two officers appointed by the Guild, the élite of merchants and traders who dominated the government of this small seignorial borough. The bridgemen administered various properties donated by townsmen and used the proceeds to keep the bridge in good repair.

Saltways

Salt was a vital commodity in the ancient world for flavouring and even more for preserving foodstuffs, especially meat and fish. Roman soldiers had an allowance of salt called 'salarium'; later this was commuted to a money payment for services in general and so the meaning 'salary' has emerged.

The expression 'worth his salt' derives from this. Salt was produced by evaporation all round the east and south coasts, but Oxfordshire drew most of its supplies from a land-based source in neighbouring Worcestershire around Droitwich. Salt was distributed by pack-horse along a network of roads radiating out from Droitwich. Our earliest knowledge of these saltways is contained in Pre-Conquest charters which refer to salt streets, salters, fords and so on. Domesday Book gives us the names of sixty-eight manors which had the right to receive a certain amount of salt. Thirty-eight are in Worcestershire, eleven in Gloucestershire, ten in Hereford-shire, six in Warwickshire, two in Oxfordshire (Rollright and Bampton) and one in Buckinghamshire (Princes Risborough). This information is supplemented in the Middle Ages by documents referring to saltways, salters barns, salters mills, and if all these places are plotted on a map it becomes possible to reconstruct the salters' ways with some confidence.

One of the saltways which crosses Oxfordshire leads out from Four Shire Stones on the north-west boundary with Gloucestershire and Warwickshire and points in a south-easterly direction. It ran through Little Compton where there are Salters Barn and Salters Mill. A road ran off left to Rollright, one of the Domesday settlements having salt rights. The road runs through Salford (referred to as Salteford in an Anglo-Saxon charter) to Chipping Norton. From here one road heads south towards Bampton, fifteen miles away, via Shipton-under-Wychwood and Widford, where there was a Salter's Corner. Others led south-east. There is an old track leading towards Stonesfield where it joins Akeman Street. This is a broad green lane with wide verges and ancient hedgerows and is known as the Salter's Way. The Roman road, Akeman Street, was used for four to five miles at this point to a point five miles east-south-east of Bicester where there is an almost uninterrupted course along minor roads leading fourteen miles to Risborough.

An alternative route from Droitwich to Bampton goes through Maugersbury and along Salt Street to Icomb, the western boundary of which is stated in an eighth-century charter to pass through a Saltwelle. From Icomb, the route cuts through Idbury and Widford where, as we have seen, was a Salter's Corner, and so to Bampton. A third possible route connecting Droitwich with Risborough leads by way of Stratford-upon-Avon, through Tysoe to Wroxton and North Newington, where there is another Salt Way. Thence, by Adderbury and Aynhoe to Akeman Street, and so to Risborough.

Turnpike Roads

The original liability for the repair of medieval highways in each manor lay upon the holders of land. Townships were called on to maintain works adjacent or beneficial to the common fields. The lord of the manor was liable when the work benefited or was situated near the demesne land. Heavy use of roads and bridges caused a breakdown in this system and it was replaced by the Highway Act of 1555, whereby the manorial duty was transferred to the parish. For every ploughland in tillage or pasture he occupied within the parish, each parishioner had to provide for four days in the year 'one wain or cart furnished after the custom of the county ... and also two able men with the same'. Every other householder, cottager and labourer had to put in four days labour or send 'one sufficient labourer in his stead'. Unpaid surveyors of highways, an unpopular and unwelcome task, at first appointed by parishioners, but after 1691 appointed by the Justices of the Peace, were entrusted with the supervision of this 'Statute labour'.

The parish system failed to work out well in practice. The surveyors were untrained and their gangs of labourers reluctant and inefficient. Householders who might have injected some energy into the system preferred to buy their way out by commuting their statute labour for cash payments. Since the tenure of the office of surveyor lasted only one year it meant that any practical experience gained would be quite wasted when another inexperienced surveyor took on the job. Little was understood of scientific road repairs. Work was limited to scouring of ditches, cropping of hedges and throwing rocks into the deepest of the potholes. Cottagers, who were supposed to do the work, spent their time soliciting alms from passers-by or drinking ale at the expense of the householders. The roads which were the object of the surveyor's efforts were often limited to the lanes and byways used by the locals, the through routes were neglected.

Among the worst roads in the pre-turnpike age in Oxfordshire was that between Oxford and Banbury. This was damaged by heavy wagons bringing malt and hops to the Oxford breweries. Arthur Young, writing in 1813, stated: 'I remember the roads of Oxfordshire forty years ago, when they were in a condition formidable to the bones of all who travelled on wheels.' In 1779 he described the Witney–Northleach road as the worst he had ever travelled 'so bad that it is a scandal to the country ... they mend and make only with local stone, in pieces as large as a man's head'. Before the Enstone–Bicester road was turnpiked in 1794, it had high sloping banks 'along which stood very lofty trees, growing in such a manner that their roots spread from one side of the road to the other, intertwining in the middle, so any vehicle passing up or down was severely tried or bumped'.

Drove roads, used for the long distance movement of animals from Wales and the West Country to London and other urban areas, further contributed to the problem. The road surfaces rapidly deteriorated with the pressure of thousands of animals' hooves. Clearly, if the full economic potential of the early modern age was to be realized, something radical needed to be done about the road system.

The turnpike trusts were an attempt to improve the roads through private enterprise and investment capital in place of statute labour and the parish system. They were based on the common sense principle that the users of the road should pay for its upkeep. Those who wished to set up a trust had to get an act of parliament. They were groups of men, usually local landowners, farmers and merchants, who had a vested interest in road improvement. They acquired responsibility for a stretch of road, set up gates, charged tolls to travellers and with the money so gained carried out repairs; investors could expect a dividend if the traffic brought in enough tolls.

The turnpike system brought a number of new changes in the physical appearance of the county. To begin with, swinging bars – tapering counterbalanced beams, pivoted to swing in a horizontal plane in order to block the road – were placed at strategic points. These were the turnpikes. Later, these bars were replaced by wooden gates on the main road, but the bars were retained to block off minor roads. Toll-houses were built at each of these gates; again, to begin with, these were temporary wooden structures. When the increasing volume of traffic looked like ensuring the continuance of the turnpike trust, more substantial and distinctive houses were built of brick or stone. They were small: their size is an interesting indication of what was thought appropriate to working-class accommodation when nearly all such housing has otherwise disappeared. They were often semi-octagonal in plan, with the bayed front containing windows in its angled sides. This enabled the toll collector to view the road in either direction from within the house. Each toll-house had to display its charges on a painted wooden toll-board mounted in front of the building. Swinford Bridge toll-house still has its tariff displayed in this way. The improved road itself was a further and most noticeable feature. It often cut off corners, included new straight stretches, and involved improved or newly built bridges. The bridge at Long Hanborough, for instance, was rebuilt in 1798 at the cost of the turnpike trust, the parish of Hanborough and the Duke of Marlborough. It is still there, a handsome two-arched structure with additional flood arches. It was bypassed in 1952 when a new bridge was built improving a dangerous corner. One final feature of the turnpike trusts were milestones. An act of 1775 ordered that all turnpike trusts were to provide milestones and guideposts along all their roads. The milestones in Oxfordshire are highly varied in design, many being unique to a particular trust. A veterinary surgeon, Mr Keith Lawrence, has recorded all of them and put the information into the archives of the County Museum. Some are straightforward, round-headed blocks. Some are faceted, some cylindrical. Many have or had (because they were removed in the war) iron plates with information about mileages to nearest towns.

The effect of the turnpike system was not immediately felt because the growth of the system was gradual. The main roads in Oxfordshire formed parts of the through routes from London to the Midlands and North Wales via Stokenchurch, Wheatley, Enstone and Chipping Norton. Along this road in the late eighteenth century moved a great volume of traffic; twenty-two farm horse coaches passed through Enstone every day and night; and at least half a dozen heavy wagons did likewise. There was also the London to South Wales road via Henley, Abingdon and Faringdon. These were among the earliest roads turnpiked in the county between 1718 and 1740. Thereafter, the network grew rapidly and by 1830 there were thirty trusts controlling 434 miles of road.

There is no doubt that the trusts improved the quality of the roads they controlled. George Cave was surveyor to a number of the county trusts and he followed the methods devised by John MacAdam. This was cheaper than Telford's technique of an expensive base of hand-placed large stones. Instead, a layer of small irregular-shaped stones, ground together by the wheels of vehicles resulting in a fine gritted surface, was employed. A slight camber and ditches on both sides resulted in a hard, well drained surface. The actual course followed by most turnpiked roads was that of the ancient thoroughfares. Occasionally, however, they were straightened and short cuts adopted. The medieval highway between Woodstock and Chipping Norton was replaced by a new road (the A34). The method used by the new roadmakers was not very promising. It consisted of ploughing up the whole length of the road; the furrow thus ploughed was six miles in length from end to end.

The re-alignment which took place at Burford had an adverse effect on some of the trade of the town. To begin with, the original coach road from Oxford to Gloucester, turnpiked in 1751, entered the town from White Hill and Witney Street and left via Sheep Street and Upton Lane. Several inns such as the Bull Hotel (which acquired a new eighteenth-century brick front) benefited from the travellers along the route. They stood to lose, however, when in 1812 the track along the top of the ridge above the town was turnpiked. Coaches on the way to Gloucester now no longer needed to descend the difficult steep hill and a new inn, the 'Bird in Hand' (now renamed the Cotswold Gateway), was built at the top of the hill in the 1820s.

The road leading west out of Oxford, leaving the city at George Street and going across Botley Causeway, was turnpiked in 1767. The plan of Sir William Blackstone, the administrator of the estates of the late Earl of Abingdon, was to repair the derelict causeway and replace the ferry at Swinford, near Eynsham, with a toll bridge. The new bridge was probably designed by Sir Robert Taylor and was opened in 1769. The road over Wytham Hill was improved but remained steep and difficult and, it was said, a haunt for highwaymen. In 1810, the lower road through Farmoor to Botley was built, but the old road over Wytham was not given up by the trustees until 1835.

The turnpike age wrought great changes to the city of Oxford. It was said in the early nineteenth century that 'Nearly a hundred coaches came every day to and through Oxford posting to and from London'. This, of course, encouraged the multiplication of inns with ample stabling for hundreds of horses which needed to be groomed and fed. The Clarendon Inn in Corn Street (pulled down in a fit of philistinism to be replaced by a brutal concrete store), the Golden Cross (now lovingly restored and used as a pizza parlour), the Angel and the Star were all part of a galaxy of inns. Hundreds of people, grooms, grocers, vintners, carters, farmers were involved directly or indirectly in the transit trade. Much of this collapsed with the coming of the railway age.

The turnpikes enjoyed a period of prosperity and then, like

the canals and railways after them, experienced a long period of decline. The most prosperous period was the late eighteenth and early nineteenth centuries. In 1821, thirteen trusts in Oxfordshire were in difficulties. By 1837, fifteen trusts, controlling 208 miles, were no longer profitable. The competition of the railways, which provided faster and cheaper transport for both passengers and goods, certainly contributed to their decline. Many of the county's roads were disturnpiked in the 1870s. The Oxford–Banbury road was disturnpiked in 1875, the Oxford–Woodstock road in 1878. Judging from old photographs, they were still dusty in summer and muddy in winter before the motor-car age, but at least the turnpikes had preserved the road system intact and had served the early industrial age well.

VI
Rivers and Canals

The River Thames

The Thames has exerted a lasting fascination for my family. My father, the son of an ironmonger and oil merchant in London's Lambeth Walk, moved with his parents to Maidenhead before World War I. Here, he grew up to enjoy all the sport and recreation the river could offer in the halcyon days before 1914. When he married my mother in 1923, it was natural that he would think of taking his new wife for a week-long cruise in a camping punt from Maidenhead to Reading and back again. Our family photograph album has faded sepia snaps of my mother, in flowery hat and full muslin dress, reclining among the cushions under the canvas-covered frame of the punt; my father, in shirt-sleeves and straw hat, manfully poling. The memory of this honeymoon trip with its tranquil days of slowly punting through rush-lined meadows remained green throughout my parents' lives. After World War II, my father's favourite family outing was to take his wife and two sons on the river and punt us from Richmond to Kingston and back. Fortified, I recall, by homemade bacon pasties, we boys used to fend off the banks with paddles while my father sought a gravelly bottom with the forked end of his punt pole.

The Thames in 1995, was still bedecked with pleasure craft. Visiting Pinkhill lock (near Eynsham), Godstow and Oseney locks (near Oxford), and Iffley lock, to the south of the city, in that drought summer, I was struck by the enormous numbers of people attracted to the river who congregated at these points for pleasure. Their various activities are not always compatible. The banks are made inaccessible and positively dangerous by steel pins driven in for temporary moorings. Long stretches of otherwise beautiful, leafy and quiet water are hidden behind a continuous range of motor boats, yachts and launches, many of them rotting away, the fluvial equivalent of a linear caravan park. Joggers lope by. Litter, old tins and worse bob up and down among the reeds. At times, large launches, clearly breaking the four miles per hour speed limit and churning waves which quickly erode the gravel and clay banks of the river, pass by, clambered over by bronzed lager louts, yelling insults and playing ghetto blasters in defiance at the Thames Water Authority's very reasonable regulations. Their vulgar presence rocks the passage of single sculled rowers; or those novel phenomena on the Thames, the women's eight, the mixed eight, or the male eight coxed by a woman.

The function of the river to provide pleasure came late in the history of the Thames. From the earliest documentary records the river is seen in its business capacity, providing water for the mutually conflicting demands of fishing, milling and navigating. These obviously required some degree of governmental regulation. By the twelfth century, the city of London is reputed to have exercised jurisdiction over the whole of the Thames, but in fact it is more likely that this only extended up to London Stone, a marker at Staines. Royal water bailiffs were appointed by the Crown to supervise the river west of this point. The statute book throughout the Middle Ages is littered with fierce but ultimately ineffective orders to keep the navigation channel free of the impediments constructed by millers and fishermen. These impediments took four main forms: fish weirs, mill dams, locks and bridges. Fishermen congregated round weirs, which were artificial barriers of stakes, stones and brushwood, constructed to hold the water of the river back. They caught the fish by means of bucks and weels, or by nets. These techniques continued in use up until the end of the nineteenth century; from early photographs by Henry Taunt of Oxford and others we can reconstruct the weels. They were designed particularly to catch eels and other large fish, and consisted of long vase-shaped structures made of osiers, with wide flared mouths. The eel nosed its way in through a cave of osier twigs which closed behind him and was caught in the apex. The fish were removed by means of a plug at this end which also served for the introduction of bait. Such fish traps were sunk in rows across the river or attached across to a sluice. Bucks were large permanent frames to which were connected larger versions of weels. Anglers fishing for sport of course had their rods, lines and hooks, but nets were the main method used by the Thameside fishermen in Oxfordshire. These were made of hemp steeped in preservative and were held down to the bed of the river with ponderous stone weights. The weights, pear-shaped or roughly triangular, with a hole drilled or pecked into the apex, were made of limestone throughout most of the course of the Oxfordshire Thames, but changed to brick east of the Goring gap when the stone was no longer available. They were lost in the river by the fishermen, especially near weirs, and can be picked up from the upcast of modern dredging operations. The grooves running from the perforation to the top of the weight show that they were tied rather than pegged. The nets themselves have not survived, but they were undoubtedly of different mesh sizes, as the regulations mentioning 'Tramills, casting-netts, flagnetts, trollnets, shownetts and all other nets and gynes' indicate. While poaching was undoubtedly rife, there were rules protecting fish stock just as in parks and forests the fence months, between February and June, were to protect deer. The fishermen tended to ally with the millers since it was in each of their interests to husband a good head of water at the weir and dam. The activities of both groups cut across the concerns of the navigators.

Millers built their weirs and wheels at points on the river where they were able to take advantage of a change of gradient. Domesday Book records over 250 mills within the present county bounds, many of them on the tributaries of the main rivers as well as on the Thames itself. Those recognized by archaeological evidence nearly always involve significant earthworks which were necessary to control and make best use of uncertain water supplies. James Bond, my

Deputy County Archaeologist, and I surveyed one such site during the drought summer of 1976 on the edge of the northern end of the Great Lake at Blenheim Park. We found a series of features: a stone-revetted bank, a leat directing the stream water to the pond above the mill, the rectangular shape of the mill buildings, the stone-lined wheel pit and the tail race, the grassed-over channels showing up dark green in the brown sunburned grass. Documentary evidence shows that in 1334 a mill in Woodstock Park was moved to a new site; it is likely that this is the site concerned.

Mills were highly desirable and profitable pieces of capital equipment, performing multifarious functions from grinding corn, powering the heavy hammers for iron making and replacing the labour intensive task of walking the cloth in the cloth fulling process. Early fulling mills are recorded in 1208 at Brightwell, and in 1223 two are mentioned at Witney. Their ownership led to unseemly, interminable litigious disputes between religious houses and other competing interests. Such wrangles between Oseney and Rewley abbeys, which both claimed the use of Thames water and tried to divert it from the Castle Mills, thus aggrieving the townsmen of Oxford, are particularly well documented. The fourteenth and fifteenth centuries are punctuated with the rival leat digging, sluice construction, and water diversion in the area of middle and upper Fisher Row in Oxford, as Mary Prior vividly narrates.

The millers and the fishermen had certain advantages over the navigators in the sense that they were in possession of the banks and controlled the weirs which determined the water levels over which the more transient bargemen and boat-owners wished to travel. While the king invariably favoured the latter in the interests of keeping the internal (and therefore easily taxable) trade moving, he was handicapped by an ineffective law enforcement system. To begin with, the dams and weirs built across the braided course of the Thames may have aided navigation by increasing the depth of the channel. The difficulty was passing the weirs: the 'flashlocks' were numerous, dangerous and costly. From Reading to

Oxford in the late Middle Ages there were no less than twenty-six locks. Passage through a lock meant the temporary removal of a section of the weir in the form of wooden rymers or paddles slotting into a wooden framework, causing a flash or rush of water seeking the lower level. The boat waiting above the weir on its passage downstream would be caught in the *debouchement* and as likely as not would be swirled unnavigably into the whirlpool below. Coming upstream was even worse. A winch needed to be built on the bank, and the barge hitched by cable and dragged up over the weir when the flash took place. The dangers of the cable parting or the labourers working the winch pausing from exhaustion made this all the more hazardous. The miller would make the navigator pay, not only a toll, but also in time, so barges might have to wait for days until a sufficient head of water built up or until it suited the miller to move the rymers. Robert Peberdy has calculated that the costs of providing the barge, paying the crew and the rowers, as well as footing the bills of the tolls and pontage (passing under bridges), would have made river navigation excessively expensive.

The solutions adopted during the Middle Ages were twofold: to make new cuts to ease the navigation round difficult passages in the river or to remove the weirs entirely. The first was done on a small scale, particularly in the reaches of the river around Abingdon; the second never proved practically possible. Monasteries, as in other aspects of medieval civil engineering, led the way. They had the resources, the motivation, the long-term vision and the shared experience of being part of an international order. Ethelwold, appointed Abbot of Abingdon in AD 953 had come from Glastonbury where doubtless he had experienced water management problems in the Somerset fens. 'He made a water-channel under the abbey court and built the mill there', says the chronicler. This mill worked for a thousand years. The wheel can still be seen under an inserted glass floor in the restaurant built over the site. The navigation channel was enhanced a century later in *c.*1055 when it was widened 'through the meadow to the south of the church', and passing boats had to pay a toll of herrings during Lent. This improvement was made at the request of the townsmen of Oxford and it does seem that in the late eleventh and twelfth centuries the upper Thames was in use for the bulk movement of goods such as grain, timber and wine.

Thorold Rogers in his *History of Prices* claimed that in the late Middle Ages the Thames was not navigable above Henley-on-Thames and that goods going west needed to be transhipped here and put on carts for an overland journey. This assertion is weakened by the evidence from the Public Records. The clerks of works at the royal castles of Wallingford and Windsor during their fourteenth-century rebuilding programmes were still able to rely on river-borne transport. Barges carrying stone from Taynton and Wheatley made their ponderous and halting way down river. The stone from the Taynton quarries was carried by cart to Radcot. There are large blocks still lying in a field near the medieval wharves. Some was put on boat, barge or raft at Eynsham. At Abingdon the abbey's building operations were furnished with stone carried down from their quarries at Wheatley to Sandford. Here, in the years 1375-6 and 1383-4, 120 loads were ferried across and the Abbey's ferryman earned one pound and a new tunic. Generally, however, it is true that the millers and fishermen succeeded in obstructing the navigation because time after time the Crown ordered the removal of their dams and weirs and nothing was done. Henley-on-Thames, on the other hand, became a flourishing entrepot port in the late Middle Ages. Grain that came from the Vale of Aylesbury and the Chiltern foothills was stockpiled in the warehouses and wharves of Henley. Here, grain factors bought very large quantities for the London market and sent it by barge down the river to the capital.

In the middle of the sixteenth century we have an excellent source of information about the activities of one Thames bargeman. Thomas West of Wallingford had a half share in a barge, the *Mary Grace*, and from his will and inventory of goods and debts it seems that he was a corn dealer and woodmonger with an extensive trade from London to the upper Thameside towns, including Marlow, Reading and Oxford. Even so, he was only able to use water transport up to Sutton Courtenay, Buscot and Culham. Here he had agents responsible for transhipping and sending the goods on by road. He stockpiled coal from Newcastle which had come via London at Buscot. His downward trade was chiefly in corn, malt, timber and firewood which he supplied to the court. His iron went as far as the smiths of Cassington and Wolvercote beyond Oxford. But what must have chiefly delighted the Tudor housewives of the upper Thames Valley were the astonishing varieties of haberdashery sold in his shop which are listed in the inventory of his goods made after his death. These included dress materials, Genoa fustian, mockado and camell, with trimmings of lace and buttons to refurbish dresses which must have been major investments, passed down from mother to daughter to servant. Goods in West's repertoire used to make sieves for the home brewer or to remove bran from meal, and the supply of wicks for candles and vinegar for pickling remind one of the essentially self-sufficient nature of sixteenth-century households. West's barge, moreover, was a mobile bookshop making available 'holy meditacions', 'primarellis', books of psalms and Bibles.

Despite this evidence for active river transport, Thomas West experienced difficulties. In 1567 he wrote that his barge was held up at Caversham because the winch was broken. Whether the winch was a piece of machinery on the bank as Prior surmises, or whether it was the standard barrel windlass on the bow of the barge is not clear. The result was 'there my barge was fayne to ly ther all the ester hallidayes and I was faigne to carry my winch from Wallingford to Cassvine (Caversham) in cart cost ii vid and I lost byt the meanes 24 of March 1567-vs-ob (5s o$\frac{1}{2}$d)'. Profits even from an active entrepreneur were reduced by a faulty navigation system.

A more determined attempt to improve the navigation was made in James I's reign by setting up the Oxford and Buscot commission. Eight Barge Commissioners were appointed, four representing the town of Oxford and four the university. Their task was to scour the river, which was all 'floundered up', and to make a passage through all weirs, to open up any streams which might make the river navigable and to erect pound locks, known as 'turnpikes'. This act of 1623–4 resulted in the building of locks at Iffley, Sandford and Swift Ditch. The original structures were built with timber walls which soon deteriorated and had to be rebuilt in stone. They have all been rebuilt several times over, but in the case of Iffley the remains of the old lock can be seen alongside its modern counterpart. Although these improvements seem to have been maintained throughout the Civil War period they only affected a comparatively short stretch of river. The flashlocks, weirs and obstructive millers and riparian owners remained for another century.

The Thames during the late seventeenth and eighteenth centuries saw an active traffic. It is related of Robert Burton, the Anatomist of Melancholy, that in his old age 'nothing at last could make him laugh but going down to the footbridge in Oxford and hearing the bargemen scold and swear at one another at which he would set his hands to his sides and laugh most profusely'. The appearance of the barges can be reconstructed from numerous prints, engravings and water-colours of the river. David Wilson, the lock keeper at Godstow, who has written the most convincing book on the Thames as a working waterway, describes these. They were 'large punt-shaped, largely un-decked craft with very little freeboard when laden with various cargoes of filled sacks, barrels, timber, hay or straw'. Some, Wilson states, had a stemmed, rounded bow, but some are swim-headed, with the flat bottom rising to a square cut, partly-decked bow. Such vessels were steered by huge wooden rudders which were very long so that some steerage was possible when the barge was travelling very slowly. The locomotion was provided by poling by halers (men with harness attached to the boat by cables) and, later, when the tow paths had been improved, by horses. Tall masts, which could easily be unstepped to pass through locks and under bridges needed strong sailing beams and mast cases to cope with the stresses while sailing or under tow.

Such vessels, immemorial in their design and crude in their construction, were nevertheless effective in taking advantage of the considerable improvements in navigation which now took place. The far reaching Act of 1751 set up a permanent body of commissioners to control the whole river. This body grew in number to over 600, including Members of Parliament for the riverside towns, which was unwieldy to say the least. It attempted to finance improvements through tolls, but this did not produce enough capital for the expensive building of pound-locks. From 1771, a new Act made it possible to raise loans for this purpose and the construction of a series of locks, twenty-two in number, before 1790–1. There were seven above Dorchester and fifteen between Dorchester and Maidenhead.

The Oxfordshire Thames was fitted with pound-locks during the crucially important years of 1770–90. Locks were provided at Shiplake (1773), Sonning (1773), Mapledurham (1777), Caversham (1778), Whitchurch (1787), Goring (1787), Cleeve (1787), Benson (1788), Days (1789), Abingdon (1790), Osney (1790), Rushy (1790), St Johns Bridge (1790), Buscot (1790), Godstow (1791) and Pinkhill (1791).

Among the advantages of pound-locks were that they led to a fall in freight rates owing to extra traffic being generated, swifter speed of passage, larger boats and greater intensity of use. Such a system is much more economical in its use of water than the flash lock and the whole operation was attended with orderliness and safety. The capital costs, however, were higher since more land was required and the expenses in stone and timber heavier.

Water transport was particularly suited to the carriage of bulky and non-perishable goods such as malt, grain and coal.

Malt was barley or other grain prepared for brewing or distilling. Beer, gin and whisky are all made from malt. We can trace the distribution of maltsters from excise accounts. It was possible to claim a drawback of excise when it could be proved that malt had been damaged in transit. In 1708 a boat belonging to a bargemaster called Rose sank and $382\frac{1}{2}$ quarters of malt were damaged. This belonged to maltsters who lived in the Thames towns of Abingdon and Wallingford as well as places in west Oxfordshire such as Witney and Stanton Harcourt. From such sources we learn that Oxford had five maltsters, Henley six, Bampton three, Woodstock two and a number of other places had one or two. These smallish industrial concerns each had malthouses with working floors, steeping cisterns, drying kilns and barley lofts. There was an advantage to be near a river or a canal because malting was a fuel-intensive trade and a special kind of coal was desirable. Welsh malting coal and anthracite were particularly favoured as they did not leave a smoky flavour in the beer.

Coal was therefore another staple in the river and canal carrying trade. Before the canals were built the main source of coal for the upper Thames region was Newcastle. It was carried by coastal traffic to London and transhipped into great so called West Country barges for the trip up-river to Abingdon and Oxford. The carriage of coal by water along this route cost 18s per chaldron in the early eighteenth century. The carriage by road increased its price more than threefold. This was the economic motivation behind the construction of the three pound-locks on the Thames in James I's reign. In 1771, 12,050 tons of coal were carried annually beyond Reading. 2,400 went to Oxford, 3,900 to Abingdon, 2,100 to Wallingford, 1,600 to Goring and 1,050 to Shillingford. There were thirty-three coal merchants or dealers living in Oxford, and just as barge mastering and fishing ran in families so did coal dealing. In the 1790s the coal merchants Ward and Holland had seventeen boats either on the river or canal, and Thomas Polley had ten.

The Canals in Oxfordshire

On 25 October 1768 a significant meeting was held at the Three Tuns Inn, Banbury, to discuss the possibility of building a new canal to link the Midland coalfields with Banbury and Oxford, thus giving access to London and the Thames. It was to have repercussions on the economy similar to the construction of the motorways two centuries later. James Brindley, foremost canal engineer of his day, was asked to survey the route at an annual salary of £200 and he masterminded the project until his death in 1772. The canal was finally opened through to the terminal wharves at Oxford eighteen years later. It was linked with the river Thames by two short connecting waterways. In 1789 the Duke of Marlborough, who was one of the investors in the scheme, built a private cut at Wolvercote with one lock, and seven years later the company itself built Isis lock (locally named Louse lock) allowing Thames barges access to the Oxford wharves via the Sheepwash channel.

This connected Oxford and the river Thames with the north. During these years equally important attempts were made to complete a national waterway network by linking with the west and the Severn basin. The Thames–Severn canal was opened from Stroud to Lechlade in 1789. Works round Radcot bridge were set in hand, driven by hopes of the projected increase in traffic. A new channel was cut at Radcot in the north bank by opening up a two-yard-wide stream. This now left the main river above Radcot bridge and swung round by the side of the Swan public house. The arches of the medieval bridge at Radcot were too low to accommodate large barges at times of high water. The lofty, single-span stone bridge which still stands was constructed in 1787 to take the Bampton–Faringdon road over the enlarged cut. The stone wharves had to be re-positioned. A recent decision at a public enquiry (1994) safeguarded the setting of the ancient bridge, a scheduled monument, by reducing the disfiguring moorings and removing excrescences such as a brick barbecue and a sewage station, which had a brief but unauthorized

A staircase of lynchets, ancient contoured cultivation terraces, a mile south-east of Uffington White Horse. *John Steane*

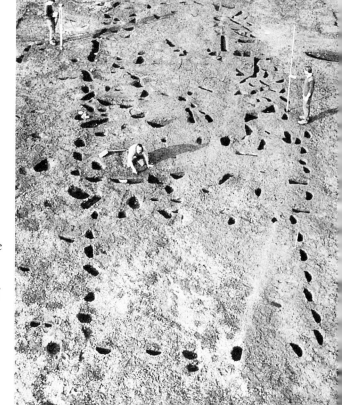

The plan of an early Anglo-Saxon hall house excavated at Yarnton, Worton. *Oxford Archaeological Unit*

The twelfth-century base of the solar tower of the Bishop of Winchester's palace at Witney. *Oxford Archaeological Unit*

The base plate and trestles of the early sixteenth-century bridge, The Vineyard, Abingdon Abbey. *Oxford Archaeological Unit*

The former Oxford City football ground, Whitehouse, Marlborough Road, Oxford. A gravel site with Middle Iron-Age (third to first century BC) settlement overlain by Medieval. The ground is surrounded by late Victorian suburbs. *Cambridge University Committee for Aerial Photography*

Three fifteenth-century alabaster panels at the Ashmolean
Museum, Oxford. *John Steane*

Iffley Church, Oxford from south-east. Victorianised west front
of Norman Church. *John Steane*

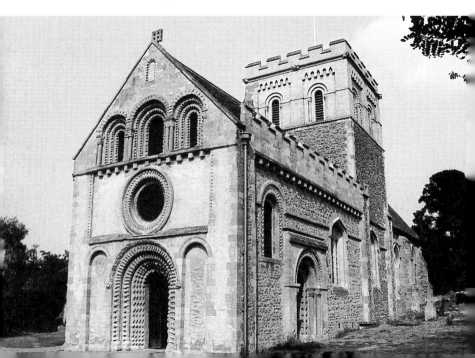

The Old School, Gloucester Green, Oxford, now part of a lively pedestrian precinct centred on an open market. *John Steane*

The University Museum, Oxford with former Chemistry Laboratory on right. A Neo-Gothic design by Benjamin Woodward. *John Steane*

The Neo-Byzantine
St Barnabas church
reflected in the
waters of the
Oxford Canal.
John Steane

Bill Bird's
commemorative
sculpture, Oxford
Canal Wharf,
Hythe Bridge
Street, Oxford.
John Steane

Chastleton House. Early seventeenth-century kitchen with serving hatch (*left*), bacon flake (*above*) and nineteenth-century range in the seventeenth-century fireplace (*right*). *Vernon Brooke*

Cogges Manor Farm. Roof *c.*1550 above hall/kitchen. Attic used by servants. *RCHM (England)*

Green College, Oxford. Octagon of University Observatory, 1770, in College garden setting. *John Steane*

Magdalen College. Bishop Waynflete's buildings in background. Remains of Magdalen Hall in mid-distance. Nineteenth-century President's garden in foreground. *Vernon Brooke*

existence on the island to the south. The river Thames
throughout its course requires constant public vigilance if it is
to continue to afford a peaceful and visually unimpaired
amenity into the twenty-first century.

During the period 1800–30 further canals were built,
providing a credible east–west passageway over the drought-
ridden chalk lands of southern England. The Wilts and Berks
joined the Thames at Abingdon in 1810, thus linking this
malting town with Semington on the Kennet–Avon. In 1819
the North Wilts canal was built to connect with the
Thames–Severn canal at Lutton. An important area, the
Somerset coalfield was linked by a local canal flowing into
the Kennet–Avon in 1794, thus ensuring that fresh supplies
of coal reached the Thameside towns.

The canal age meant that people living in the upper
Thames region could now get good quality coal at lower
prices from Staffordshire, Shropshire, the Forest of Dean and
Wales. The canals also brought a new kind of industrial
architecture to Oxfordshire. Hump-backed waggon bridges,
spanning both canal and towing path, were built of brick or
stone. The stone was often the unyielding, pink Midland
sandstone which stood up to rough treatment better than the
grey limestones of the Cotswolds. On the southern section of
the Oxford canal are many wooden drawbridges, pivoted on
a toothed segment of cast iron. They are easily operated, the
projecting fixed twin beams acting as counterbalances. There
are many village wharves along their courses. Public houses,
with stabling for the numerous canal horses, also grew up,
gaining an unsavoury reputation for fighting and drunken-
ness. Such were The Jolly Waterman, The Struggler, The
Golden Lion and The Steam Packet in Banbury, and The
Running Horses and The Nag's Head in Oxford. The canal
boatmen, as Mary Prior points out, often ran the pubs. These
were the places where they secured contracts with the agents
of the coal factors.

Such a peripatetic life as a bargee or canal boatman might
be thought to have encouraged a disorderly and chaotic
element in mid Victorian society. It certainly led to a desire

on the part of the legislators in the 1870s to register the boats and control the lives of their transient inhabitants. Living conditions aboard were indeed very cramped, and as competition increased and profits began to fall, individual boatmen's families often gave up their houses and took to the boats. Children slept under beds, in cupboards or on tables, but, paradoxically, the inspectors found that everything was done to keep the boats neat and clean: they were painted in the traditional glowing colours with roses, castles and geometric patterns. The galleys foreshadowed later built-in kitchens, with cupboard doors doubling up as tables.

Attempts were made to provide the Oxford boatmen with religion. Henry Ward, a wealthy coal merchant, built a boat in 1838 to serve as a boatman's chapel. It was moored near the terminus of the canal at Hythe Bridge and services were held there on Sunday afternoons and Wednesday evenings until one night in 1868 it sank.

The trade on the canals gradually died. Competition from the railways was recognized as being the principal factor. The opening of the London and Birmingham Railway in 1838 and the Oxford–Banbury branch of the Great Western Railway in 1850, with its continuation northwards two years later, sounded the knell of the canals. For a time, however, the actual amount and value of the goods carried by the canals increased. Proportionately, however, the railways with their greater speed, accessibility to the centres of towns and flexibility gained year by year.

The decline of the Oxford canal has brought about some interesting changes in the part of Oxford where it terminated. From the 1920s and 1930s its operating costs exceeded its receipts. Pacey's Bridge, rebuilt in 1922 to carry the increased volume of road traffic, was built lower than the old one and there was no headroom for boats to navigate through its arch. Consequently, the Castle Mill standing right under the Saxon St George's tower was isolated, ceased functioning and was pulled down. Since river transport was now in its death throes, the boatmen's pubs were strangled. The Running Horses lost its licence in 1938 and The Nag's Head was rebuilt, but with its front door facing onto Hythe Bridge Street now buzzing with motor traffic instead of the canal, the source of its former custom. The basin of the Oxford canal was sold to Lord Nuffield in 1936 and after World War II the yellow Cotswold stone walls and quadrangles of his munificent foundation began to rise. The Canal House, the fine Greek Revival, stone-built company office is left high and dry 300 yards away from the present end of the canal. To commemorate the important part the canal played in Oxford's social and economic history over two centuries, the City Council commissioned local painter and sculptor William Bird to create a monument (see plate section) to the canal which is at the same time an amenity. Its materials, old brick and cumbrous black and white painted beams, recall traditional canal architecture. Its shape, that of a capstan, commemorates the energy and effort which went into the boatmen's lives from 1790 to 1990. Its function, to provide a visual focus and a comfortable seat for those frequenting the canal bank near the middle of the city, is a winner.

One other canal feature worth a visit is Tooley's boatyard at Banbury. This stands on the canal bank near the northern end of the Oxfordshire stretch of the canal. It is a stone-built dry dock big enough to house barges requiring repair. The sluices, wooden superstructure and surrounding sheds, housing tools, paints and materials are all there. This rare survival from an earlier Industrial Revolution, whose national importance is recognized by its scheduling as an Ancient Monument, may well be integrated into a major shopping redevelopment by the time this book is published.

VII
Crafts and Industries

The high, bare Cotswold hills running diagonally across west and north Oxfordshire are composed of Jurassic limestones which have produced some of the finest building material of England since Roman times. The earliest buildings in Oxford were made of the enduring, rubbly Corallian limestone which outcrops east of the city at Wheatley. During the later Middle Ages, magnificent yellow and grey freestones from the quarries of Taynton and Burford were dug for the construction of Windsor Castle and many of the Oxford colleges, and continued to be used in the seventeenth century for the rebuilding of St Paul's Cathedral. In the eighteenth century, Headington quarry produced stone of varying quality used throughout the city. It proved unable to withstand the atmospheric pollution of the nineteenth century and accounts for the large-scale refacing of the city using other material in the twentieth century. In the north of the county, the villages are built of a dark brown, gingery, iron-rich limestone from quarries such as Hornton. Nearly all the quarries have now ceased working, but their sites are among the most evocative of the busy industries of the past.

Taynton, the site of the most famous Oxfordshire quarries of the Middle Ages, is one and a half miles north of the village of Taynton and three miles to the north-west of Burford. The stone pits are on private land and permission must be sought (in 1995) for access from the Lee brothers at Taynton Manor Farm. I came here on a raw January day in 1977 and Mr Phillip Lee, already in his seventies, showed me round. We walked up a farm track, and on the slope above the farm saw the first signs of quarry activity. The surface is littered with grey blocks, fluted with drill holes, being seasoned and made ready for cutting. The sawing shop, a single-storeyed building with walls of superb ashlar blocks and a corrugated iron roof, stands silent, its winch and crane quietly rusting. The final block to be cut stands smooth-edged in front of the circular-bladed saw. Mr Lee recalled that he had last used it in preparing stone for Christ Church some years before. Further up the hill, across a field, the irregular undulations of the old quarries come into sight. There are some two hundred acres of cratered landscape; the collapsed shafts of the medieval quarries are filled with dripping hawthorn bushes. Further boles of twisted hawthorns are seen in the gullet. Mr Lee showed me his tools: crowbars, picks, a shovel, a sledgehammer and wedges stashed under a great block he referred to as the weatherbed. On the rock, holes had been drilled, the steel plates and wedges known as plugs and feathers were in position, all set to crack another great block which would then be dragged out like stones to Stonehenge. I came again in the summer of 1994. Bullocks now graze quietly where the quarries once rang with the shouts of workers and the rumble of moving stones. The quarries were bright with flowers, purple milk vetch, bastard toad flax, orchids, flourishing on the lime rich soil.

Three miles east of Carfax and hemmed in by London Road on the north and the Eastern Bypass is the site of the former Headington quarries. Although they are now almost completely covered with urban sprawl, it is possible to detect their former existence by looking at maps and by investigating the ground. A hundred years ago there was a separate community living and working here, all involved in extracting the stone, and divided from Headington village by the space of several fields. Pitt Road, Quarry High Street and Quarry Hollow are obvious reminders. The network of paths such as Cox's Alley and Coppock's Alley thread through in between the quarries. They are walled and stand on the old ground surface, which has been dug away on either side, so we can look down on gardens and yards sited on the former quarry floors. Here are built, higgledy-piggledy fashion, the quarrymen's houses. Many of them have blocks of high grade ashlar stone built into them. Occasionally, as in the garden

Headington Quarry. Ordance Survey map 25 inches to the mile. 1st edition 1878. Holy Trinity Church has the grave of C. S. Lewis (*Centre for Oxfordshire Studies*)

wall at No. 8 Coppock's Alley, one sees a piece of carved and faceted stonework, doubtless prepared for a college or church and never so used. The little community had its own school, with ecclesiastically designed windows dated 1871, a small quarryman's church with a simple rough stone floor, and a public house appropriately enough called the Mason's Arms.

The Wheatley limestones form a ridge shaped like a crescent about a mile long with the village lying in the centre. The quarries can be traced in the western part of the village. I remember watching the school children celebrating May Day on the floor of one of the quarries. Further stone pits were on both sides of the A40 about half a mile to the north-west. Lye Hill quarry was used until recently as an overflow storage park for British Leyland cars. One quarry in Shotover Park was saved from infilling by the conservation conscious South Oxfordshire District Council. The geological circumstances which produced this shelly, hard, rubbly rock date from a period when the area was a shallow, tropical sea bed, overgrown with straggling coral reefs.

The search for stone would have been the first stage in setting up the industry. Since there were no geological maps, supernatural powers were sometimes invoked! When Battle Abbey was being founded, William I undertook to provide stone from Caen in Normandy until a woman, through a dream, located good quarriable stone on a nearby site. The seventeenth-century antiquary John Aubrey told a story, derived from the memories of old men, recording that at Bradford-on-Avon, St Aldhelm, who was riding over there, 'threw down his glove and had them digge and they should find the greatest treasure meaning the quarry'. Having decided where to dig, the second stage was the removal of the overlying layers of earth and then shovelling out the shattered weathered and fissured overburden down to the top level of workable stone. These upper layers produced useful rubble and were removed using spades, shovels, picks and pickaxes. The next stage was the winning of blocks of stone. These had to be cut vertically and split horizontally. The old method was to cut grooves and to fit wooden wedges in rows: these were then watered and, as they swelled, the stone split. During his lifetime, Mr Lee of Taynton explained that rows of holes $1\frac{3}{4}$ inches in diameter and 18 inches in depth were drilled across the top surface of the block. Into each hole were inserted a pair of steel plates and between these a plug. When these were all in place a sledgehammer was used to tap the protruding ends of the plugs and the stone split vertically. Wedges and crowbars were then driven in from the side and the block prized from its bed. Rough dressing or scappling was then applied using hammer axes with two vertical cutting edges and two equally sized blades. The blocks might be used without further tooling as was done in the cloister wall at New College in the late fourteenth century. A more precise and flatter finish would be given using a bolster, a broad-bladed mason's chisel, driven by a mallet or maul. This produced a diagonally-tooled surface such as is seen in the fifteenth-century masonry at Swalcliffe Barn. For internal work, as for highly finished dressings for windows or jambs for doorways, the surface of the blocks was drawn over with a tool known as a drag. This was made of a sheet of iron with a semi-circular top edge and a row of teeth like a curry comb. This produced a 'fair face'.

The stone was roughly worked at the quarry where waste material was taken off. It might be finished off in lodges set up on the building site itself. I remember watching rough masons preparing the squared stones used in the repair of Swalcliffe Barn. They set up their tables next to the building. Medieval mason's lodges were temporary wooden buildings where masons worked and met one another. Much of the stone used for Merton College bell tower in the 1450s was quarried at Taynton and taken to Burford to be worked. A hut was hired from 1 March to the Feast of St John the Baptist (24 June) for 12d. A man called Wymer Web paid 8d for straw to roof it. The 'face moulds', presumably templates to guide the masons, were brought here and officers came from the College to Burford to pay them. Masons looked after one another. A man insured during the building of the cloister at All Souls College was treated by an apothecary.

The medicaments cost 20d and a further 20d was expended on making him well.

How was the stone industry organized? The ownership of quarries might be in the hands of local families. In 1395-7, when New College bell tower was under construction, John Cooke of Taynton provided 2,681 feet of freestone including 1,357 feet at 2d, 1,324 at 1½d, and 267 'talstones' at 1d. To provide the material for Merton College bell tower, Thomas Brewys produced 38 feet for 6s 4d, John Hokes 111 feet for 18s 6d and John Athers 44 feet for 7s 4d. The stone from Taynton cost more in freight charges than at the quarry face – the carriers were frequently the quarriers themselves. The regular rate was 2s a load. The carriage from Headington to Thame worked out as 1s 2d a load. Axles and wheels had frequently to be mended and on occasions the roads were specially repaired to take the additional traffic. The colleges might buy a quarry to supply its stone needs. Dean Higdon of Cardinal College bought half an acre of quarry from Fyshe of Marston and paid 8d on deposit for £3 6s 8d to be paid at a subsequent manor court at Headington. A third way of proceeding was for the master mason to gain a lease or ownership of the quarry and exploit it by selling the stone. William Orchard, the master mason at Magdalen College (*fl.* 1468–1504), leased land at Barton in Headington parish and carried out stone quarrying. He contracted to supply stone to Magdalen and to Eton College. Similarly, Robert Janyns appears to have had trade connections with Taynton quarries.

Once the stone was cut it was brought to the building site and stockpiled with the other materials, scaffolding, lime for mortar, timber for centering and lifting gear. The site had to be cleared. In densely urban Oxford this might mean that churches and houses had to be taken down to produce a vacant site. Merton College chapel, for instance, could not be started until the Church of St John the Baptist was demolished. At Cardinal College (later Christ Church) the church of St Michael was dismantled; its cure of souls was handed over to St Aldate's. Magdalen College was laid out on top of, and surrounded by, the buildings of the Hospital of St John the Baptist. The Hospital's drains and wall foundations were recently laid bare when the new kitchen was under construction. The earlier building had influenced the layout of the College in a number of ways.

In medieval Oxford, as in present Third World countries, the scaffolding was of timber; willow and alder were preferred: the platforms were made of unstable hurdles. The bell tower of Merton was scaffolded using twenty-four hurdles at 3d each and four at 2d. The timbers and hurdles of the scaffold were bound with rope. Lifting gear involving cables and pulleys was used to haul up the stone to the mason's working platform. During the construction of the vault in the Divinity Schools in the 1470s, a *magna rota* – a large crane worked by a treadmill – was used (like those still surviving at Salisbury and Peterborough Cathedrals, and at Tewkesbury Abbey).

Once the scaffolding was set up the building of the walls could commence. Scant attention was paid to the provision of deep foundations. At Swalcliffe, the bulk of the great barn raised by New College (1400–9) was built on rock, but the slope involved the building-up of the foundations at the east end. Damp courses were sometimes supplied by loads of oyster shells. Seventy loads of bitumen were provided for the building of Queen's College chapel at a cost of 68s 9½d.

The master mason was responsible for overseeing the complexities of the building process. At Magdalen College, William Orchard conscientiously carried out this task. He had contracts with the college in 1475, 1478 and 1479 for the provision of buttresses, masonry for the chapel, hall, library, two towers and the cloister chambers at 1d and 2d a foot. The pinnacles were to be 11 feet 6 inches high and Orchard received 11s 1d for each pinnacle. He employed rough masons such as Thomas Edward who was paid 13s for polishing 100 loads of 'walstan' at the quarry. The pay differentials were considerable. Among those working on the bell tower of Merton College was Henry Prendergast, who also served as rough mason and quarryman. He worked for twenty-four weeks at 16d a week (32s) and received 24s for commons. His colleague, John Taylour, worked for 24 weeks at 9d (18s) and received 24s for commons. Other men were paid piecework. Thomas Wykes, mason, was paid £4–9s–0d by William Orchard for cutting and shaping 'great table' in Wheatley Quarry, 540 feet at 2d a foot.

A large structure such as St George's tower in Oxford Castle took a number of seasons to complete. The 'lifts' are clearly visible in its tapering profile. Each winter the unfinished walls of a structure were thatched with straw to prevent frost damage. As a building neared completion we hear of scaffold holes being filled in with plaster. They could thus be easily unblocked when maintenance work required the replacement of scaffolding. Once the walls were completed the carpenters took over; they inserted the floors and staircases and built the roof framework. It was then the turn of the plumbers, who came in to deal with the guttering and roof coverings.

Oxford was sited at the junction of the stone-producing zone of the Cotswolds and the brick, tile and timber areas of the clay vales and the major river valleys. The historic core of the city is largely built of limestone. The building stone industry, just described, continued to flourish during the eighteenth and nineteenth centuries as the colleges regularly added to and altered their buildings. With nineteenth-century industrialization, smoke pollution attacked the external stone surfaces. The novelist, Thomas Hardy, an architect by training, looked on the consequent damage with a practised eye. He pictures Jude the Obscure, the would-be scholar and cleric, but actually a stone mason, commenting on Oxford's buildings. 'Cruelties, insults, had, he perceived, been inflicted on the aged erections. The condition of several moved him as he would have been moved by maimed sentient beings. They were wounded, broken, sloughing off their outer shape in the deadly struggle against years, weather and man.'

After World War II, Oxford launched a great appeal to restore its buildings, threatened not only by continuing atmospheric pollution, but also by vibration caused by an enormous increase in traffic. Patching was abandoned and systematic refacing, often with stone from France, was tried. The result is that the air of hoary decay has vanished to be replaced by a cleaned and often bland exterior to the city's famous buildings.

The unexpected sight of a bottle-shaped brick pottery kiln among the well manicured gardens of the Chiltern village of Nettlebed, half-way between Henley-on-Thames and Wallingford, reminds us of a formerly important but now extinct industry. Bricks and tiles were made at Nettlebed from the fourteenth to the nineteenth centuries. The clay-with-flints, which was the basic raw material, was found smeared in pockets over the chalk at Nettlebed, Russell's Water, Shiplake and Woodcote: sand was also needed for brickmaking, to temper the clay and to line the moulds. At Nettlebed, the clay and sand rights on the common went together. The surrounding woods provided coppice timber, a naturally regenerating fuel. The 1877 Ordnance Survey Map of Nettlebed shows a wilderness of abandoned and water-filled clay pits, a tramway connecting the diggings to the works, and a scatter of workshops and clamp kilns. Here, census returns show that considerable specialization prevailed within the industry; specialist brick, tile, pottery and drain-pipe burners were employed in addition to carters, clay diggers and general kiln labourers.

The bottle kiln at Nettlebed, so reminiscent in shape to those of the potteries in Staffordshire, was a type of updraught kiln. The outer brick 'bottle' is likely to be of eighteenth-century date, though the interior arrangements have been modified later. The unfired but sun-dried bricks were trundled in, using a specially designed sideless 'crowding' barrow, and stacked inside the square chamber; the entrance was then bricked up. The fuel was timber and the heat came from three stoke holes below ground level, fuelled from within a shed built up against one side of the kiln. After the fire had completed the initial drying of the bricks for about two days, coal was added to drive up the heat to higher temperatures needed to cook the bricks properly. Each kiln load fired about 12,000 bricks. Tiles had been made and used in Oxfordshire since the early fourteenth century. The manor of Cuxham, belonging to Merton College, used 15,000 flat peg tiles and 150 crests and ridge tiles for its new byre built in 1312–13. Nettlebed made 35,000 tiles in 1365 for building works at Wallingford Castle. Since the county was well endowed with stone and timber resources, it was slow, compared with eastern England, to incorporate brick into the stock of traditional building materials. The quadrangular moated castle at Shirburn built c.1379 was the first documented example of brick building. Bricks also seem to have been used in the towers of the small castle at Rotherfield Greys built in the middle of the fourteenth century by Sir John de Grey. In 1416–17 Thomas Stonor made a payment of £40 to Michael Warwick for making 200,000 'brykes' and a further £15 for their carriage from the kilns at Crocker End (a significant place name), three miles through the Chiltern Woods to Stonor House. The chapel tower at Stonor with its diaper decoration of green glazed vitrified headers was probably built of this consignment. During the next five centuries, Stonor became a veritable museum of brickwork. In 1758–9 additions were made to Stonor House and bricks were supplied by Catherine Shurfield 'kiln woman'. Kiln books from eighteenth-century Nettlebed survive amongst the Stonor papers. The warm red/orange façade of Stonor glows, cupped as it is against the dark Chiltern woods.

The finest complex of early brick buildings in the county is at Ewelme. Here one of the most powerful magnates of the period, William de la Pole, Duke of Suffolk, set up house with his wife, Alice Chaucer, granddaughter of the poet. The de la Poles had come from Hull, where they had started off as fishmongers and became financiers to King Edward III. They had built in brick in Hull and carried on using the material in Suffolk, where they had great landed estates. In the 1430s the Duke and Duchess built themselves a brick palace at Ewelme of which a fragment remains. More noteworthy, and well worth a visit, is the complex of school, almshouse and church; all using red brick and all dating from the middle years of the fifteenth century. Some of the masons who rebuilt the church must have been brought from Suffolk. The brick masons, however, copied the latest Netherlandish fashions. The crow-stepped gables, the cusping in the arch above the porch door, the ready use of moulded and cut bricks (there are no less than twenty-three different moulded brick types) are all paralleled in contemporary Bruges. Not surprisingly, 'Les Flemyngges' is a common name found round about Crocker End in the fifteenth and succeeding centuries.

Brick spread slowly across the county from the south-east, which was most open to outside influences and was lacking in a locally won, enduring building stone. By the seventeenth century, it was being used as infill (known as 'nogging') to timber-framed buildings, particularly almshouses in Thame, Watlington, Wallingford and Abingdon. By the eighteenth century, it was being used to reface the fronts of Georgian houses throughout the region to the east and south of the stone belt. Wantage is full of buildings using the chequer pattern of orange brick and grey and green vitrified header bricks. From being a high status fashion used only on the show fronts of houses it gradually became a more workaday material. Oxford, Banbury and Bicester were ringed round with brickworks, fuelled by Midlands coal, brought in first by means of the canals and latterly by the railways. The canals were important in bringing coal as fuel and in transporting the bricks and tiles when sold. By the 1820s, there were yards along the length of the Oxford canal from Barton in the north, through Adderbury, Somerton and Bletchington, to Oxford. Similarly, there were yards sited along the Wilts and Berks canal in the Vale of the White Horse at Uffington and Drayton.

The industry reached its apogee in the period 1860–80 when eighty-three yards were in operation and 266 people were employed. The agricultural depression, the falling housing market from 1901 onwards, and the development of the highly competitive brick industry using deep Oxford clays in Bedfordshire, hit the Oxfordshire brickmakers hard.

Brickyards went out of business rapidly during World War I and were again vulnerable during the Depression of the 1930s. The small yard at Chalgrove struggled on, but sold only 7,500 bricks in its final year of business in 1954. I remember visiting the works in the late 1970s; it was like a ghost town. Creaking timber, empty hacksteads where the bricks used to dry, crumbling kilns, rusting pugmill. The last load of 16,000 Oxfordshire bricks still lies unfired in the Chalgrove kiln. All over the county, pits were infilled, chimneys demolished and the trucks and mineral lines sold for scrap.

The industrial archaeology of the brick industry may be defunct, but the brick buildings live on. They vary from the polychrome brilliance of Butterfield's Keble College to the rich redbrick villas of north Oxford; the plain brick nonconformist village chapels, the rows of urban workers' dwellings; humble farm buildings and country labourers' cottages. The enduring nature of brickwork, its ability to withstand atmospheric pollution, the delightful colours, variety and textures have enriched the Oxfordshire scene.

The basic skills of building in stone and brick began relatively late in the archaeological and historical record in Oxfordshire. Far more ancient, and stretching back into the second millennium before Christ, is evidence for the craft of making cloth. Physical traces of flax have been found in Bronze Age contexts; the distinctive tools used in the various processes associated with woollen textile making have also been found in prehistoric occupation debris. At the Roman villa of Shakenoak, near North Leigh, combs were recovered which were used for freeing raw wool from tangles and foreign matter caught in the fleece. This process was necessary before the next stage, spinning an even yarn, could be attempted. Until the advent of the spinning wheel, perhaps in the twelfth century AD, spinning was done by means of twirling the woollen fibres round a spindle, a wooden stick weighted by a whorl. These whorls were perforated objects of bone, stone, ceramic or glass and they are frequently found trodden into the floors of early houses or cast out with the rubbish into pits. With a plentiful supply of spun wool the weaving process could begin. Double post holes excavated in Saxon sunken-floored huts are interpreted as the framework of vertical warp-weighted looms. Credence is given by the presence of rows of perforated clay-shaped buns (sometimes of stone) found nearby: the loom weights. Double-pointed, bone implements, known as 'pinbeaters' and 'sword beaters', were employed to ease the weft into place. One inscribed with a legend in Old English EADBURH MEC AM (Eadburh owns me) was found in the destruction level of a house dated *c.*1150 at Wallingford. Such finds presuppose the existence in Romano-British and Saxon Oxfordshire of many self-sufficient economic units producing their own cloth.

The making of woollen cloth encouraged the breeding of sheep, and here Oxfordshire had a distinct advantage over other areas of England. The dry hill pastures of the Cotswolds were particularly suitable for sheep farming; the so-called Cotswold breed are seen on the fifteenth-century monumental brasses of the Fortey family in Northleach church in Gloucestershire. The type is that of a large polled animal with a clean face and its fleece depicted by short curls like those of a shorn longwool. The actual size of the sheep has been calculated from bones found in such sites as Oxford, All Saints and the Hamel. They seem in general to have been small in the Saxon period and gradually enlarging as the Middle Ages advanced.

That sheep were bred all over the county in the early Middle Ages seems likely given the wide distribution of place names with an element referring to sheep; Shipton-under-Wychwood in the Cotswolds and Shipton-on-Cherwell are obvious reminders. Shiplake was the stream where sheep were washed; Shifford, the sheep ford. There were Sheep-bridge Copse in Great Haseley, Sheepcotes, a farm dating from *c.*1551, in Postcombe, and Tag Green was a dialect term for a young sheep. Sheep required less in the way of housing than did cattle, although long, single-storey buildings were sometimes erected, and New College Farm at Swalcliffe had an eighteen-bay sheephouse. There were

Sheephouse Farm in Harpsden and Sheephouse Barn in Chislehampton. The market towns of Bicester and Burford each had their Sheep Streets. The Ridgeway was used for driving sheep along in the eighteenth and nineteenth centuries to the great markets at East Ilsley in Berkshire.

If the place name evidence suggests that wool production was widespread in the county, the textile industry in the early Middle Ages seems to have become concentrated in the rising towns. By 1130, guilds of weavers had been established in Oxford. Henry II and King John both bought cloths in Oxford, and seven times between 1230 and 1263 the town weavers supplied cloth, mostly the coarser russets and tweeds, for the King to give in alms. Oxford merchants are found at the fairs of Northampton, St Ives and Boston selling wool and cloth. Gradually, however, the industry began to decline in the thirteenth century as entrepreneurs became increasingly aware of the advantages of rural cloth production. In some places this was to benefit from water-powered fulling mills. One of the earliest recorded fulling mills lay on the town's boundary at Seacourt by *c.*1200. It is likely that the weavers' guild was felt to hamper the trade by its demands and restrictions. Cloth production seems to have been established in many Oxfordshire villages by 1275. As the number of weavers in Oxford itself fell so there is evidence for a rise in those coming from the Bampton and Witney area.

Witney was particularly well sited to profit from the woollen textile industry. Bishop Peter des Roches showed the same financial acumen he used in running Henry III's treasury when he founded his new town beside the river Windrush, a good mill-stream with clear, soft water in a parish near the Cotswold wool supplies. Witney also had efficient communications to Oxford, London and to the south, via Abingdon, to Southampton and thence to the textile markets of Europe. The mills were an essential part of the venture. In 1210 money was paid out to restore one or more of these; and in 1223 there were not only three grain, but also three fulling mills, evidently in the same location as in the sixteenth century.

Wool for the Witney weavers was collected from a wide radius. The bishopric wool was stored in Witney from 1370, sometimes for a period of years, awaiting sale. When, by 1453, the bishops gave up their interest in sheep farming, there were plenty of local energetic farmers and merchants profiting from the brisk wool trade along the Cotswolds willing to take over. Such woolmen were the Elises of Thame and the Standlake family; they were joined in the fifteenth century by John Hood of Witney and the Wenmans and the Fermans. Easily the most wealthy of the Witney woolmen and clothiers in the sixteenth century was Richard Wenman, merchant of the Staple, who paid four-fifths of the tax for which the town was assessed. On his death he made cash legacies of over £2,000. Edward Wilmot was the richest man in the town after Wenman. His family had engaged in enclosure at Stadhampton and Chislehampton.

Witney did not turn to a specialization in blanket production until the seventeenth century. Until then it produced narrow cloth and broad cloth. The narrow cloth was made on a narrow loom and was of finer quality. The broadcloth was a heavy, felted material used for all kinds of clothing, covers, awnings, tilts and house cloths. It was normally white or undyed, but some was apparently dyed in the town. We hear of red cloth taken as a distraint in one of the cases brought up before the borough court.

Despite the wealth they accumulated, Witney clothiers were mostly independent masters with only two or three looms. The richest of them, like Walter Jones, owned only five looms, two in his shop and three in his house. His brother Henry had four looms in his shop. They relied on their families for additional labour and took on apprentices who were attached to them for seven or eight years. Their access to capital meant that they had the ability to store quantities of yarn and wool and they had cloth lying idle in the finishing processes or on sale in London and were still able to keep the looms going. The richer clothiers also controlled the finishing processes including the fulling (or tucking) and shearing. In some instances, one member of the family might be the clothier, another the fuller: John Collier was the clothier and Stephen the fuller. After finishing came the business of selling. Witney merchants are found mingling with those from Shipton-under-Wychwood, Wootton and Banbury in the cloth halls of London.

The result of this is that the cloth industry dominated life in Witney to a greater degree than in other Oxfordshire towns. In Witney 248 men were clothiers, weavers, clothmen, clothmakers, coverlet makers, blanket makers, warpers, wool winders, cardmakers, dyers, fullers and felt makers, accounting for forty-six per cent of the work force. In Banbury between 1590 and 1650 only sixteen per cent of the occupations were in the cloth trade. Neither Henley-on-Thames nor Thame developed a comparable weaving industry. Bicester and Charlbury were ordinary market towns.

The prominence of the cloth industry in Witney's economic life is still reflected in the vernacular buildings of the town. The houses of some of the wealthier clothiers and woolmen flanked Church Green, the huge triangular space between the parish church and the market at its apex. Dame Emmote Fermer bought a house here in 1494. In 1591 Henry Jones, clothier and bailiff, was a tenant of the Wenman's house next to Shaw the butcher. Nicholas Gunne, another clothier and bailiff, possessed a shop on the north side of Church House. Along Corn Street were houses belonging to wealthy clothiers such as the Joneses, the Yateses and the Bringfields.

The comparative size and richness of furnishings of these houses can be gauged from the probate inventories. Although they have been refronted in later periods, many of the surviving houses in Witney's town centre have a sixteenth- or seventeenth-century core. Nicholas Gunne, a clothier who died in 1602, had two main living rooms on the ground floor and a separate buttery, kitchen and dairyhouse. In his shop he kept three looms and a warping house for the preparation of yarn. His house was two storeyed: upstairs were two main bedrooms; his hall had a carpet on the floor and wainscot on the walls. Together with the window glass, the interior reflected rising standards of comfort. This was borne out by the furnishings which included ten jointed stools and a comfortable feather bed with twenty sheets, fine and coarse, feather pillows and bolster. The kitchen equipment was lavish enough for its owner to entertain on a large scale: twenty-five large pewter platters, two dozen of the lesser sort, a dozen dishes, half a dozen plates, half a dozen porringers, and the same saucers, fifteen candlesticks, five dozen trenchers (wooden dishes) and numerous pots, pans and kettles.

At the other end of the scale is the house of a poor broadweaver called Gregory Merryman. He had a hall or living room furnished only with a table, bench and form, a cupboard and a chair. The glass in his window was valued at 13d. His chamber or bedroom, which led off or was reached by a ladder, had a jointed bedstead and a press or clothes cupboard and an old copper. In a little chamber there was a bedstead, a flock bed, a pair of hempen sheets, two pillows, a pair of blankets and a white coverlet. In the buttery and kitchen were a few dishes and pots. Merryman's apparel amounted to a cloak, a coat, a doublet and a pair of breeches.

The fame Witney gained in the production of blankets really started in the seventeenth century. The reputed origin goes back to the year 1320 when a certain Thomas Blanket at Bristol is said to have invented a woollen fabric with the nap raised and of a length hitherto unknown. Blanket makers from Witney are known from the reign of James I, and Dr Plot in his *Natural History of Oxfordshire* (1677) expatiates on the trade. He attributes 'the excellency of these blankets to the abstersive nitrous water of the river Windrush where they are scoured ... but others there are again that rather think they owe it to a peculiar way of loose spinning the people have hereabout'. He reckoned there were '150 looms, employing near 3,000 poor people, from children of eight years old to decrepit old age, to work out above a hundred packs of wool per week'. He further explains that the blankets are made of 'head wool and bay wool' and of this they make blankets of '12, 11, 10 quarters broad'. Of the 'ordinary and middle wool they make blankets of 8 and 7 quarters broad.' He has interesting observations to make on the marketing:

> they make in pieces about 30 yards long and one yard ¾ broad and dye them red or blue which are the colours best please the Indians of Virginia and New England, with whom the merchants truck them for Bever, other Furs of several Beasts etc, the use they have for them is to apparel themselves with them their manner being to tear them into gowns of about two yards long, thrusting their arms through two holes made for that purpose and so wrapping the rest about them as we do our loose coats.

Other products included blankets of six quarters broad, commonly called cuts, which served seamen for their hammocks. The worst wool was used for collar makers, wrappers to pack their blankets in and tilt cloths for bargemen. Dr Plot describes how they sent the blankets in waggons up to London which then returned laden with fell wool from Leadenhall and Barnaby Street in Southwark.

The blanket industry received a boost from royal patronage in 1687 when, according to Wood, James II went to Witney where they presented him with a pair of blankets with golden fringe. Another indication of their prosperity and power was the charter granted to the Company of Blanket Weavers in 1710. In 1712 there were 115 members and from 1700 to 1730 the industry employed 3,000 persons from eight years old and upwards, and 150 looms were in use. A Blanket Hall was erected in 1712 and at this hall all the blankets made in Witney were weighed, measured and marked.

Machinery was brought into use in the late eighteenth century. In 1782 the Court Book of the company recorded that 'it is unanimously agreed to purchase, erect, and set up an engine for rowing Blankets upon the same construction as the Company are informed are used at Colchester'. It seems clear that the people in the villages for fourteen miles around Witney went on spinning by hand. Many small capitalists employed a few weavers each and sent the wool out to the cottages in the neighbourhood to be spun. With the advent of more machinery such as the 'spring loom', by which one man was able to do the work of two, the industry soon devolved into the hands of about five major manufacturers. By 1852 these were dominated by the Early family: they were John Early and Co., Richard Early, Edward Early, Richard Early junior, Early Brothers and Horatio Collier.

A record in speedy textile production had been set in 1811 by Sir John Throckmorton of Buckland. John Coxeter, manufacturer of Greenham Mills, Newbury, took wool from his patron's Southdown sheep and had the cloth woven and a coat made in thirteen hours twenty minutes, thus winning a 1000 guinea wager.

Early's mill bettered this record in 1906. As Bloxham describes:

> At 3.46 am as the sun rose the men began to shear the sheep (which had been kept inside overnight to prevent the fleeces from being drenched with dew). By shearing only the wool actually required for making the blankets – probably that from the back and shoulders, they left rather strange-looking partially shorn and rather confused animals. The wool was then willeyed, (blended), dyed, carded, spun and woven before being rushed to the tuckers who completed the finishing processes of washing, shrinking, drying and raising the nap. The entire process was completed in a mere ten hours twenty-seven minutes.

Oxfordshire was famous for another type of textile, this time produced in the Banbury region. The tradition of woollen textile weaving went back as far as the sixteenth century in this area, though the wool trade was never as important in north Oxfordshire as in the Cotswolds or Stroud valley. Plenty of coarse wool was available from the sheep in the surrounding hills, which also provided ample water for fulling and dyeing. Banbury itself served as a wool market. The corporation put up a wool hall in c.1610 of which part survives as Nos. 2 and 3 Market Place. It apparently had an open ground storey which was walled in c. 1646 when money was spent on rebuilding the gaol. Banbury and several other local towns became the foci of a considerable horse-drawn traffic, which created a large demand for webs, girths, horsecloths, wednal for lining horse collars and tilt cloths, or awnings for carts and waggons.

From the middle of the eighteenth century, Banbury weavers also made a narrow fabric of wool or worsted with a long nap of hairy pile called 'shag'. It acquired the name 'plush', from the French word *peluche*, in Victorian times and was a kind of coarse velvet.

To begin with plush was a home-based industry with handlooms to be found in cottages in a number of villages such as Bloxham, Bourton, Wordington and West Shefford. When Banbury church was pulled down in 1799 it is said that the massive timbers were much in demand for the making of hand looms of which there were some five hundred in the district employing about a thousand people. There was a long, low building with large windows at the top of Cook's Hill, Shutford which once housed a dozen or so hand looms.

In the nineteenth century the plush industry was encouraged by fresh inventions. Steam looms came to Banbury and three fairly large firms came to dominate the trade. In 1838, Gillet, Lees and Co. of Banbury acquired Sir Henry Bessemer's embossing machine. Rather like a mangle with the rollers heated internally by gas, this machine cut into the material a design so that the pattern stood out on the surface of the plush. Plush rapidly secured an expanding place in the market. Victorians prized it highly for curtains, tablecloths, upholstery, overmantles – even picture and mirror frames were made of plush. All manner of fibres created a great variety of finishes: wool, mohair, silk, cotton, artificial silk and a mixture of these. One could buy no less than 122 shades of silk plush as a shade card in Banbury Museum demonstrates. Plush embossed on the Bessemer machine was used to decorate Windsor Castle and provided the furnishings for the Houses of Parliament when they were restored after the fire of 1834. It was used for the state liveries of royal courts and noble houses throughout Europe. Scarlet plush for the English court, 'Italian blue' for the house of Savoy, special green for the Royal Foresters at Windsor, scarlet, blue and black for Spain, cream for the Netherlands, green and purple for the palaces of the Persian Shah. There were also more workaday uses. When the pile was left uncut it was used as fustian or corduroy for workman's clothes; this lasted for years and trousers were reputedly handed down from father to son. A similar type was used to upholster railway carriages. It was even used by the natives of Africa once a waterproof version was developed to deal with tropical rain storms. It was used for panning for gold (black), covering machine rollers (green), powdering ladies' noses, and scrubbing the bodies of athletes and those taking Turkish baths.

World War I seriously injured the sales of plush, though it has to be admitted that fashions had been changing and the use of livery decreasing since Victorian times. John Hill of Banbury ceased plush manufacture in 1900. Cubitt, Son and Co. closed in 1909 and its good will and machinery, including the Bessemer embosser, were bought by Messrs Wrench of Shutford who prolonged the life of the Oxfordshire plush industry until 1948. The problem at Shutford was to find craftsmen and apprentices who would be prepared to live in a rural village and resist the temptation of going to work in one of the large engineering concerns in Banbury. Oxfordshire plush is now only a textile memory.

Beer originally meant a drink made of malted barley and flavoured by hops; it was virtually unheard of in England before 1400. The medieval drink was ale, drunk universally by all classes of men, women and children. Water supplies in the Middle Ages were notoriously unsafe being largely polluted so ale, which was boiled and contained preservatives, was safer. It was thick, sticky and rather sweet, but could be clarified by the addition of herbs and spices which might have the additional advantages of preserving it and disguising its flavour if it became sour. Cultivating barley, the 'drink corn', was one of the chief tasks of the medieval farmer. Hopped beer was introduced into England c.1400 by Dutch brewers and hops began to be cultivated in south-east England. It took about two centuries for the bitter taste to be widely appreciated, but the better keeping properties reduced the necessity for frequent brewings and together they encouraged its adoption as the national drink.

Domestic beer making was widespread in the sixteenth and seventeenth centuries. Some two hundred inventories from Oxfordshire have survived for the period 1550–90, and of these well over a quarter included brewing or malting equipment normally listed in the kitchen, buttery or bakehouse. Thomas Taylor, a Witney yeoman (d.1583) had a 'yeling howse' (yelling is a corruption of gylling – an old term for brewing). This building contained an assortment of brewing utensils:

A Flaskett and foure Wyrgen Baskettes	1–4
a sowing baskett & another wyrgen baskett	0–8
9 Barrelles Twoo ollde buttes Two Rundlettes	
& one lyttle olyfe barrell	9–6
3 payles three Mallte seeves one heare	
seene foure Treene platters & a payre of	
wooden tongues	2–9
a bread grate and three little keevers	1–4
Twoo Boosshelles & one pecke	2–0
a shelfe & settles	1–8
fyve brasen woort pannes	2–0–0
fyve ollde sackes	2–0

His yeowting (soaking) vat in which the barley was steeped in preparation for malting was in a separate 'well housse' with the 'heave clothe' on which the malt rested over the fire during malting.

The malting process is described well by Gervase Markham, an early Stuart writer on husbandry:

They take a good quantity of Barley and put it into a Cesterne or vat and so steepe it in water the space of 3 nights, then drain it from the water and let it drop a day, then lay it on a fair floore in a great thick heap or centre, and let it soke 3 nights more in which space it will sprout at one end (for it must not sprout at both). Then they spread it very thin over the flower and either with a shovell or the hand it must be turned and tossed twice or thrice a day for the space of 14 days more ... then they drie it upon the kilne with a gentle fire, of swete straw, (for any other fuell yields too strong a smoake and gives the Malt an ill taste) after the Malt is dried, cooled, rubbed clean, skreened or winnowed, then it is sent to the mill and ground according to the proportion of the Brewing.

Clearly a yeoman farmer like Taylor was self-sufficient in most of his foodstuffs. Larger households similarly had the capacity to brew for family and servants. Chastleton House, built by Walter Jones, a successful wool merchant and clothier, had a compact plan with the innovative feature of the main service including buttery and beer cellar being located in the basement. To the side of the house, in a wing attached to the stables was the building adapted in the eighteenth century to become the brewhouse. A chimney with fireplaces was inserted in the two-storey building. Malt was delivered through first-floor loading doors and stored in the specially strengthened upper floor.

We know the sort of equipment the seventeenth-century brewhouse had from Walter Jones's inventory of 1633.

> Item one brasse furnace, three great massive vates with two hoops two coolers xii Item fower cowles two kevers one still and one board, one brasse kettle and other necessary implemts thereunto belongeing iili In the sellars.
> Item twenty fower hogsheads six rundlets three skooles and settles for beare vii

A minute examination of the now empty brewhouse has produced evidence for beer making. Aided by Markham we can reconstruct the process:

Water was first heated at the main fireplace in a cauldron supported by a suspension crane still *in situ*. The hot water was carried up the steps to the mash tub situated in the alcove to the south of the fireplace. 'After the malt is ground they put it into a mash vat and the liquor in the lead (cauldron) being ready to boyle put it to the malt and mash together. Then drain the liquor from the malt and put it in the lead againe and ad to it for every quarte of malt a $1\frac{1}{2}$ lb of hops and boyle over for the space of an houre. Then cleanse the liquor from the hops throgh a strait sive into the cooler.' The seatings for the trough and the cooler can be traced on the floor slabs of the Chastleton brewhouse. 'Then put in your barme (yeast) and after they have wrought, then heat them together and doe this so: divers times together.'

When the yeast was added the mixture began to ferment so it was drawn off into a vat. It was then emptied into buckets and poured into casks to complete the process of fermentation. The bungs were driven home and the casks were carried to the beer cellar under the house. Trundling such heavy materials resulted in the fracturing of floor slabs and these heavily worn areas were repaired with a non-slip surface of end-set bricks. The floor of the cellar was provided with channels to deal with spillage; the barrels were set on their sides in racking, traces of which are still visible.

Brewing was done monthly throughout most of the year at Chastleton in the 1770s and 80s judging from the purchases of malt and hops. Casual labour was employed to carry out the multiple operations.

July 27 Pd Jenny which she pd Baker for	
5 peck of malt at 3d per bushell	3–9
Do Mr Winslow for a pd hops	9
Pd Rose brewing	6
Aug 19 Pd Mr Winslow for 5 lbs hops @ 9d	3–9
Aug 20 Pd Baker Davis for 10 bushels	
of malt at 3s	£1–10–0
Pd Rose Brewing out of grains	——

The last is a reference to Rose being paid by being allowed to take the spent malt in lieu of payment. This would have made a valuable source of animal feed.

The communities of scholars in Oxford colleges were commensurate in numbers with the occupants of great country houses. About a dozen brewed beer for themselves. The Queen's College listed a brewer among the college servants at the time of the foundation of the college 1340–1. The accounts survive from 1691–1977. The College brewed 'strong and small beer', 'double' and 'middle'. In 1690 barrel purchases are recorded from coopers as far away as Thame and Blewbury. The brewhouse still stands on the west side of the Fellows' Garden. Its louvred windows for emitting the heat and steam of the brewing process survive, but since brewing ceased after World War II it has been converted into a carpentry shop above and a garage below. The College steward has in his keeping malting shovels and a paddle used for stirring the wort. Faded sepia photographs show the brewers at work amid the steam and the smells, surrounded by mighty vats and barrels. The beer was proverbially strong.

In the 1700s brewing on such a small scale became very expensive. High taxes were levied on malt and hops; fuel whether wood or coal was also costly. William Cobbett deplored the extent to which people gave up home brewing and turned to the drinking of tea: 'a destroyer of health, an enfeebler of the frame, an engendere of effeminacy and laziness, a debaucher of youth and a maker of misery in old age'.

As domestic brewing declined so the fortunes of the common brewer grew. Great brewing families all closely related – the Halls, Treachers, Morrells and Tawneys – emerged to dominate the trade in Oxford. These common brewers were concentrated in the town centre. Henry Drought and Charles Moore were in the St Aldate's/Brewers Lane area from the 1750s to the 1780s. Morrells' brewery site was in St Thomas's. This had passed through the hands of the Tawney family until 1803 when it came under the control of Mark and James Morrell. Other towns gained common breweries in the eighteenth and nineteenth centuries. By 1860 every Oxfordshire town had at least one. There were fourteen in Oxford, ten in Banbury, seven in Bicester, five in Abingdon, four in Deddington, three in Witney and Wantage, two in Eynsham, Wallingford, Watlington and Henley. Competition was intense and those that survived owed their success to a combination of good business sense, good brewing methods, capital to invest in new plant and the acquisition of tied houses to ensure distribution and sales. The demand for beer was unprecedented in the first half of the nineteenth century; it used English malt and hops and, despite the temperance movement, sales rocketed, as beer was considered superior to gin.

Industrialized brewhouses and malthouses became distinctive buildings (and among the largest) in the Oxfordshire landscape. Thomas Hunt built a new brewhouse in Banbury and then took into partnership William Edmunds, who brought an injection of capital into the business. A valuation of 1858 gives some idea of the new machinery being invested in; it included large cast-iron vessels, a Capital Refrigerator, a malt dressing machine and a Tizard's Patent Mashing Machine with revolving spurgers. A similar programme of modernization by building onto and adapting older buildings was carried through by William Brakspear of Henley. He installed a refrigerator in 1836 and employed steam power for milling and pumping. In particular, the pure water gained from sinking an artesian well on the premises, plus the purchase of the best quality barley and hops, ensured a high reputation for Brakspear's beers. Others solved their technical problems by building tower breweries between 1870 and 1912. Philips in Oxford, Townshends and Morlands in Abingdon, and the Hook Norton Brewery all built these distinctive towers which were prominent landmarks useful in advertising the product.

The Hook Norton brewery remains in operation. It is an extraordinarily compact building performing the complex processes of beermaking under one roof. Steam power pumps the water from deep wells up to the cold water tanks at the top of the fifth floor of the tower. The sacked malt is similarly powered up to the malt store from where it is transported to the grist mill for crushing. Using gravity feed, the liquor (the brewers' term for water) is transferred down a stage to the hot liquor tank where it is heated and mixed with the malt in the mash tun. The starch of the malt is converted into soluble sugars and after sparging (sprinkling with more hot liquor), the sweet wort is run off. The wort is now boiled with hops in the copper; this provides the preservatives and the flavour. Once on the hopback the wort is separated from the spent hops. There are two by-products; the spent hops are a useful fertilizer for market gardeners and the spent malt is used for cattle feed. The process continues by the wort being pumped up to the fourth floor of the tower to be cooled. It passes through a refrigerator and makes its way into the fermenting tuns where yeast is added. The fermentation takes four or five days as the yeast multiplies, turning the sugar in the wort into alcohol. The beer now is stored and rests until it is put into casks or bottled.

Hidden from view of Harrison's Lane, behind the County Museum in the little town of Woodstock, is the building which housed the last glove factory in Oxfordshire. It is a single storeyed structure with three large, well-lit, white-washed rooms, heated either end with fireplaces, ventilated from louvres piercing the red tile roof. It stands on a long, asphalt-covered slope which reminds one of a school play-ground. This surmise is a correct one; the Woodstock Gloving Factory occupied the premises built for an Industrial School c.1870–1910. Here, until 1987 when it closed, I used to buy gloves for my mother; she was fond of gloves, fur gloves, kid gloves, gloves which matched her numerous handbags. Here I watched the glovers at work, cutting, grounding and sewing.

Making gloves in such factory conditions was the last stage in a long history of gloving in the county. In the early Middle Ages it was concentrated in Oxford itself. Adam, the glove maker, was living in the parish of St Clements in 1279. Regular glover's shops were to be found on the High Street frontage near the present Mitre Hotel. Several of the city officials in the later Middle Ages were known as 'gaunters' or glove makers. The Ashmolean Museum has a richly embroi-dered pair presented to Queen Elizabeth I when she visited Oxford University in 1566. Judges were similarly honoured by being presented with a pair of white kid gloves from the University and a second pair from the City on the Commis-sion Day of each assize.

By the sixteenth century, gloving had spread into west Oxfordshire. Among reasons put forward to explain this is that deer skins from Wychwood and sheepskins from the Cotswolds were plentiful sources of raw material. Certainly Bampton and Burford were known for tanners and leather dressers. Witney had a series of tanner's pits by the Windrush which I recorded in the early 1980s. The royal court at Woodstock may have boosted local demand for gloves by its requirement for hawking and hunting gloves. Perhaps the most plausible reason for its growth is that gloving offered an alternative or supplementary occupation in an area, the Forest of Wychwood, where the possibilities of agricultural employment were restricted.

The industry went through domestic and factory phases in its history. Arthur Young in 1809, in his *View of the Agriculture of Oxfordshire*, coupled breeches making with glovemaking; they both used leather. In the eighteenth and nineteenth centuries small family businesses grew up in Woodstock, Charlbury, Hanborough, Stonesfield and other villages in west Oxfordshire, employing two or three journeymen, 'grounders', and 'cutters'. These skilled artisans sorted the skins, dyed them, pared them down to ensure even thicknesses and cut them into glove shapes. This last involved using shears for slitting the skins or (from the early nineteenth century) knife-edged templates (the 'webs'). The cut-outs were bundled up and taken by cart (or later by van or bicycle) to be sewn together in the homes of the outworkers in the villages around. Each firm would rely on the labour of dozens, if not hundreds, of women and children for whom the wages acquired by piecework were a vital addition to the family economy. In 1851 in Leafield, in the depths of Wychwood Forest, there were 153 gloveresses; sixty-nine were under the age of twenty-one and a child of five was even listed. In the village of Hanborough there were 149 females engaged in gloving, fifty-two of whom ranged in age from eight to nineteen years.

Gloving was a comparatively healthy occupation in that none of its processes involved toxic materials. Also, in fine weather the gloveresses could sit outside to sew where the light would be better and they could escape briefly from the severe overcrowding of eight to ten people crammed into a four-roomed cottage. Hand sewing was superseded by treadle-operated Singer sewing machines, but these tended to be owned by the operators and this did not by itself signal a move to the factories.

Foreign competition in the second half of the nineteenth century led to many of the smaller firms disappearing. Samuel Pritchett of Charlbury employed in gloving twenty-eight grounders (rubbing down the tough backs of the skins with emery-covered hand blocks), eight bleachers, sixteen cutters, eight layers-out and ironers, eight boys, and no less than 850 females. The railways brought new sources of raw material, such as hides from South America and South Africa, barrels of egg yolk used in leather dressing from Russia, and Singer sewing machines, invented in the USA in 1850. Increased industrialization also led to greater variety of product: motoring gloves, military gloves (which could be blancoed white), motor-cycling gauntlets, wicket-keeping gloves, also prize-fighting gloves, described lyrically by an old grounder as 'beautiful leather the colour of port wine, with white facings and stuffed with kapok'.

The final stage of the industry was when a few large concerns set up factories where all the processes were concentrated. While electricity was used sometimes to power the webbing process and almost universally to drive the sewing machines, the basic skills of cutter and maker remained handcrafts to the last. Mr Ival Hornbrook, for many years Records Officer in the County Museum Sites and Monuments Record, was a renowned glover at an earlier stage in his life. He was entrusted with the task of introducing the craft into the island of Malta, when the economy of the Crown Colony was thought to be in need of a boost. By 1973 only four west Oxfordshire gloving firms were still in business. Glovemaking had become part of the county folk memory.

VIII
Towns

Twenty-five years ago, a seminal work was published entitled *Historic Towns in Oxfordshire*, edited by Kirsty Rodwell. The genesis of this book was the realization that modern development was destroying the historic core of towns like Gloucester and Hereford and that the nation was thus losing vital knowledge about the origins of towns and the way of life of their inhabitants in the early periods, when there was a lack or a scarcity of documentation from the written records. As I write, a new intensive urban survey of the City of Oxford is under way, funded by English Heritage, organized by the City Council, strengthened by a battery of computer-driven aids, which will act as a pilot scheme for a new generation of historic town data-bases. Planners are now constrained to take the historic environment into consideration. Mitigation strategies that allow the conservation *in situ* are the ideal; excavation, an expensive last resort, is recognized as being essentially destructive. Survey, mitigation, excavation have all contributed to the historic town scene. How far have they altered our perception of Oxfordshire's historic towns during the years 1975 to 1995?

Concerning the origin of towns, archaeologists are now beginning to recognize that late in the Iron Age certain religious, political and economic foci had already begun to develop proto-urban features. These include good communications, fortification and a certain level of occupation density, characteristics easy to demonstrate by digging. Less easy to display is specialization of function, the existence of craft industries and retail facilities which go with towns. Abingdon is a conundrum, as we have seen. On the Vineyard site, even on this restricted area, there was an extensive settlement of at least nine circular houses in the late Iron Age. Iron-Age material has been found all over the historic town core and a ditch ten metres wide, cut three metres deep into gravel, dated *c.*50 AD, has been interpreted as providing the defences for an 'oppidum'. There may have been similar but less well defined 'oppida' at Cassington and Dyke Hills, Dorchester, but only Abingdon has produced sufficient evidence for claims to be put forward that it is 'Britain's oldest town'.

If this is so, Britons in the upper Thames Valley were no strangers to the idea of urban life, heretofore assumed as being introduced by the Romans. Oxfordshire has two walled Roman towns, Alchester and Dorchester, as well as several smaller unwalled urban centres. Alchester is seven miles north of Oxford and in an area which was quite heavily Romanized. It was fortified with a rampart and wall, added at the same time (an unusual feature) in the second century AD. Excavation in advance of roadworks has shown the existence of a Roman industrial suburb half a mile north of the town.

The site of the town itself was a marshy one, requiring radical drainage and artificial building up of the ground level. This seems to have gone hand in hand with the drainage of Otmoor, a large flat circular area five miles by seven miles, surrounded by a rim of higher land to the south of the town. Alchester failed to attract continuing urban settlement probably because the drainage system broke down in the last four decades of Roman rule and the Saxons settled at Bicester, a drier site a mile to the north. The banks of the Roman defences can just about be traced in the ground today. Metal detector users are in process of riddling the field surface where once Roman craftsmen worked. Scheduling the ancient monument here simply seems to act as a challenge to law breakers.

Dorchester-on-Thames was altogether a more significant site for a town. It lay at the junction of the rivers Thame and Thames, in the centre of a rich corn-growing region. There are slight signs of a military outpost within the first century of the Roman occupation. The buildings continued to be mostly timber in construction, as excavations by Professor

Frere on the former allotments have shown. The town was fortified in the second century AD with an earthen rampart, later fronted by a wall and, it has been claimed, with towers which would have held 'ballistas'. The altar set up by M. Varius Severus, a Roman officer concerned with supplies, is a good indicator that Roman Dorchester was of some strategic and economic significance. Graves found in the vicinity contained late Roman military equipment of the sort issued by the administration to Saxon *foederati*, mercenary troops, who took on the policing and defence of parts of the province when Roman rule began to collapse.

Dorchester was evidently in a flourishing state late in the fourth century, since quantities of small change dating from the Theodosian period have been found, indicating large pay-outs or an active market. The 64,000 denarii question is, however, the extent of continuity between the Roman town and the missionary centre set up by Birinus in the mid seventh century. A Saxon sunken hut was found by Frere which apparently respects the line of the Roman gravelled road surface. Other Saxon timbered buildings dug up in the 1970s did not. It seems in fact as if the Saxon settlement pattern in the area was dispersed. They appear largely to have avoided dwelling in the stinking ruins of the abandoned town. It was robbed extensively for building materials. The abbey church, with presumably the site of the Saxon cathedral under it, was *outside* the defences of the town to the east.

Oxfordshire cannot furnish us with any other examples of towns which have a Roman origin unless the Roman settlement at Abingdon is proved to have been urban in nature. When then was the network of market towns, that are such a characteristic feature of the landscape, established? There seems no doubt that the Church played a leading part. Monks and bishops can be credited with the foundation of a number of Oxfordshire's towns. A minster or abbey already existed at Eynsham when its foundation was confirmed in 1005 by King Ethelred. It lost its rich endowments for a time, but by the early twelfth century had recovered its property and set about optimizing its income. The Anglo-Saxon abbey, foundations of which began to be uncovered in the late 1980s, stood south of the market place. A church of St Leonard was provided for the parishioners. Acre End was built up with tenements fronting on it and was followed by Mill Street which had been developed as far north as Newland Street by the thirteenth century. Here, in 1215, the abbey attempted to encourage late new development by founding a new borough with a charter. This provides significant topographical information: the monks grant

> all that land which was of our demesne and lies without [outside] the town of Eynsham, to wit between the same town and the great street towards Cassington bridge to the south and likewise all that land which was of our demesne towards the north, in length 20 perches from the same street towards the north: on this condition that whoever holds an acre of these lands shall pay us 4s yearly (and lesser areas $\frac{3}{4}/\frac{1}{2}/\frac{1}{4}$ acre at the same rate ie 3s, 2s, 1s) to hold by hereditory right etc.

Newland was certainly laid out in this way. The street, and the burgage plots behind it, is straighter and wider than the other thoroughfares in the town.

The monastic borough of Eynsham was not a wild success; in the mid fourteenth century it was still smaller in population than Tilgarsley, a village to the north. But the Black Death struck here and the shivering survivors were accommodated at Eynsham which lived on to acquire a 'New Row' in the fifteenth century and even to have its Market Square encroached on by building in the sixteenth century. Far from killing off the town, the dissolution of the Abbey stimulated its growth. Its buildings profited by absorbing the great resource of construction materials. Moulded stones can be found built into houses all over the town. The market, begun by the monks, continued into the eighteenth century.

Another example of a town which benefited from monastic patronage, even if its origins predated the monastic connection, is Faringdon. Described by Ashmole in *The Antiquities of Berkshire* (1719) as 'pleasantly situated on an eminence', it was the site of a royal residence in the late Saxon period. Edward the Elder died here in 924. An adulterine castle here was stormed by Stephen in 1145 and King John granted the site of the castle to the monks of Citeaux to found an abbey. The monks decided the location was unsuitable and moved to Beaulieu in Hampshire. They encouraged the development of the small market which was laid out on the slope to the south of the minster church and to the east of the Westbrook. The market was held on Mondays in 1218, and in 1313 a license was obtained to change it to Tuesdays. Fairs were held on the Feasts of St Luke, the Purification of the Blessed Virgin Mary and St Bartholomew's Day. Faringdon, like Eynsham, never prospered. Leland, the antiquary of Henry VIII, said 'some call this town Cheping Farington but there is none or very small market now at it'. Throughout the Middle Ages the burgesses retained strong interests in farming. Their rights in manure, the folding of sheep and pasture for cows interested them more than urban crafts or buying and selling.

Faringdon's situation on the main road from London to Gloucester (until the nineteenth century) ensured its significance in the coaching age. In 1681 it was described as 'pretty well built with some good inns for entertainment of which the Crown is chief'. A remarkable feature in the largely Georgian town of Faringdon is the way in which local builders have clearly been influenced by the notable design of nearby Coleshill House, the brainchild of Sir Roger Pratt (1620–85). Tragically burned down in 1953, Coleshill's hipped roofs, jutting eaves, prominent chimneys, denticulated cornices, long rectangular windows and pronounced quoins are found immortalized in diluted form throughout the town. In particular, the late seventeenth-century Market Hall and Bell Inn are microcosms of the now vanished great house.

Witney, six miles to the west, was also the creation of the Church, this time in the persons of the Bishops of Winchester. There had been Saxon settlement on the meandering core of the river Windrush called Wittas' island (Anglo-Saxon 'ey'). The Bishops of Winchester obtained a large estate of four parishes as a gift from Queen Emma in 1044. Next to the church, on a site afterwards known as the Mount, they built a great house in the early twelfth century. Excavation by Brian Durham and the Oxford Archaeological Unit in 1983 exposed the massive foundations of a 'solar tower', the private chambers of the owner. Linked with it was an antechamber which was no doubt attached to a great hall now buried deep under the present Victorian Mount House. Durham also found a gatehouse to the north, a length of thirteenth-century curtain wall, a long building with a hearth constructed leaning against the curtain, a chapel and garde-robes attached to the tower. Most interestingly, the tower was surrounded with a stone-revetted clay bank, probably in response to a worsening military situation in the Civil War of Stephen and Matilda. This last work was during the episco-pacy of Henry de Blois, an ambitious builder and art patron who 'built six castles' in 1137. Unique among Oxfordshire's recent excavations, the site has been consolidated, covered by a huge Teflon tent (which looks like a medieval tournament pavilion) and explained with the help of an interpretation centre. It is a monument to the co-operation of English Heritage, the County and the District working in imaginative partnership. It is also a tourist draw sited next to a supermarket!

The medieval market of Witney was a long narrow triangle with its base at the church and the Bishop's House stretching 400 metres to the north, to the crossroads formed by a junction of an ancient east–west route with the curving High Street. On either side of the market and High Street are long burgage plots with old stone walls bounding them. These contained the houses, workshops, tofts (yards) and crofts (paddocks) of the medieval inhabitants of the bishop's town. Unfortunately, they have been all but eliminated in the intensive redevelopment of the historic core of Witney, led by the energetic District Council. This means that the material evidence for reconstructing the town's past has been swept away without very much recording and with no large-scale excavation. Some green shoots are now visible in this desert of lost opportunities. The town Historical Society has recently started a museum. The local branch of the Council for the Protection of Rural England stoutly defended the last burgage plot at a recent Local Plan Enquiry.

One of the ways that the historic importance of the site was brought home to the inspector at this enquiry was the measurement and analysis of the slow-growing lichens on the walls of the long plot. Dr Vanessa Winchester of the Oxford University School of Geography was able to point to parts of the wall having started life around 1500. The western wall, bounding Puck Lane, and the lower courses of the northern boundary wall would seem to have been built about 1740; the upper courses, although constructed in the same style, were dated to the 1860s because the lichens were not so well developed. In this way the different growth rates of the silver-grey *Aspioilia calcarea* and the orange *Caloplaca flavescens* are brought to bear on a heritage problem!

The Bishops of Lincoln in the Middle Ages had an even greater interest than the See of Winchester in encouraging urban development. They had important estates in and around Dorchester, Thame and Banbury. When seen from the air, the town of Thame clearly has two town centres. There is an irregular skein of streets around the church, formerly an Anglo-Saxon minster, but rebuilt in the Perpendicular style by the prosperous merchants of the town in the fifteenth century. Here the bishops sited their moated prebendal house. One of the canons, a rich ecclesiastic on the way up in his career in the medieval Church, would have lived, and farmed, here. A thirteenth-century chapel survives, complete with its grouped lancet windows and simple roof of trussed rafters, collars, soulaces and ashlars. The prebendal hall, seen in eighteenth-century watercolours in the Bodleian Library, has disappeared, but the solar, with its splendid fourteenth-century crown post roof, still stands.

Attached to this more ancient focus is the planned element of the town, its remarkable fish-shaped market place swelling out in the middle, with the burgage plots running off almost at right angles. Close inspection shows they have a slight reversed S-bend, so that this new adjunct is likely to have been cut out of the town's open fields. Lining the market place are timber-framed houses of the sixteenth and seventeenth centuries, many of them brick-fronted to bring them into accord with eighteenth-century fashion. Behind their façades are rooms with painted wall decorations imitating plaster and textile surfaces. One such room has been taken out and re-erected in the County Museum, Fletcher's House, Woodstock. I recorded another painted on boards, dated 1590–1610, in the Swan Hotel.

Banbury has the distinction of being the most studied town in the county after Oxford. It had a notable early Victorian historian, Alfred Beesley, whose *History of Banbury* (1841) set a high standard of documentation, maintained through the next century by the publications of the Banbury Historical Society. In the Saxon period, Banbury was the site of a minster church and a centre of an important estate belonging to the Bishops of Dorchester. When the see was removed to Lincoln in 1072 by William I it continued to act as a power base for the bishops. Alexander (1123–48), a prelate who was a prodigy of building ambition, ordered the castle to be constructed and laid out a new town, complete with market-place, between the river Cherwell and the older settlement. The tolls of the market are mentioned from 1138 and a fair was granted in Henry II's reign. The castle now lies under pedestrian walkways and supermarkets but much information was recovered by Peter Fasham and Kirsty Rodwell in excavations prior to redevelopment. Bishop Alexander's curtain wall castle was proved to have been replaced by a thirteenth-century concentric version complete with drum towers, a gatehouse, inner and outer wards. It was so strong that, when helped out with earthen additions to take the impact of cannon shot, it resisted manfully two Civil War sieges. Another medieval building flattened in Banbury was the old parish church; this proved similarly resistant to demolition in 1793 and had to be blown up by gunpowder! It was replaced by a vapid Classical design which is crumbling into rusty decay after less than two hundred years.

The nascent town secured a double benefit from castle and church; merchants and farmers gained security for the storage and display of valuable goods, and the facility for quick and even-handed justice in the bishop's market court. The presence of the church nearby reminded them of the sanctity of oaths and the desirability of honesty in transactions. The bishop profited from tolls and the fines levied. By the sixteenth century the burgesses took over from the bishop and built themselves a town hall, ceremoniously transferring the wooden cage (for prisoners) and the other instruments of law and order from the castle to the town hall.

When one looks at a map of the market towns of medieval Oxfordshire, they are so thick on the ground (there are twenty altogether) that one questions whether there was enough trade to go round. Oxfordshire, in fact, was the richest rural community among the counties of medieval England as judged by the assessed wealth in the lay subsidy of 1334. It was not evenly distributed, however: central Oxfordshire was worth more than £30 per square mile; northern, £20–29 per square mile; and southern (the Chiltern region), was rated at only £10–19 per square mile. Consequently, some towns like Oxford and Banbury succeeded and went on growing; others stood still at certain periods and then declined (Wallingford is an example), while a few never really fulfilled their lordly founder's expectations. These included Charlbury and a string of failed markets in the Vale of the White Horse like Baulking, East Hendred, Hinton Waldrist, Kingston Lisle, Shrivenham and Stanford-in-the-Vale.

The oldest were the most prosperous. Oxford and Wallingford were both burhs, fortified centres, effective in their opposition to Viking incursions by virtue of their strong defences. Oxford's markets, held in midweek and at the end of the week, followed markets in the surrounding area. Both Oxford and Wallingford declined in the later Middle Ages for reasons explained elsewhere. Eynsham's market was established on Sundays in the reign of Stephen, Abingdon's was the creation of Edward the Confessor. All of these prospered at least up until the end of the population boom in the thirteenth century. Tensions between townsfolk and monks at Abingdon led to rioting in 1327 when it is possible that the timber campanile to the north of the abbey was destroyed. Its foundations were dug up in the late 1980s. Serving other parts of the county were Bampton, a hundredal manor and market of Pre-Conquest origin and Burford, also in Bampton hundred, which had a market from the late eleventh century. Deddington and Chipping Norton each acquired their markets in the twelfth century.

Burford is particularly interesting in that it preserves the form and plan of its medieval origins with hardly any accretions. It has one wide street which is half a mile long and climbs the slope towards the present Oxford–Gloucester road. In the Middle Ages the main road ran east–west through the centre of the town, past the Tolsey (the sixteenth-century market hall). There are no less than six houses or parts of houses of the fourteenth century, two of the early fifteenth, and as many as twenty-two houses, or parts of houses, surviving from the late fifteenth to early sixteenth century. The relatively wide plot frontages meant that few houses were built gable-end on but the gables on timber-framed houses were treated decoratively. Below the sixteenth- and seventeenth-century gables is a wealth of medieval doorways, some leading through to the long yards, the remains of burgage plots. Their thresholds well below street level are a reminder of the constant rise in street level at the bottom of Burford High Street, matched by the continuous hollowing process of the traffic in the upper part of the High Street. Many of the shops have built out on to the pavement. These recall the temporary nature of medieval shops, open fronted, made of wood and leaning like pentices against the side of the houses. The Borough charter of Wallingford protected the burgesses from 'picage' and 'pannage' and 'stallage'. 'Picage' *et alia* were dues for breaking ground in markets and fairs for the erection of a stall.

The rights to hold markets and fairs are easy to document and date, and the market-places are usually still recognizable in the townscape, although at Thame, Witney and Woodstock they have all been encroached upon by building in the Middle Ages. How can one work out the distribution networks and the evolving pattern of exchange in commodities over different periods? Archaeology is beginning to give answers because it deals with a universally used and indestructible medium: pottery. The intensive study of medieval pottery in the Oxford region is now far advanced. Maureen Mellor has mapped the chief production centres over six centuries. Some of Oxford's Late Saxon pottery came from the north-east, from the Cambridge and Huntingdon region. These St Neots wares were supplemented by bright glazed pottery from the Stamford area. They were overtaken in the thirteenth century by material seeping in from the east, the so called Brill/Boarstall wares of Buckinghamshire. To begin with, quality wares were brought in, by cart and pack horse, to penetrate the market in a limited way – about a twelve-mile radius. Then a much wider variety of pots flooded in and a greater distribution area was defined. In turn the pinkish/yellow fabrics of Brill/Boarstall were replaced as the focus of the ceramic industry shifted south and east to the forest environs of Nettlebed and Crockerend. Here, the potters allied themselves with tilers and brickmakers. It was from this area, as we have seen, that 'Les Flemynges' (presumably immigrant workers from the Netherlands) made 200,000 bricks for the building of the chapel tower at Stonor Park in 1416. In the fifteenth century the Surrey whitewares successfully took over a share of the market in south Oxfordshire and increased their domination in the early modern period.

The picture just painted in broad brush strokes is a gross simplification of a much more complex story. Take the influence of rivers. They do not seem to have acted as arteries for the free movement of pottery. In fact the Thames could act as a barrier. The tolls collected at Folly Bridge, the southern gate of the town of Oxford, inhibited the pottery made in the kilns in the south of the county from reaching the Oxford markets. Similarly, the products of north Oxfordshire potteries failed to penetrate markets south of the river. Despite Oxford's international academic connections, remarkably little in the way of foreign imported wares has been found.

Pottery was supplemented by glass which is known to have been manufactured at Benson in 1441-2 and is mentioned by Dr Plot in the mid seventeenth century as being made at Henley-on-Thames and other places in the Chilterns. 'The invention of making glasses of stones ... carried on by one Mr Ravenscroft who has a patent for the sole making them ... (of) the blackest flints calcined and a white cristalline sand'. Disappointingly, no material evidence has come from Henley-on-Thames over the last twenty years for this interesting industry.

In reviewing the changing fortunes of Oxfordshire towns perhaps undue emphasis has been given to ecclesiastical foundations. Other towns had lay lords from the Crown downwards as founders. Woodstock, seven miles to the north-west of Oxford, was a royal foundation. It was a hunting lodge of Edward the Confessor and a favourite resort of the Plantagenet kings. Henry II is credited with the foundation of the town, allegedly to house his court while he conducted an illicit affair in the park with Rosamund Clifford. The layout of the town relates to access to the manor rather than to the highway from Oxford to Chipping Norton. The only regular and apparently planned element is the block of tenements, dating to the thirteenth century, running between (the present) Union Street and Oxford Street. It must have been a curiously insecure commercial existence for the burghers of Woodstock: the King's itineraries brought him and his court, which, over the period 1100-1500, could number anything between 120 and 800, at irregular intervals, sometimes for two days, sometimes for a fortnight at a time. Certainly, Woodstock was a favourite royal house in Edward III's and Richard II's reigns. The court held the great ecclesiastical festivals such as Christmas here. The occasions of royal baptisms and the churching of queens (the ceremony of recording the return to normal life of the royal spouse after childbirth) were celebrated with feasts, tournaments and hastiludes (pageants). All would have required the services of vintners, victuallers, embroiderers, glovemakers, tailors, goldsmiths, painters. But what did these craftsmen do for the rest of the year? As hangers on to the court they would have had a thin time moving from one religious house to another, or living in tents or villages within ten miles of the king's person.

Unfortunately, throughout the sixteenth century the royal manor decayed and the town was forced to fend for itself until in 1705 the Churchill family, the Dukes of Marlborough, arrived and occupied the new palace in the park. Once again there was work for stone-masons, plasterers, plumbers. Woodstock, with ducal patronage, prospered in the eighteenth century. The Marlboroughs gifted almshouses and a town hall, and the local gentry built up-to-date Georgian houses, a number of them such as the Bishop's House showing scaled down versions of Vanbrugh's architectural style.

Woodstock, for many people, calls to mind Fletcher's House, a gracious eighteenth-century building set in a lovely garden, since 1965 the headquarters of a model and modern County Museums service. To begin with, its collections comprised the objects which other museums did not collect – those associated with the county's agricultural and industrial past – but latterly it has become the main repository for the astonishing stream of artefacts which have poured out of archaeological excavations. After thirty years ambitious plans are in the offing to refurbish, with the historic building itself forming a key element in the display, and new galleries, as well as the indispensable coffee room constructed around the garden. Like this book, the approach in the displays will be thematic; unlike this book, the experience will be three-dimensional. It is hoped that a heightening of perception about the county's past will lead to an enrichment of life for Oxfordshire people and their visitors in the future.

IX

Oxford

As yet there is little evidence for a Roman settlement in central Oxford. The Ordnance Survey Map of Roman Britain shows Roman roads converging on the river Thames crossing, but there is no agreement among archaeologists as to where this was exactly. The causewayed Abingdon road which leads out of medieval Oxford to the south, has forty-two arches built into its course, as we have noticed, and at Redbridge (near the Park and Ride) it has been suggested that several of these arches may be Roman in date. The two long, straight roads leading out of Oxford to the north, the Woodstock and Banbury roads, again look as if they could be Roman. They keep to the long, low gravel ridge between the Thames and Cherwell. On the eastern heights below Shotover, where the Churchill Hospital now stands, dozens of Roman pottery kilns have been located. Evidently this part was a major industrial area in Roman times, sending pottery along the river Thames to both east and west, and by pack horse to the north. Recent housing developments at Blackbird Leys have shown that the Roman settlements here were spread over a wide area.

All this however does not amount to a Roman occupation of the site of Oxford. There was certainly human settlement here from the Bronze Age. A Beaker burial was located at the Hamel, dug deep into the clay of the valley bottom. There was also a religious centre from the mid Saxon period. An eighth-century minster associated with a Mercian princess called St Frideswide was founded along the edge of the gravel terrace overlooking a now lost channel of the Thames. In the mid Saxon period the river constituted the boundary of two kingdoms, Mercia and Wessex. 'Oxenford', where Saxon herdsmen guided their animals across the braided streams, was at the point where the north–south road which bisected Anglo-Saxon England crossed the Thames. Whether the ford was on the site of the later Grand Pont and Folly Bridge or whether, as John Blair has postulated, it may have been south of Christ Church on the line of the present Parks Road, Schools Street (subsequently Catte Street) and Oriel Street is a moot point. There is even lack of assurance about whether the primary mid Saxon settlement at Oxford was to the north or south of the Thames crossing. Professor Biddle in a lecture in 1995 suggested that it might have begun as a 'wic' or market centre just inside Wessex on the slightly higher land above the flood-plain near East Wyke farm and the former West Wyke. Blair, Hassall, Durham and others prefer an origin for Oxford to the north of the river. This proved more defensible and Blair thinks there may have been a line of churches growing up in the late Saxon period, St Frideswide's Priory and the parish churches of St Aldate's and St Ebbe's.

So Oxford began as a religious focus, on an important road, near a major river crossing. It acquired burghal status AD c.900 when King Alfred's surveyors began to lay out a rectilinear grid of streets and ordered the raising of an earthen enclosing bank. A coin of Edward the Elder was found lying on a primary road surface in New Inn Hall Street. Whether the town was 'laid out' in one go, or whether it was developed bit by bit over a long period, is not clear. Certainly the largest 'insula' between the modern George Street and Pembroke Street was built up along the street frontages *and* in the middle by the late Saxon period. The Saxon town flourished and was extended to the east and west of the early defences in the early eleventh century. It was attacked and burnt by the Danes in 1009, a sure sign that there was something worth pillaging. The Normans immediately recognized the strategic significance of the place and ordered the destruction of the western part of the Saxon town to accommodate a motte and bailey castle. There was some reshaping of the streets. Saxon cellar pits have been found well in front of the present street lines in the city centre. Perhaps the Normans, expecting more traffic, set back the

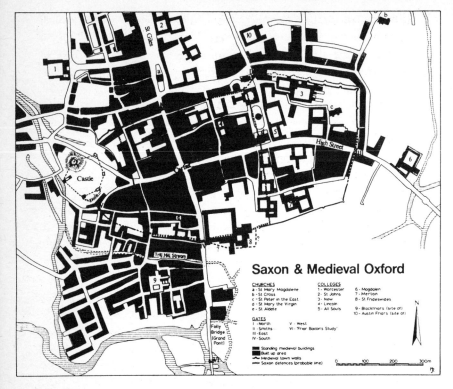

Saxon & Medieval Oxford

CHURCHES
a - St Mary Magdalene
b - St Cross
c - St Peter in the East
d - St Mary the Virgin
e - St Aldate

COLLEGES
1 - Worcester
2 - St Johns
3 - New
4 - Lincoln
5 - All Souls
6 - Magdalen
7 - Merton
8 - St Frideswides
9 - Blackfriars (site of)
10 - Austin Friars (site of)

GATES
I - North
II - Smiths
III - East
IV - South
V - West
VI - 'Friar Bacon's Study'

■ Standing medieval buildings
▪ Built up area
∿ Medieval town walls
▬ Saxon defences (probable line)

Plan of Saxon and Medieval Oxford (*after Rodwell 1975*)

building frontages of the Saxon streets. With the increased width, temporary stalls could be built for marketing. More constructively for the economic life of the townsfolk, the first Norman constable Robert d'Oilly put in hand the building of the great causeway with stone arches where the bridge crossed the main channels of the braided Thames, as mentioned above. This was one of the earliest stone bridges of Western Europe. It has recently been scheduled as a government-protected ancient monument to protect it from the depredations of bodies such as British Telecom who cut service trenches willy-nilly across it.

Oxford now had good communications with the rest of England. It was in fact bang in the middle as the Revd H. E. Salter, Oxford's greatest local historian pointed out. In the fifteenth century the abbot of Eynsham bought his wine and Spanish iron from Bristol. Robert Walford, mayor of Oxford and a vintner, acquired *his* wine regularly from Southampton, while John Langdon, a Canterbury monk, celebrated his award of a degree of DD by bringing four pipes of wine from London, up the Thames to Marlow and then overland. Oxford was equidistant from these three great ports of southern England.

The central location undoubtedly favoured the beginnings of a university here, but the actual circumstances are still unclear despite nine centuries of imaginative fantasy and intensive research. It certainly was not King Alfred who founded Oxford University, a spurious tale put about by University College from 1380 onwards. It may have had something to do with Henry II's wars with France in the 1160s when he forbad English scholars to go to the University of Paris. Certainly, there had been *magistri* teaching or learned men living here since *c.*1120. From the start, successive monarchs have favoured the University. Its trained scholars provided the Crown with a pool of potentially experienced and talented government employees. Moreover, the many benefices accruing in the endowments of the colleges provided royal civil servants with lucrative incomes at no cost to the Crown. Oxford also became a forcing ground for episcopal and clerical administrators. Oxford men like Robert Kilwardby and John Peckham occupied the highest ecclesiastical and secular offices in the land in the thirteenth century. The fourteenth and fifteenth centuries produced a series of top-notch bishops: Walter de Stapledon, Bishop of Exeter and Treasurer to Edward II; William of Wykeham, Bishop of Winchester and Clerk of Works to Edward III; Henry Chichele, Archbishop of Canterbury and a distinguished diplomat and lawyer; Richard Flemyng, Bishop of Lincoln; and William of Waynflete, Bishop of Winchester and Chancellor of England in Henry VI's reign.

Successive kings intervened on behalf of the University in its violent confrontations with the townsmen, fining the latter when rioting and wenching scholars were killed on the streets, protecting them from traders trying to make an honest living, and remorselessly adding to the privileges of Gown at the expense of Town. The Chancellor's swollen jurisdiction meant that the urban community was no longer in charge of its own affairs. Consequently, as the town declined economically in the later Middle Ages, the University ever strengthened its grip. It was a powerful employer and consumer of goods and services. Through its control of the assizes of bread and ale it had a stranglehold over the victualling trades. Increasing jurisdictional powers were accompanied by an extension of its landholdings. The newly founded colleges bought up run-down and tenantless land in the eastern part of the town and thus created the most compact academic quarter in all the world's cities.

I have begun to mention colleges, but the most important institutions in Oxford during the period 1100–1530 were not the colleges but the academic halls. These were buildings scattered round the streets of the walled town with a few outside. They were houses belonging to prominent citizens and clergy with livings in the Oxford area, leased out to masters who provided students with board and lodging and taught by lecturing Canon and Roman Law, Liberal Arts and Theology. The University established control over their unruly inmates only slowly and with the greatest difficulty. Gradually, during the thirteenth century, it began to regulate rents and to promote security of tenure for the proprietors of the academic halls. They in turn were responsible to the Chancellor for the good behaviour of their registered bodies of scholars. At their most numerous, in the fourteenth century, the academic halls numbered 120. They were thickly concentrated to the north-west and south-east of the University Church of St Mary the Virgin, in areas marked out by the modern Merton Street, Oriel Street and High Street and in the area between what is now Turl Street and Catte Street. They took their names from ancient local families, saints, trades or inns. Such were Woodcock, Broadgates, Bostar, Hert Hall, Hare Hall, Glasen Hall, Mummer Hall and so on.

These academic halls were scarcely distinguishable, architecturally speaking, from normal town houses. They were usually of two storeys, with a hall rising over from ground floor to the rafters. Off the hall, would be smaller rooms. The pressure of urban living meant space was at a premium and the frontages of such halls were often narrow with a long plot behind. Hinxey Hall, so called, has been excavated and proved to have been occupied from the fourteenth to the sixteenth centuries. It was connected to Fish Street (later St Aldates) by a walled passage and consisted of hall, buttery and kitchen and cross ranges containing chambers for student accommodation. The street frontage of academic halls might well be occupied with shops. Access was then by means of a long narrow passage known as the entry. A number of these entries exist still on the north side of High Street, between St Edward's Street and Carfax. Most of the halls have gone, superseded or absorbed by the colleges. Only eight survived into the reign of Elizabeth: Broadgates, Gloucester, Hart, Magdalen (hall not college), St Alban, St Mary, New Inn and St Edmund.

Forty years ago, the presiding genius over Oxford's ancient buildings and documents was Dr W.A. Pantin ('Billy' to his countless friends and students), Fellow of Oriel and Keeper of the University Archives. His stout form, pink faced, sweating and sterterously breathing, but bubbling over with enthusiasm, was a familiar figure in the schools lecturing on Franciscan schoolmen or the medieval town house. He examined, measured and analysed dozens of Oxford's town houses practically single-handed and then extended his studies to priests' houses and chantry houses, looking at their functions as well as their features. His rooms overflowed with books and papers. Billy, hard at work and too busy to go to hall for dinner, called his scout (college servant) to bring him a ham sandwich and a pint of beer. This was done. Half an hour later Billy called again – where was his provender? It had disappeared among the accumulation of scholarship. Months later, we are assured, the sandwich was found serving as a bookmark!

Dr Pantin recognized in Tackley's Inn, 106–7 High Street, 'one of the very few examples of a medieval academic hall still surviving sufficiently for us to be able to trace its plan and arrangement'. It can be seen (by application); the present High Street front was occupied by a row of small leased shops. Behind is the hall, its early sixteenth-century roof intact and lit by a transomed Gothic arched window. Billy spent much of his last few years travelling the county with Peter Spokes, a former town clerk and Lord Mayor, photographing listed buildings and making a huge contribution to the National Monuments archive. I remember visiting Ashbury Manor, a fine late medieval house built by the Abbots of Glastonbury in the far south-western corner of the county. I enquired as to the whereabouts of the famed fifteenth-century garderobe seat. I was told that Billy and Peter had come several years before and the owners had handed it over to their visitors: the last they had seen of it was Billy and Peter driving off waving the article in triumph. Since we were putting on an exhibition on sanitation in the County Museum at the time, I tried to track it down in Oriel College. Billy's scout remembered it well but a search in Oriel's vaults yielded nothing. The Ashbury lavatory seat has disappeared, reputedly chopped up for firewood. Memories of Billy are still green. His disciples are still to be met in roof spaces and on building sites, measuring, sifting and re-living the city's past.

One of Pantin's great contributions to the history of the University was to point out the importance of the monastic colleges. Great Benedictine houses sent small groups of monks to Oxford to extend their education in the schools. Canterbury College (now absorbed by Christ Church) provided for the needs of Canterbury Cathedral priory. Gloucester Hall (Worcester College since the eighteenth century) still has a series of small fifteenth-century houses in its front quad bearing the coats of arms of Glastonbury, Malmesbury, St Augustine Canterbury and Pershore. Each unit or *camera* was one monastery's responsibility. More significant in the intellectual life of the nascent university of the thirteenth century were the friars. They come here early on at the beginning of the century, attracted by the emerging town and the vigorous intellectual life. A site was found for the Greyfriars which actually included a piece of the southern town wall and so down-slope to the floodable river. The Blackfriars arrived in Oxford in 1221 and originally settled on a plot to the south of what is now Blue Boar Lane. In 1236 they moved to the more spacious but less salubrious large island outside the walls south of Littlegate Street and west of St Aldate's.

Very extensive urban renewal and city centre redevelopment in the late 1960s and 1970s involved the destruction of large areas of St Ebbes the south-western corner of the walled town. The Oxford Archaeological Excavation Committee was set up to respond to this challenge in a series of 'Rescue' digs. Despite this epithet, there was plenty of time to excavate before building work began, because of the size of the projects. Consequently, Tom Hassall and his team were able to recover the complete plans of the Pre-Reformation Greyfriars and the Blackfriars as well as the plans of town houses as they had developed over 700 years.

The Westgate centre with its department stores, local government offices and supermarkets now straddles with concrete piling and underground servicing the church where the friars prayed, preached and promoted religious debate.

An archaeological discovery only becomes an historical fact when it is published. Fortunately, the high academic standards set by the first director combined with a tenacity of purpose and a ruthless drive towards corporate promotion, has led the Oxford Unit to be among the most successful professional archaeological bodies in the country. Their prompt and detailed publications illumine many dark tracts of the county's and city's past.

We had little idea of what the layout of the buildings of the Greyfriars comprised apart from a description by William of Worcester, Britain's first architectural historian, who in the fifteenth century measured buildings not with a tape measure but his feet! Buried under five metres of debris, the much robbed-out wall footings were painstakingly uncovered. Gradually, the plan emerged of a huge church ideal for preaching to large numbers of pilgrims and townsfolk. Attached to this at right angles was an extraordinarily long (100 feet) transept which had a row of ten chapels. Attracted by the sanctity of their lives and the power of their preaching, lay folk vied with each other to be buried within the Greyfriars' precinct. Their skeletons were found in the cemetery to the north of and in the church itself. We know that notable people like St Agnellus, the leader of the first Franciscan group of friars who came to Oxford in 1224, and the heart of Richard Plantagenet, Earl of Cornwall, King of the Romans and brother to Henry III, were buried here. At the other end of the social spectrum, the diggers found the bones of one unlucky man, no doubt a felon, his left ankle shackled in iron fetters.

The contribution of the friars was not limited to their social and pastoral work among both the fashionable and less prosperous townsfolk. They also took a leading part in the intellectual life of the University, producing in the thirteenth and fourteenth centuries some of the leading teachers and thinkers. Such scholars included Friar Roger Bacon, the founder of Modern Scientific Method, John Duns Scotus, a notable theologian, and William of Ockham, a prolific writer of philosophical and theological tomes. Oxford-trained friars were much in demand as ecclesiastical administrators. The Blackfriar, Robert Kilwardby, as arch-bishop of Canterbury, crowned Edward I. The Franciscan, John Peckham, succeeded him at Canterbury. Both took a leading part in the political and religious controversies of the day.

When did Balliol, New College, Magdalen and the rest come into existence? Early on in the thirteenth century it was realized by would-be benefactors that if they left their money to the loosely organized shifting University it would be frittered away. A body of scholars, known as the fellows (Latin *socii*) under a principal, warden, master or president, tied closely to a set of rules (the statutes), had a much better chance of carrying out their benefactors' purposes, so a college was an autonomous, well-endowed community of scholars. What was there in this arrangement of benefit to the founder? Founders insisted in return that regular prayers should be offered up for their souls and those of their families. Their kin moreover was to be preferred in new admissions, followed by the sons of tenantry. This explains the curious system (now phased out) of scholarships and exhibitions tied to various schools and parts of the country. Economic sustenance was guaranteed the gift of landed estates and by appropriations of benefices which ensured clerical jobs for former collegiate members.

The atmosphere of medieval Oxford was overwhelmingly religious. The scholars, whether teachers or learners, were all *clerici*: not necessarily bound to become priests, but certainly they were unlikely to forget that their lives were to be spent in the service of one or other aspect of the universal Catholic Church. They worshipped daily in the college chapels, which in the case of Merton could reach cathedral-like dimensions. Theology was the culmination of studies in the schools. Lectures and disputations were ranged round points of theological interpretation. Theological treatises poured forth from the fertile minds of the Oxford schoolmen. The books written by the scholars and copied by the scriveners were nearly all connected with the study of the Bible and the Early Fathers. The first University library, housed above the Convocation House, built to the north of the chancel of the University church, was given by Bishop Cobham in 1329; although its books were pawned to pay for the donor's debts, the intention was clearly to provide clerkly scholars with clerical books. The founders of the early colleges were nearly all bishops. Stapledon founded Exeter, Wykeham New College, Chichele All Souls, Waynflete Magdalen, and Wolsey, cardinal and archbishop, founded the college afterwards called Christ Church. Chichele is a particularly interesting example. A New College man himself of the first generation, he rose rapidly in the uncertain world of Lancastrian politics. He saw the need for a clergy dedicated to Church and State, established a loan chest to help poor students, and being a lawyer himself he understood the importance of securing good titles to land. He gave land to St Bernard's College on the site where St John's College now stands and in 1438 persuaded the King to act as co-founder when he established All Souls College. This was planned to be a Lancastrian chantry, an ideological and spiritual prop to the damaged monarchy. A warden and forty graduate fellows were to study for degrees with higher faculties of law and theology. No mention was made of undergraduates. It was left to educationalists such as Wykeham and Waynflete to found feeder schools at Winchester, in the case of New College, and at Wainfleet (Lincs), and in Oxford itself in the case of Magdalen, which guaranteed a flow of students well versed in grammar and studious habits. Gradually the idea caught on that colleges would do well to nurture undergraduates within their controlling walls rather than pick them off the streets. This process doomed the academic halls to extinction in the long run.

So a college was a continually evolving organism. It was a site, usually several house-plots covered with buildings, some of which were adapted and some purpose-built for the functions of eating, sleeping, studying and praying in common. The most important building was the chapel. The chapel absorbed a goodly proportion of the total expenses of the college, being decorated with images, stained glass, painted wall surfaces and elaborate service books, as well as expendables such as candles and bellropes. It might also double up as the parish church. Merton College chapel was built on the site of the church of St John the Baptist. It began as a magnificent choir of the 1280s, its lateral windows decorated with stained glass bearing the images of Henry de Mamesfeld, Fellow of the College 1288–96, dying in 1328. It is a piece of self-advertisement which vies with the immortalization in their own lifetimes of Lord Nuffield and Messrs Kellogg and Green. The roof timbers are part of the original structure. In the mid 1980s I remember crawling along the planks suspended over the collars of the thirteenth-century

trussed rafter roof above the painted boards supplied by
William Butterfield – a perilous journey – accompanied by
the plump but indomitable photographer, the late and
lamented Cynthia Bradford. She had learned her craft with
Helen Muspratt, who set up a studio in Oxford in the 1940s
and whose superb portraits recorded a whole generation of
Oxonians. Cynthia's contribution to museum photography
will long be remembered.

Merton College chapel, magnificent though it is, is only a
fragment. It never acquired a nave. Its transepts were added
in the fifteenth century and it thus became unusually shaped
with an antechapel crossing the T, particularly convenient for
additional altars, for housing monuments, and for providing
a space for disputations (the formal oral examinations).
Other college chapels, such as New College, Magdalen and
Wadham were built T-shaped *ab initio*. Henry Janyns, master
mason, built Merton's tower, completed in 1450, from which
a melodious and sonorous set of bells chime the quarters. The
blocked-up arches which would have led into the nave can be
seen on the western front. Even the site was lost in an ill
considered sale to Corpus Christi College early in the
sixteenth century.

Merton College is also significant architecturally in that it
invented, by accident, that most typically Oxford of architectural characteristics, the 'Quad'. Roman villas had been
arranged round courtyards; medieval monasteries grouped
their buildings round cloisters; but it was not until the middle
of the fourteenth century at Merton that the quadrangular
form was used as a collegiate building. Merton had already
built an L-shaped library; further ranges were added at
intervals including a treasury and a stone-vaulted and roofed
monument tower to house the College's invaluable deeds,
titles to its landed endowment. The result was the quadrangle; convenient for security, it was enigmatically called 'Mob
Quad' in the eighteenth century. Its windows opened
inwards: for silence, a vital requisite for study and thought.
Furthermore, it could be enlarged by building upwards: each
of its staircases gave access to sets of rooms where a more

senior member of the college supervised the life and work of the juniors. The quadrangle was ideal for linking communal buildings like the chapel, hall and library. New College quadrangle was made up on one side with the T-shaped chapel fronting onto the first-floor hall. Here, the cloister was built separately on this long and narrow site to the west of the chapel, next to the town wall. At Magdalen, on an extensive site formerly occupied by the hospital of St John the Baptist outside the east gate of the town, Waynflete laid out an untramelled plan round a great cloistered quadrangle with hall and chapel in series on one side, a library and tower on another, and accommodation provided via staircases on the other two. The quadrangular plan proved so successful in educational institutions that it was extended to hospitals and almshouses in the county and beyond. An early Oxfordshire example is Ewelme, where in the 1430s the Duke and Duchess of Suffolk founded an almshouse, with an adjoining school and a rebuilt church, near their rural palace. The almshouses are grouped round a courtyard, the staircases connected by a continuous covered way or pentice, all constructed in timber-framing and brick-nogging. The accommodation block for the retainers with its Gothic timbered hall also still survives. Buck's drawing of the early eighteenth century shows it to have been larger and accessed by an external staircase and gallery. It was probably laid out down one side of great court – another variant of the quadrangular plan; this plan went on being used in the Henrician palaces at Bridewell, Hampton Court and Nonsuch.

A good summing up of the position of the University of Oxford in 1470 is found in the Magdalen College Fastolf papers: 'the université beying a grete tresour for the Churche and for the land is gretely minysshed [diminished] and in decay, and by liklyhode shuld sone almost perish if it were not supported by the halp of colleges which supportacion is more of merite than many older dedez of pyeté.' (*Paston Letters and Papers of the 15th Century*, ed. Norman Davis, Oxford 1976, 589)

Oxford has lent its name (and fame) to a series of products during the ages. When I came up as an undergraduate in the 1950s, I had heard of Oxford marmalade and Morris cars – the Morris Oxford was one of the range. I was also aware that an earlier generation of male undergraduates had disported themselves in a species of wide-legged trousers known as 'Oxford bags'. If one had asked commercially minded travellers in the Middle Ages what Oxford reminded them of the answer might well have been 'books'. From the twelfth century, the town was a resort of book writers, copyists or scriveners, parchment and paper makers, leather workers and binders, and bone and metal workers, who provided the clasps, the styli and the parchment prickers. Archaeology has contributed towards an understanding of the mechanics of book production because many excavations in the historic core of the city have produced these objects. A surprising number of the manuscripts made in the town and used in the University have survived, many kept in the Bodleian but some are in the college libraries, including a choice few in Keble College – an unlikely location given the College's late start and Low Church tradition.

The first step in the production of a manuscript was to arrange for the loan of the book (the so called 'exemplar') to be copied. The library, college, or individual would generally require a pledge – perhaps a volume of equal value – and this was placed in a lockable chest. Such a strong-box, c.1300 in date, made of oak planks bound with iron bands, still stands in Merton College library. The volume was handed over to the scrivener, unlikely to be a monk or even someone in priestly orders, but certainly a man with clerical education. He was equipped with a desk, pens (goosequills), a penknife, and ink made of oak gall or soot and gum arabic. The distinctive Oxford ink was dark brown with a pale yellow/green metallic reflection. The parchment, the whole skins of sheep or calf, would be purchased from the parchmentors; each pair of folio sheets would require a whole skin. There was a hair side and a smooth (facing the guts of the animal in life) side. Quartos were a page folded four ways and octavos eight ways. Each page would be prepared by using a parchment pricker, a pin made of ivory with a bronze spike on one end. With this and a rule, the position for the lines could be marked by a series of minute perforations penetrating several sheets at a time. These would be joined up using a lead stylus and the rule. Having decided where to leave spaces for the frequent illuminated letters and the much rarer illustrations, the scrivener could get to work copying. It is clear that such manuscripts (the word is Latin for 'written by hand') took a long time to make. Several hands may be evident in the same book. Also the rapid improvement over several pages of the work of an apprentice can be recognized. The parchment is extremely durable providing it does not get gnawed by rats; the inks on the other hand do fade if they are not protected from the light. Keeping a book closed is an excellent preservative and libraries do not willingly allow the unscholarly to handle their wares promiscuously! All these stages of book production can be illustrated in the collections in the museums of Oxford (St Aldate's) and the Ashmolean. Candlesticks and shell-shaped lamps were doubtless used by the scriveners and binders when working late to copy, finish or repair a book. Artificial light was forbidden in the Bodleian and other college libraries; even today the would-be reader has to undertake not to introduce any fire into the library building. Consequently, the scholar's reading day was restricted to the hours of sunlight.

When portions of the book had been written the folios were taken along to the limner or flourisher who would add the illuminated letters and other decorations. Their work is even more distinctive than the copyist's hands. At some point the master in charge would check the text and erase mistakes with a knife, or simply put a line through them and add the correct version. Finally, the book was reassembled and handed over to the binder. Tawed leather was used up to the fifteenth century, but thereafter tanned leather with a smooth, polished surface which could be decorated using separate blind stamps. Since each binder used a set of tools peculiar to himself the surviving medieval bindings have been recognized as being the stock of such individuals bearing such names as John More, Thomas Hunt and Thomas Uffyngham.

Examples of the books are sometimes exhibited in deliberately darkened rooms in the college libraries and public displays are usually put on each year by the Bodleian Library. Not all undergraduates in the medieval University required to use let alone own books. Although they were said to be 'reading' for their first degree in the Faculty of Arts, they did not need books. Instead, they were required to hear lectures (from Latin 'lego', I read); in this case it was the bachelor or the master who read the prescribed text sentence by sentence, adding his own commentary. When this was written down it was known as 'a gloss'. At Dulwich, where I went to school in the 1940s and 50s, precisely the same method was used to teach the classics once one had mastered the rudiments of the grammar. Students for the higher degrees, including Theology and Canon Law, not only had to use books; they had to swear that they owned books from which they could teach in their turn. The schools where these subjects were taught had to be supplied with desks to accommodate their books as well as benches. The Arts schools however only needed benches for the students to sit on as they listened to or disputed with their teachers.

For the economic use of a scarce commodity like books libraries were needed. We have noticed Bishop Cobham's munificence in leaving the University his library, which was planned to be accommodated in the upper room above the vaulted congregation house, built alongside but not attached to the north side of St Mary the Virgin, the University church. Although it is no longer used as a library, it is worth gaining permission from the verger to view this, the earliest library building in Oxford. Other medieval libraries are to be seen at Merton College, Trinity College and Magdalen College. The first academic library to be built on the ground floor, defying rats and mould, was the Codrington Library at All Souls (1720), financed by the profits of West Indian sugar plantations. Medieval libraries were secure places – hence the tortuous approach and the lockable door: they also needed to be protected from the damp – thus they were on the first floor. The books themselves were stored in chests, flat, or were propped up and chained to lecterns. They relied on natural light, hence the single windows at Trinity, Magdalen and Merton strategically placed between each bench, with the light falling on the sloping surface of the book. It was only the development of printing and the invention of paper which led to cheaper multiple copies that forced colleges, schools and universities to invent new ways of storing books. Presses for housing the books vertically instead of flat were built, first at Merton College in the 1580s and then twenty years later at the Bodleian. For a time librarians couldn't make up their minds how to entitle them or accession them. The titles were sometimes written on what we would call the side of the book. Then the binders stepped in and began stamping the titles in gilt lettering on the spines. For many years yet they were classified by size; big books of whatever subject at the bottom, little books at the top, a recipe for confusion in the twentieth century!

One of the most magnetic spots in the city of Oxford is the schools quadrangle of the Old Bodleian Library. Here, throughout the summer, there is a constant stream of tourists, in the main obeying the strict rules of silence, quietly going past the bronze statue of the Earl of Pembroke (attributed to Lesuer) in and out of the glass door and so into the stone panelled lobby or *proscholium* and the Divinity Schools beyond. It is a very special place: a great rectilinear space lit from floor to ceiling with straight, mullioned, four-centred windows and plain glass, the intervening walls panelled and cusped in cream stone. The lower part of the building *c.*1420–30 was designed by Richard Winchcombe, a quarry owner and master mason who had worked for New College on its barn at Swalcliffe and church at Adderbury. The design proved too richly moulded (and therefore expensive) for his University patrons. The work languished until Duke Humfrey of Gloucester (d.1449) left his library to the scholars. A further storey was added and what had been a timber roof of the Divinity School became the floor of Duke

Humfrey's library. A new master mason, William Orchard, was brought in to the Divinity schools to design the superb stone vault, decorated with the shields of arms of the university's friends and benefactors of the day (the 1480s). Lecterns were supplied in this first floor, rat-free, well lit space and Duke Humfrey's books, chained to the furniture, were installed. A hundred years went by and Oxford was in the turmoil of the Reformation. The books were now in confusion. The King's officials plundered them; manuscripts, representative of the old Catholic order, were thrown out. The printing presses of Protestant Europe were now churning out new books on new subjects. Sir Thomas Bodley, whose Devonian family had made a fortune from the fish trade and who had enjoyed a not very distinguished diplomatic career (sent by Elizabeth to negotiate in Holland without knowing Dutch), stepped in to help the University which was in dire need of books. He paid for the quadrangle which was attached to one end of Duke Humfrey's library and the Divinity School. On the top floor was a huge (for the day) book room going round three sides. Below were offices, and on the ground floor the teaching rooms of the various faculties. Reading their painted labels over the doors one gets a good idea of the curriculum of the sixteenth-century university: Geometry, Arithmetic, Languages, Metaphysics, Logic, Astronomy, Rhetoric, Law (Jurisprudence), Music, Natural Philosophy, Grammar, History, Moral Philosophy and Medicine: the books and catalogues have now invaded the first floor and the old faculty schools have been converted into offices of the Library and an exhibition space. From the tower of the five orders (with superimposed pillars of Classical architecture), James I, enthroned like God, presides over the Library in sculptured splendour. In fact, he contributed nothing to the Bodleian: his interests were in the hunting field, not in supporting the Library, despite the fact that he wrote books on witchcraft and against tobacco.

Accompanied by a guide and member of the University, the visitor (in small groups at one time) is able to climb the creaking staircases of Bodley's building and look into the book-lined interior of 'Duke Humfrey'. Bodley's bookcases replaced the lecterns (whose shadows stained the walls between the windows), and scholars, bent over their studies, still sit in the alcoves, lit by the cross-light from large perpendicular windows. The lateral pressure of the weight of books has necessitated the construction of deep buttresses to support them and the stone vault lying beneath. The simple, braced tie-beams add a vernacular touch to this splendid room: the boarded ceiling in between is powdered all over with the arms of the University.

Go to Merton College chapel and there on the north transept is the alabaster and marble monument to Thomas Bodley MA, 1612, by Nicholas Stone. His half effigy in a gown sits in an oval niche flanked by two pillars of bound books with ornate clasps piled upon one another. I like the 1613 poem written by V.I. (whoever is he?) of Christ Church who says that the only book not in Bodley's Library is the Book of Life and that, in consequence, Bodley has now gone to heaven to take care of that ('*nunc curaturus*').

A hundred years passed and again the Bodleian was bursting at the seams. Dr John Radcliffe, a successful London medical man (and surgeon to Queen Anne) devoted £40,000 of his fortune to the University and paid for a new extension. Nicholas Hawksmoor, pupil of Wren, designed a cylindrical library with a dome to be attached to Bodley's cube. Eventually more land between the Bodleian and the University church was acquired and cleared of tenements. The Radcliffe Camera (Latin for a 'room') was redesigned to be majestically free-standing in the hub of the University. The architect, inspired by Hawksmoor's plans, was James Gibbs.

The dome of the Camera is the most distinctive attribute of the Oxford skyline. Like St Paul's, London, it is a double dome with a thin skin of decorated plaster covering the complex series of king-post trusses which meet in the centre in a great mast of timber. Covering the whole is a coat of lead and the Camera is capped with a cupola. I know all this because Julian Munby obtained permission from the University surveyor during the quinquennial survey of the structure in 1985 for us to climb the vertical scaffolding and penetrate the windows of the dome. The view, as you would expect, was staggering. A hundred feet below, the steeples of All Souls rocket up towards you. The readers and the tourists scurry over the cobbled surface like ants. All round are roofs of emerald green copper (the Bodleian), grey Stonesfield slates (New College), grey/green Westmorland slates (roof of Hertford College), the spiky and crocketed pinnacles of the old Bodleian and the University church of St Mary. It took ten minutes or so before I was sufficiently composed to note the measurements of the timbers I had come to record! We found that the carpentry design actually used differed markedly from Gibb's published plans so the adventure was well worth while. It led to a new piece of information about one of Oxford's best known buildings.

The Radcliffe Camera was originally three things: a public monument to the munificence of the good doctor whose statue graces the staircase; a covered walkway, because the ground floor was arched and open of access; and a circular reading room for Georgian gentlemen who were more conscious of their noble surroundings than desirous of acquiring learning. What it was not was an efficient book store. There was a tremendous waste of space in the circular plan, also the echoing tread of would-be readers was a distraction. However, beneath the grass and pavements of Radcliffe Square are well organized vaults containing copies of all Britain's State papers.

Oxford still is a byword for books. Nowadays, apart from the University Press, which no longer prints its own books, the main trade lies in selling books in retail outlets. The principal Oxford bookshops (as distinct from multiples, which sell books like vegetables) are situated around Broad Street. Here are the world-famous B.H. Blackwell and Parkers (now absorbed by Blackwell), and Dillon's (a welcome competitor to Blackwell's with fresh ideas about bookselling). An enormous, friendly second-hand bookshop is Thornton's of Broad Street. Robin Waterfield has a shop like a Middle Eastern bazaar in Park End Street, but I must

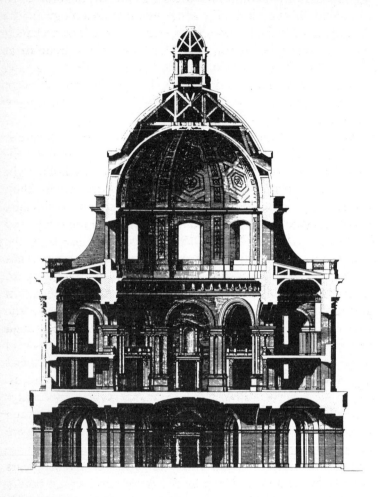

Radcliffe Camera, Bodleian Library, Oxford. 'A section showing
the inside of the library' designed by James Gibbs. The ground
floor was open until mid nineteenth-century. The carpentry was
built around a central mast (*Bodleian Library*)

confess that my favourite bookshop is Oxbow, the brainchild of David Brown, formerly a keeper of archaeology in the Ashmolean Museum, who has set up a marvellous archaeology and history bookshop in the third floor of a warehouse at the back of Waterfield's in Park End Street. With strong links in the United States and Europe, David also publishes an archaeological series as well as making available the fruit of world scholarship.

The Reformation traumatized the University severely. Ideologically, it became a battleground for contending religious orthodoxies. The protagonists on the Catholic right wing and Puritan left wing lost their jobs when their respective religious policies were out of favour. Politically, Oxford continued to throw in its lot with the monarchy, and when the government bewilderingly changed direction, the University, in general, followed. The townspeople were not so pliant, and conflict waxed and waned according to whether there was congruity of religious views between town and gown. Physically, the dissolution and destruction of the monasteries left gaping holes in the townscape. Although new colleges, founded by lawyers and merchants, arose in their place the grip of the clerical estate did not relax. During the sixteenth century colleges increased in number and status. Academic halls declined. The populations of undergraduates shot up, putting pressure on buildings which expanded laterally and vertically to accommodate them. Cocklofts were inserted in the roofs of college quadrangles. When we compare Oxford in 1600 with the situation seventy years before, the wounds inflicted by the Reformation have hardly begun to heal. The tensions within this small society would burst out in the violence of the Civil War, forty years ahead.

In a nutshell, Henry VIII's break with Rome and assumption of Royal Supremacy heralded the largest upheaval of land-ownership since the Norman Conquest. Within a few years of either side of 1540, as a result of the royal policy backed by a subservient parliament, Oxford saw the demise of Oseney and Rewley abbeys, Greyfriars, Blackfriars and the Carmelites. The monastic colleges were absorbed into new more secular foundations, their possessions, briefly in the hands of the Crown, passed to gentry and merchants. On the Greyfriars site much of the land was quickly possessed by property developers, who in turn sold it on to speculative house-builders. Some of the walls of the Greyfriars remained to demarcate properties, but most were stripped of their usable stone and robbed right down to the bottom of their foundations. It is from the ghost forms of robber trenches that archaeologists have to reconstruct the buildings. One or two of the ancillary buildings of monastic sites survived because they had a use. The end of a fifteenth-century barn, its roof a complex mass of timbering and props, stands forlornly among industrial dereliction; it is the only roofed remnant of the once proud Augustinian abbey of Oseney. A single door in a wall by the Oxford canal is the only upstanding piece of the Cistercian Rewley Abbey.

Equally worrying for the participants in this drama were the sackings of recalcitrants, the promotions of radical supporters of the new orders, exile for the dispossessed and sometimes imprisonment and even death for those of whom the government of the day wished to make an example. Heads of colleges were particularly liable to be moved on if they were not considered to be sufficiently supportive. Merton College furnishes some good examples of those profiting from the changes. Robert Serles, a fellow, was one of the leaders of the Marian attack on the Protestant Archbishop of Canterbury, Thomas Cranmer. William Tresham was a member of the commission appointed by 'Bloody Mary's' government to examine Cranmer and Bishops Ridley and Latimer. Richard Smyth, another fellow, after holding the post of Regius Professor of Divinity, gave evidence against Cranmer. Cranmer, Latimer and Ridley were, of course, burned at the stake outside Balliol College. A cross in the street marks the spot. A very spiky memorial in Victorian Gothic was raised ineptly at the south end of St Giles to commemorate these Protestant martyrs. Smyth, however, was a marked man when the Protestant religion was brought back by Elizabeth. He fled to Douai and there became chancellor of the new Catholic university. The Reformation could make or break the careers of Oxford men.

It was not only personalities who were affected by the ups and downs of the Reformation. The chapel buildings similarly went through a phase called by a recent Cambridge historian, Terence Duffy, 'the stripping of the altars'. Again taking Merton as an example, the College replaced its Catholic Latin missals with others in English in 1547–8. A copy of the royal injunctions and homilies was purchased. A painter was paid 18d for blotting out certain things, presumably pictures, voiding outworn decorative schemes. A carpenter earned a day's pay for removing images. The subwarden bought for 10s two books of the new public prayers only a few days after Parliament had accepted it. The interior of the mighty thirteenth-century chapel was brought in line with the austerity of the Edwardian regime by removing the altars and statues. Even the stained glass was whitewashed, but miraculously not smashed unduly. Destruction was not limited to chapel fittings and furnishings. Libraries were also cleansed of writings representing the old order. Dr Thomas Layton, sent by Thomas Cromwell to New College in 1535 to carry out royal orders, wrote exultantly that he had found pages from the works of Duns Scotus (one of the principal theologians of the Middle Ages) flapping about in New College quad, like so much litter. It was being collected up for use in deer management. Also, in 1965, in the course of repairs to chambers on the south side of New College quad, it was found that the beams had been lined with the leaves of manuscripts.

Other colleges have produced physical traces of the Marian Counter Reformation of the period 1553–8. Sir Thomas Pope, a strong supporter of Henry VIII and Treasurer of the Court of Augmentations, the great department created by Thomas Cromwell to handle the monastic land take-over, decided to take advantage of his position by acquiring one of the monastic colleges and refounding a college which he dedicated to the Trinity. He obtained a charter in 1555 from Philip and Mary and for a hundred years Trinity was content to use the old buildings, the chapel, hall and library of the former Durham College. A discovery was made in 1986 when a ground floor in the south-east corner of the Durham quad was stripped of panelling, uncovering a painted scheme of decoration which probably dates from the time of Pope's refurbishment of the college buildings. It encapsulates the political affiliations and religious susceptibilities of the founder. Red and white roses are of course a loyal affirmation of the Tudor dynasty, but painted over them was the insignia in three large black letter initials IHS (*Iesus Hemispheris Salvator*, Jesus the Saviour of the World) which indicates the leaning towards the Roman Catholicism of the founder. The painted room at Trinity provides a vivid illustration of the 'right about turn' (Bindoff's phrase) of the short-lived period of the Marian reaction.

Sir Thomas Pope may have had the strong religious feelings of a Catholic but he was a layman. He set the pattern for lay involvement in the foundation of colleges for the next few centuries. Sir Thomas White, a Reading clothier and Merchant Taylor, founded St John's College, again using the site and buildings of a former monastic college, St Bernard's. Jesus College, started by Hugh Price, treasurer of St David's Cathedral, received moral if not financial support from the Queen. It was the only college to be founded in the reign of Elizabeth. Nicholas and Dorothy Wadham, rich and childless Somerset gentry, devoted their considerable fortune to building Wadham College in the first years of James I's reign. A civil servant, a clothier, a royal personage, a treasurer, gentlefolk – they mirror the way power and influence were shifting in Elizabethan society away from the Church into the world of laymen.

During the Middle Ages noblemen and those aspiring to nobility sent their sons to be trained in the martial skills, in sports of all kinds and to acquire the social graces in the households of their peers. Increasingly in the sixteenth century the aristocracy and ambitious gentry sent their sons to Oxford and Cambridge to absorb a smattering of scholarly education before leaving, for the most part without degrees, to pursue legal studies in the burgeoning inns of court in London. This influx helped to swell the undergraduate population at Oxford and colleges began to make special arrangements for teaching ('tutorials') and for housing these 'gentlemen commoners' as they were called. Many colleges (New College and Corpus Christi are good examples) enlarged their student capacity simply by building another storey on top of the ranges round their quadrangles. In parallel with these developments was a determined attempt to admit bright sons of poor men by offering what has been called 'a system of quaintly termed scholarships – battelships, sejarships and servitorships' by which in return for some menial duties such as serving at table, the holders paid lower fees.

The Elizabethan Church settlement was accepted in Oxford. It is nevertheless clear that there was support by some individuals in some colleges for a religious position rather closer to the Catholic tradition, but they still declined to brave the penal legislation which made life for Catholic recusants like the Stonor family so difficult. Thomas Laud, fellow of St John's College, Bishop of London and Archbishop of Canterbury, pushed ahead with his stringent ideas for reforming the Church of England. He, and King Charles I who supported him, grew steadily out of touch with the radical, Puritan left wing. Laud paid for a quadrangle to be added to his college which with its use of beautiful, classically composed doorways and Italianate loggias brought to Oxford a more refined and elegant classicism than it had previously experienced. The 'frontispieces', so called, of Wadham, Oriel, Merton and the Old Bodleian had been derived in design from the title pages of Renaissance books. Their piling of superimposed orders of classical architecture was crude, top heavy and unharmonious. Laud's work at St John's College was of a different and superior quality and augured well for the triumphs of Oxford's classical architecture in the eighteenth century.

Laud's contribution to the intellectual life of the University was beneficial. An instance is the care with which he founded and endowed a chair in Arabic first occupied by Dr Pococke, a remarkable Arabist who for six years was chaplain to the Levant Company at Aleppo. We have an account of a seventeenth-century lecture and tutorial when Pococke is described:

> Upon this Book ... he spent an Hour every Wednesday in Vacation time, and also in Lent explaining the sense of the Author and the Things relating to the Grammar and Propriety of the language, and also showing the Agreement it hath with the Hebrew and Syriac ... the Lecture being ended, he usually tarried for some Time in the public School, to resolve the Questions of the Hearers and satisfy them in their doubts, and always, that Afternoon gave them Admission to his chamber, from one o'clock till Four, to all that would come to him for further Conference and Direction.

Laud's zeal, efficiency and acerbity made him highly unpopular in the Church and in the country and undoubtedly contributed to the outbreak of the Civil War. During the first years of James I's reign Oxford college halls and libraries had been furnished with splendid wooden screens deeply carved and ornate with swags, fluted columns, grotesques, and capped with obelisks and fretted strapwork. Now, at Laud's insistent will, chapels were similarly provided with screens and reredoses, raised communion tables, scarcely distinguishable from altars, decorous paving and organs. Such finery was offensive to the Puritan minded. Even the University church did not escape censure. The most baroque architectural feature in Oxford, looking as if it has stepped straight out of an Italian city, is the porch of St Mary the Virgin dating from the 1630s. Its broken pediment, barley-sugar columns and statue of the Virgin Mary and Child made it a target for the puritanical townsmen. When the Parliamentary soldiers marched out of Oxford at the beginning of the Civil War, one of them raised his musket and took a pot shot at the sculpture. The mark of the ball is still visible from the top of a passing red bus.

By virtue of its central position in the kingdom, its command of the Thames crossing, the Royalist sympathies of its University and the wealth of the colleges in plate (which could be turned into coinage) Charles I made Oxford his centre of government and the base from which to launch attacks on London during the first Civil War (1642–6).

Oxford's defences were put in order. The Saxon burh with its eleventh-century extensions had been strengthened by a free-standing stone wall in the thirteenth century, paid for by murage grants. This can still be traced on foot in more or less disjointed fashion for almost the complete circuit. The finest stretch, complete with bastions (horse-shoe shaped projections designed to provide enfilading fire), wall walks, gateway and bell tower, built on one of the bastions, may be seen at New College. William of Wykeham in acquiring this elongated site had taken on the responsibility of maintaining the wall. An idea of the breadth, if not the depth of the ditch, can be seen in the sloping, cobbled surface of the entry leading down to the Turf Tavern which actually sits in the ditch. What is not visible at New College is the buried face of an outer lower wall at this point running parallel. This is the remains of an abortive and unfinished attempt to equip the thirteenth-century town with concentric fortifications in the Carcasonne manner. The wall now turns south and bounds St Edmund Hall. The east gate was destroyed in 1771, but the public house of the same name records its site. A fourteenth-century misericord (wooden tip-up seat) in New College chapel shows a gatehouse of two towers and a semi-circular arch. A long stretch bounds the town on the south. Here the countryside laps the wall as it did in Rome when I was there in the 1950s. There is a curious change of direction to the south when the wall meets the *enceinte* of St Frideswide's Priory (now Christ Church). Here an angle bastion, part of Corpus Christi College seems to have defended a postern gate tucked into the corner. The south and west gates disappeared in the seventeenth century, but Tom Hassall's diggers of the Archaeological Unit found the remains of Littlegate and traced the wall foundations for most of its way to the castle.

The castle, from being an impressive statement of Norman and Plantagenet royal power, had declined by the seventeenth century to an outdated fortification and inglorious prison. True, its great Norman mound was still there (and still is) crowned by a decagonal shell keep (of which the well chamber remains and is visitable when not vandalized).

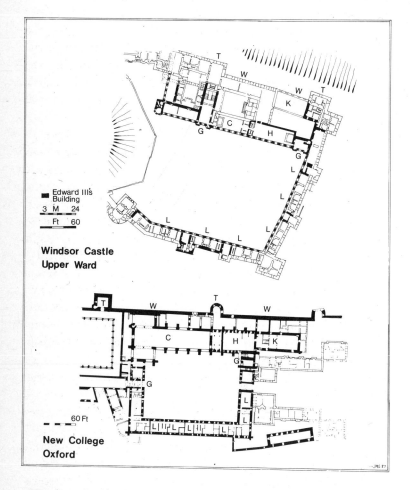

Windsor Castle, Upper Ward and New College, Oxford. The influence of Wykeham's work at Windsor on his own foundation at New College, Oxford. Key H: Hall, C: Chapel, L: Lodgings, W: Wall, T: Tower, G: Gateway (*see Steane 1993*)

Ralph Agas's map of 1578 shows that the complete circuit of the curtain walls with internal towers stood in Elizabeth's reign, accessed by a wooden trestle bridge to a street just outside the West Gate. But his depiction of the interior is blank apart from a goal-post-like structure which may represent the gallows and a freestanding building which is probably the Sessions House. Prisoners from both sides were kept in unspeakably bad conditions in the towers during the Civil War. The most impressive bit of the castle left is the massive, knobbly, tapering St George's tower adjoining the town corn mills which may predate the Norman castle. Derek Renn has suggested it may have started life as the defender of the Saxon west gate of the town.

An extraordinary continuity of land use from the eleventh to the twenty-first century (as seems likely) has characterized the castle site. Below the motte of the Norman defences are the concrete and glass offices of the County Council, the local Kremlin. Burrowing deep underground and within spitting range of the walls of H.M. Prison are the vaults containing the County Records. The gaol itself, rebuilt within the tight constraints of the medieval bailey in the nineteenth century, holds the county's criminals fast as it has done so for 700 years. What will be done with this piece of administrative and governmental archaeology when the prisoners are moved to more salubrious and, one hopes, more reformative surroundings? It could of course be displayed as a tourist attraction in this city already suffering from the effects of being on the so called London–Stratford axis. It might serve as a diversion from obsession with the colleges which are now more reluctant than they used to be to open their gates to large visitor numbers. The Centre for Oxfordshire Studies could be re-housed here. Perhaps the rest could be leased out to firms, such as the Oxford Archaeological Unit, interested in Heritage management. I have just heard that St Peter's College would like to take some of it over; surely the castle could perform all these functions?

Continuing round the curving course of the city wall to the north there is a convincing stretch of its grey, Corallian, rubble masonry punctuated by a bastion base bounding the garden at the rear of the City of Oxford High School (where T.E. Lawrence studied as a boy). There is a gap where Frewin Hall Street breaks the line; it can be traced at the rear of the houses in St Michael's Street. St Michael's Church tower, of similar build and material to St George's tower is late-Saxon in date. It was incorporated in the defences as a watch tower and the defences diverted round to the north, thus providing the church with a little churchyard.

The city wall by itself, despite the fact that its ditch was re-cut, would have offered little opposition to a besieging army of the mid seventeenth century, so Bernard de Gomme, a Dutch military expert, was employed by Charles I to design an elaborate scheme of earthern bastions and outworks to cover the suburbs and keep the Parliamentary artillery at a distance. Those to the north-east were still partly visible when David Loggan drew his bird's-eye view in *Oxonia Illustrata* (1675).

The most obvious and lasting effect of the Civil War on Oxford was the disappearance into the royal mint of much of the college plate. Some was kept back but the King was well informed and insistent. The buildings, too, were used for war purposes. Magdalen tower served as a point of observation during the ineffectual siege of fifteen days in the summer of 1645. New College tower was taken over as a powder magazine. The Grove at Magdalen became an artillery park. The King graced Christ Church with his presence; its palatial scale appealed to his absolutist tendencies and his aesthetic sensitivity. The Queen had her apartments in neighbouring Merton College. The undergraduates joined up, forsaking their studies, and the intellectual life of the University dimmed as the town was given over to the roistering soldiery. After the war, Magdalen's earthwork defences on the east side of the town, where Elias Ashmole had served as 'a Gentleman of Artillery', were reshaped to provide water walks. What had been described during the war as 'works in the river', approached by 'a high and strong causeway' probably to be identified with 'Dover pier', were now paved with gravel. The bowling greens were re-turfed. The scholars returned to their books and their games.

War had meant much enforced leisure. King Charles, following his predecessors, was enthusiastic for hunting, hawking and even bull and bear baiting. He continued to hunt while at Oxford, nonchalantly disregarding the fact that half the country was in civil turmoil. In 1635 he had authorized the handing over of 'Henry the 8 his Stirrups, Hawkes-Hoods, Gloves' and 'Henry 8 hawking glove, hawking glove, hawks hood, dogs collar' from the Hampton Court wardrobe to John Tradescant for display at his cabinet of curiosities at Lambeth. These objects were among those given by Elias Ashmole to the University in 1683. They can still be seen in the new Ashmolean Museum in Beaumont Street (see p. 91).

The scholars of the University showed a similar propensity to hunt. Through the Middle Ages there are constant complaints of their poaching affrays in the royal forest of Shotover which came to the eastern bounds of the city. Bishop Waynflete, drafting the statutes for his Magdalen College, ruled that 'no member of the college should keep a Harrier or other Hound of any Kind, or Ferrets, or a Sparrow Hawk, or any other Fowling Bird, or a Mavis or any other song bird'. Dr Routh, president from 1791 to 1854 (a record for longevity of a head of house), called his dog a cat to comply with the founder's statutes. The problem continued in the twentieth century. A special meeting of College officers was called at Magdalen on 25 June 1941 to consider whether to rescind the permission granted to members six years earlier to read in the Grove, which acted as the College's deer park, in view of instances of undergraduates chasing rabbits, disturbing the deer etc.

During the late seventeenth and eighteenth centuries the student body (and the dons – from Latin *domini* – masters), also disported themselves at real tennis and at cock fighting. Reminders of this have come from recent archaeological excavations. While Oriel College was refurbishing its student accommodation in the early 1990s the remains of its indoor tennis court came to light. Brian Durham and his team uncovered a series of superimposed floors of different materials, the walls with numbers painted on them for scoring and the remains of flanking viewing galleries. While recording the early seventeenth-century roof of the hall at Wadham College I picked out from the wall top a number of soft sewn leather balls, together with dried-up orange and lemon skins. Doubtless they had been thrown there by high spirited gilded youths during some long forgotten and uproarious college feast. At Holywell, outside the city walls on Balliol College land, Brian Durham also found the circular base of a structure interpreted as an eighteenth-century cockpit: chicken leg bones trimmed to take spurs had previously been found in medieval deposits in the west of the town. Loggan shows bowling greens at New College, Magdalen (re-turfed in 1636) and Holywell.

Old antagonisms died hard. Speaking of the gravel walk in Magdalen in 1680, Anthony à Wood commented that the walk had originally been planted before the Civil War in 1637, but the trees were 'caused to be plucked up' by Abraham Forman and Edward Draft 'because planted in fanatick times'. Magdalen College had not in fact suffered so severely as might have been expected considering its position outside the walls and the known royalist sympathies of its governing body. J.R. Bloxam, a fellow in the 1830s, who was a zealous historian and recorded the building history with assiduity, recorded some destruction of the chapel ornaments in 1649 and 1651, but it was less drastic than the iconoclasm of the Edwardian reformers a hundred years before. The figures of the Virgin and Child were pulled down from the gateway erected in 1635 at the height of the Laudian revival. A pulpit for Puritan sermons was erected in the choir and the organ was removed. It was purloined by Oliver Cromwell himself for use at Hampton Court Palace. The Restoration of Charles II resulted in its return to the College in 1660.

More devastating was the effect of the Civil War on the intellectual life of the University. For six years scholarship languished. The colleges were choked with Cavalier courtiers,

the town bursting with billeted soldiers. Pamphlets prolifer-
ated, books remained unread. The undergraduates drilled
with pikes and muskets. The townsfolk sullenly and reluctantly worked on the fortifications. Money was mulcted from
all, from colleges to paupers.

It is all the more amazing that within a few years of the
Restoration Oxford experienced an astonishing flowering of
intellectual talent. In particular, scientific studies took off.
Astronomy and Mathematics (Wren), Chemistry (Boyle),
Experimental Philosophy (Hooke) all made great strides. The
Royal Society, encouraged actively by the King, contained in
its early membership a galaxy of Oxford scientists. The
University acquired its first scientific collections when Elias
Ashmole, an otherwise repellent and fame-seeking Comptrol-
ler of Excise, got control of the Tradescant collections and
presented them to the University in 1683. A special building,
restrained Baroque in style, small but somehow monumental
in proportions and impressively sited in the centre of the
University buildings, was erected to house the gift. These
natural and man-made objects occupied the top storey; the
middle one provided a lecture room and, more significant for
the future, was the fact that in the basement there was a
laboratory for scientific experiments. This had a specially
strengthened vaulted roof to resist chemical explosions!
Tradescant's rarities were split in the nineteenth century
between the new Ashmolean, formed by an amalgamation
with the University Galleries in Beaumont Street, and the
University Museum in Parks Road. The old Ashmolean today
houses the University's stunning collection of early scientific
instruments. The laboratory is presided over by the portrait
of Robert Plot, the first keeper of the Museum.

Oxford now had a library (the Bodleian), a great church
(St Mary the Virgin), lecture rooms in the Bodleian quadrangle and the Divinity schools, a laboratory and a museum. It
was fitting that it should also have acquired a ceremonial
centre: a theatre. The young Christopher Wren was commissioned to design the Sheldonian (1664–9). Modelled on a
Roman prototype and paid for by an archbishop, the

Sheldonian Theatre is not the most beautiful building in Oxford. Its exterior was described as being like a man in a bowler hat with the brim pulled down over his eyes and his trousers drawn up under his armpits. The roof was formerly pierced by a range of outsize dormer windows, the light from which poured onto the compositor's trays of the University Press. Their heavy printing machinery was kept inopportunely in the dark basement. The intervening horseshoe-shaped auditorium with its hard bench seating, notoriously uncomfortable for concert addicts, is used for degree ceremonies, encaenias (when honours are heaped on the good, the powerful and the rich) and musical events. Working in Duke Humfrey's library one can hear bursts of heavenly music from next door! For all its strangely disproportionate exterior, within it is arguably the most splendid public space in England. Here is vigorous carving, pillars painted to resemble marble superimposed on each other, lavish provision of galleries and windows, plush velvet thrones for the Vice-Chancellor and the proctors, and, crowning it all, a painted *trompe l'œil* ceiling purporting to be an awning in the Roman manner, but in fact canvas suspended on battens from a timber floor. We know that Wren's design for the upper floor, illustrated in Robert Plot's *Natural History of Oxfordshire*, failed and had to be replaced using Baltic softwood during the Napoleonic Wars. But the form was retained, a masterpiece of interlocking ingenuity which mirrors the new scientific age of the late seventeenth century.

An interesting insight into the standard of life of an upper class academic household in Oxford in the late seventeenth century was gained when excavations were made at Oriel College in 1982. Here a stone chamber within the Provost's lodging which had been used as a cess pit produced at the bottom of its fill the remains of grapes, raisins, raspberries, black pepper, strawberries, apples, plums, figs, mulberries and a walnut. All these were recognized as having passed through the alimentary canal (apart from the walnut!). Equally interesting was the evidence for squalor in the Provost's way of life. The deposit contained numerous puparia of *sphaeroceridæ* (sewage flies). The only opening to the chamber was in the house and as Brian Durham, the excavator, commented 'there were sufficient fly puparia to say that for every seed that went down, one fly came up'.

The eighteenth century registered a sad decline in the reputation of Oxford as a university. In politics its rabid Tories, often flirting with Jacobitism, were out of kilter with the Hanoverian dynasty. Consequently, the Whig politicians who moved the levers of power in Church and State alternately ignored Oxford or were suspicious of its agenda. In religion Oxford remained a creature of the unreformed Anglican church and produced droves of unspectacular and often pretty unlearned clergy who occupied the parsonages and episcopal palaces of Georgian England. They did little to provide for the spiritual welfare of the teeming masses peopling the growing industrial towns. In scholarship Oxford failed to live up to the promise of the last thirty years of the seventeenth century. Liberal thought was frowned upon. John Locke, for instance, was excluded from Christ Church. The University Press, despite its handsome new buildings, published only fourteen new books between 1713 and 1755. It is not surprising that some of the greater minds Oxford helped to nurture during this period tended to bite the hand that fed them.

Take Edward Gibbon, author of *Decline and Fall of the Roman Empire*. He gave a damning description of the dons of Magdalen: 'The fellows of my time were decent easy men who supinely enjoyed the gifts of the founder ... from the toil of reading, or thinking, or writing, they had absolved their conscience ... their conversation stagnated in a round of college business, Tory politics, personal anecdotes and private scandal: their dull and deep potations excused the brisk intemperance of youth.' Doubtless, Gibbon embroidered his recollections, but Samuel Johnson, who spent four unhappy terms at Pembroke College before going down degree-less, gives a less varnished version. Of his tutor he said that 'he was a very worthy man but a heavy man, and I did not profit much by his instructions. Indeed I did not attend him much.'

Sent for to explain why he had absented himself from four successive tutorials, Johnson impudently explained that he had been sliding in Christ Church Meadows. He shared the eighteenth-century prejudice against dissenters. Religious tests were maintained to keep them out of the University. In 1768 six dissenters were expelled from St Edmund Hall. Boswell thought the measure harsh, claiming that they were 'good beings'. Johnson replied: 'I believe they might be good beings, but they were not fit to be in the University of Oxford. A cow is a very good animal in a field, but we turn her out of a garden.'

This doesn't present a very balanced view of the University at this time. The recent publication of the *History of the University of Oxford* shows that things were not as bad as Gibbon, Johnson or ill-disposed satirists such as the Whig Nicholas Amhurst made out. Colleges were supervising reading of their undergraduates more closely. The books recording the college 'collections' (internal examinations held at the beginning of the term to test work done in the vacations) have survived in some instances such as at Christ Church. Examinations, however, were sloppily run, degrees were given away without rigorous testing; the curriculum too remained antediluvian and heavily dominated by the classics and theology. Rowlandson's scathing cartoons of port-swigging and grossly overweight dons pursuing other men's wives were not far from the truth: his pictures of buxom wenches swinging from ropes as they were hauled into college windows by swashbuckling undergraduates persist. Even the Ashmolean Museum failed to live up to its hopeful beginnings. The specimens which Plot and Lhuyd, the two first keepers, had charge of, were neglected. 'Nothing', one visitor wrote, 'can equal the negligence with which the Ashmolean Museum was kept ... Lhuyd's fossils were tumbled out of their papers and nobody regarded or understood them.'

Whatever the low moral and intellectual tone Oxford sank to in this period there is no doubt that it was the scene of architectural triumphs of European importance. The chief movers in this were the young Christopher Wren (who had been involved in designing the Williamson Building at the Queen's College), Dean Aldrich of Christ Church and George Clarke of All Souls. Aldrich, in Colvin's words, was 'more than just an academic student of architecture ... he was an accomplished draughtsman'. A bequest of £3,000 enabled the college to rebuild the Peckwater Quadrangle. Having taught the Christ Church Summer School from 1990 to 1995, I can appreciate the lordly accommodation provided for the aristocratic gentlemen commoners of eighteenth-century Christ Church. The quadrangle is surrounded on three sides by identical façades, each dignified by an order of Ionic pilasters. Internally, the suites of panelled rooms are approached up wide wooden staircases with turned balustrades. 'Grandly classical' sums up Peckwater. The library, which closed the fourth side of the quadrangle, was designed by another amateur architect, George Clarke, for forty-six years fellow of All Souls.

All Souls College in the early eighteenth century was inhabited by wealthy aristocrats, 'a factious club of largely absentee fellow ... mutinous and politically divided', warring incessantly against their own warden and their visitor, the Archbishop of Canterbury. Nevertheless, under the influence of George Clarke, an able politician with experience from the reigns of William III and Queen Anne, and the possessor of a valuable architectural library, the College embarked on a major rebuilding programme 1703–51. They dabbled in classical designs at first, but finally opted for a more imaginative scheme combining neo-Gothic features and classical principles, the brain-child of Nicholas Hawksmoor. The younger assistant of the great Wren, Hawksmoor was in some ways more inventive than his master. He was asked to design a new quadrangle. The money came from the will of Christopher Codrington who had valuable sugar plantations on Antigua in the West Indies. The descendants of former slaves still bear the plantation name, Codrington, in the island of Montserrat. Hawksmoor's grand library occupies the whole of the north side of the quadrangle and balances with the chapel on the south side. Linking the two is an astonishing façade incorporating twin towers and steeples, looking like a Gothic cathedral west front. He completed the scheme with a Gothic, colonnaded screen facing Radcliffe Square. Although the general tone was Gothic, the symmetry of the external façades (including an odd central doorway into the library) and the interior detailing of the hall, buttery and library were all Classical. This mixture of the two styles had been brilliantly foreshadowed by Wren who crowned Wolsey's Gothic tower base at Christ Church with his classically flavoured and ogee-domed tower. Hawksmoor welded Gothic and Classical together at All Souls and produced something startlingly original.

Another of Hawksmoor's designs was used in the Clarendon Building. Here profits from the Earl of Clarendon's *History of the Rebellion* were ploughed back into a monumental design which was to house the University's printing and publishing house: on one side the Bibles, which were pumped into the British Empire over the next hundred years, were made; and on the other, learned books in Arabic, Latin, Greek and Hebrew were to be set up and printed. Despite its poor publishing record the building itself is a great success with its giant columned portico, perfectly proportioned windows and a skyline punctuated excitingly with lead statues. These, after travelling up the Thames to Oxford, 'were at first refused and suffered to lie at the Wharf for close two years' before being heaved into position.

Dr Clarke, while initiating and encouraging the building programme at All Souls, eventually grew impatient at the behaviour of the fellows who were feuding with their visitor, and left his fortune to build Worcester College. On this westernmost site of the eighteenth-century University a symmetrical range consisting of the library, over a colonnade, and two projecting wings containing hall and chapel was built in the Classical style. The library contains Dr Clarke's superb collection of architectural drawings. Worcester College has suffered more than most from the depredations of ceaseless motor traffic, which make it virtually inaccessible to the pedestrian. Its romantic grounds, laid out by a perceptive bursar around a curving lake and lined on one side by the Oxford canal, are among the delights that Oxford offers; more a park than a garden, *rus in urbe*.

Both at All Souls and at Worcester new Classical components were tacked on to pre-existing late medieval college buildings which were retained. At the others, the break with the past was considered and final. The constricted site of the Queen's College along the High Street was cleared of houses and a congery of medieval collegiate structures to make way for a thoroughgoing Classical design of buildings round two great quadrangles. Despite its uniform appearance the Queen's College was in fact built over a period of forty-five years between 1692 and 1738, each component designed by different architects as various sources of funding became available. The library, a magnificent first-floor room with majestic book presses, a blaze of windows and a richly plastered ceiling was first in 1692–5. Wren's Williamson building of 1672 was re-cased and enlarged upwards. The front quadrangle certainly involved Hawksmoor, but William Townsend probably adapted his plans to meet a more restricted collegiate purse. There is a great sense of theatre in the rusticated screen, the base of which is in Headington hardstone, pierced centrally by the entrance surmounted by an open arched dome. The visitor penetrates the colonnade and is faced with the hall, backing up against the chapel, crowned with a copper-roofed cupola. Although, like most other Oxford buildings, it has been completely refaced, in this instance by orange Axminster, Bath, Clipsham and white Portland stones, the symmetry and monumentality are stunning. What is not so pleasing is the fact that the sculptures in the major pediment were unnecessarily removed and replicated. Because of their wealth, the autocratic and autonomous habits of colleges tend to ride roughshod over planning laws, designed to protect historic buildings.

Oxford was now graced with a plethora of buildings gleaming in the new and fashionable Classical style, but, like the rest of early nineteenth-century England, it required radical reformation. Its administration, almost unchanged since the Laudian statutes of the 1630s, was oligarchic and college-led. A new impulse was needed to energize its flagging academic life. One reason for its uninspiring reputation *c.*1800 was that it had cut itself off from the steady and increasing supply of able young men. In 1581 a regulation had banned Roman Catholics from admission. In 1661 the Dissenters were similarly excluded. Student numbers dropped significantly, reaching a nadir in the 1750s. Recovery increased the pressure for reform. The entry averaged 234 in the years 1800–9. After the reforms inaugurated by the Royal Commission in 1850, the numbers had more than doubled in the decade 1860–9. By the end of the century, after a second bout of reform, it averaged 821 annually. This had been accomplished in three ways. The abolition of religious tests (such as submission to the thirty-nine articles of doctrine of the Anglican Church) allowed non-Anglicans to be admitted. The heady brew of Oxford graduates now included Jews, Catholics and Nonconformists. Secondly, a broader cross-section of society was represented. The scholarships and exhibitions were now impartially competed for by students from state secondary schools. The traditional recruiting ground had been the long-founded grammar schools, lately turned into middle-class preserves and renamed public schools. Entry requirements were tightened up and a uniform examination imposed on all entrants before matriculation (a ceremony of admission undertaken in the Sheldonian Theatre at the start of a student's university career). Moreover, serious attempts were made to reduce the cost of expensive collegiate living and to encourage non-collegiate and therefore cheaper institutions which were now allowed to admit students who worked towards degrees awarded by the University. Oxford also took a lead (over Cambridge) in offering adult education opportunities to non-University based students.

This enlarged entry was not going to be satisfied with a fossilized curriculum and outdated teaching methods. Here certain colleges like Oriel and Balliol led the way and reformed themselves. Oriel College, in particular, under the influence of John Keble, John Henry Newman and Hurrell Froude undertook effective pastoral care of their undergraduates. Written college examinations 'for the improvement of the college discipline as well as to ascertain the progress of the undergraduate members' became the norm. The quality of college tutors (still largely responsible in Oxford for individual teaching) was raised. Before the reforms only twenty-two out of 242 fellowships were decided by open competition. These were now thrown open to all comers. Furthermore, fellows were no longer obliged to take Holy Orders. They could devote themselves to a lifetime of teaching and research rather than being obliged to bury themselves in country living while still in their prime. The rule about celibacy was relaxed, first of all for professors. They could set up house (with plenty of servants) in the smart north Oxford villas William Wilkinson and Frederick Codd were designing in the St John's College garden suburb. By the end of the century, fellows could marry, and gradually the common rooms lost their misogynist spirit.

The colleges, kicking and struggling to keep their independence, were persuaded to help pay for the salaries of professors who, it was hoped, would inspire the faculties and departments to undertake research as in contemporary German universities. Slowly the University, which had been largely impotent in the eighteenth century, began to wrest some powers from the colleges.

The tremendous strides taken in the nineteenth century that increased human knowledge in biology, physics and chemistry meant there was a widening gap between such advances and the Oxford curriculum, which was deep frozen in classics, mathematics and theology. Honour schools in such science subjects, in modern history, English literature and modern languages were now established. The facilities for science teaching, improved as they were when the University Museum was built, remained absurdly inadequate. Colleges such as Magdalen and Trinity set up their own laboratories while Professor Daubeny paid for the equipping of chemistry laboratories in the Botanic Garden buildings out of his own pocket. It was not until World War I was almost lost through insufficient numbers of chemistry and other science graduates that the government of the day set up the Asquith commission (1922) resulting in a greatly improved resourcing for sciences. Oxford's production of science graduates increased from 100 to 200 per year and this was considered (by the *History of the University: the Twentieth Century*) to be just sufficient – but only just enough – to ensure the successful outcome of World War II.

The building which enshrines in visible form many of the aspirations of the Victorian scientific establishment is the University Museum. The University granted £30,000 for the shell leaving for the moment the question of internal fittings. Of thirty-two designs submitted, the Gothic plans of Messrs Deane and Woodward were chosen. Ruskin, in the main, approved, but there were serious miscalculations including an error in the calculated elasticity of the wrought-iron supports for the roof. The interior of glass, cast-iron pillars and wrought-iron vaulting ribs was very advanced for the day. H.W. Acland, the main mover behind the scheme, described as *desideranda*: 'a workroom where the student may see and work for himself; the lecture room where he may see and be taught that which by himself he can neither see nor learn, and, as an adjunct to these, a room for more private study for each; thirdly a general space for the common display of any illustrative specimens capable of preservation ... and lastly a library'. Most visitors nowadays are there to enjoy the 'common display of illustrative specimens', yet it is from this remarkable building that Oxford science developed until it covered the fifty-acre site to the north-east of the city, swallowing up a corner of the University Parks in the process.

It was in the lecture room of the University Museum that the celebrated meeting of the British Association took place in 1860. A year before Charles Darwin's *Origin of Species* had been published, arousing a furore of opposition from the fundamentalist, and in their own eyes, orthodox, members of the Church of England. The Bishop of Oxford, 'Soapy Sam' Wilberforce, was opposed by a leading scientist of the day,

Thomas Huxley, a follower of Darwin. 'Turning to his antagonist with a smiling insolence', the bishop begged to know was it through his grandfather or his grandmother that he claimed his descent from a monkey? On this, an onlooker reported that 'Mr Huxley slowly and deliberately arose ... he was not ashamed to have a monkey for his ancestor, but he would be ashamed to be connected with a man who used great gifts to obscure the truth.' It seems that for most of the audience the Darwinists carried the day.

All this frenzy of scientific activity occurred in early Victorian Oxford against a background of religious turbulence. A number of Oxford-based clergymen in the Church of England including Edward Pusey, John Keble, John Bloxam and John Henry Newman launched a powerful Counter Reformation known as the Tractarian or Oxford Movement. They wished to return to the conditions of the early Church and to arrest the creeping control of their institution by irreligious, laicizing politicians. They were fearful of the progress towards disestablishment as seen in Ireland and Wales and suspected that the State was planning a takeover of Church property. They claimed to offer a middle way (*Via Media*) between the evangelical tradition and Roman Catholicism. The Oxford Movement exercised a powerful influence over many of the clergy who, roused from their torpor, undertook a crusade against the religiously indifferent mass of the English working class. Victorian churches in Gothic style sprouted from many industrial towns. Ecclesiastical interiors became more mysterious and dim with stained glass, gleaming brass lecterns, pews arranged as in monasteries, altars at the head of flights of steps – 'smells and bells'. As for Newman, he retired from Oriel common room and the pulpit of St Mary the Virgin to the monastic seclusion of the parish church he had built at Littlemore and went over to Rome in 1842. The Oxford Movement had certainly deepened the religious life of the nation for a time, but it did not arrest its comparative decline. The days of Anglican control over the University were over.

Although its power had begun to disintegrate, the Church

of England still retained a lively influence over the Oxford scene. Take the foundation of Keble College in memory of John Keble (d.1862), a key figure in the early Tractarian movement. William Butterfield, one of the most original Victorian architects, designed the magnificent chapel and two large quadrangles between 1868 and 1882. The design is distinctly bold in a number of respects; the use of polychrome brickwork, orange, yellow and blue in bizarre patterns, chequers, chevrons, and trellises, which have earned epithets ranging from 'holy zebra' to 'streaky bacon', is alien to Oxford's largely limestone building tradition. Keble is also unusual in collegiate planning terms in that it adopts the corridor rather than the more traditional staircase for accessing its accommodation. This means that the rooms are less private, more noisy and therefore less suitable for prolonged and uninterrupted study. Keble's third characteristic was that it was cheap and offered a cut-price university education suitable for the sons of indigent clergy. It has an enviable collection of medieval illuminated manuscripts and Holman Hunt's *The Light of the World* glows in a side chapel. Keble has now largely lost its theological college flavour; its modern buildings, all glass internally and presenting a yellow-brick, heavily fortified exterior is one of the most arresting pieces of modern architecture in Oxford, not otherwise noted for the originality or quality of its recent building. It is sad that the latest addition, an emasculated red brick effort in Keble Road, only serves to emphasize the richness of Butterfield's imagination.

A second college which indulged in major rebuilding in the Victorian Gothic style was Exeter. This college founded by Walter de Stapledon, Bishop of Exeter in 1314, helped to educate William Morris, the notable designer of textiles and wall coverings, and Edward Burne-Jones, the painter and designer of stained glass. Their rooms have regrettably been rebuilt but the College holds on to various memorabilia including Morris's spectacles and his pipe. The early seventeenth-century chapel was demolished in the year Morris entered the College and was replaced by George Gilbert

Scott's design, roughly based on the Sainte-Chapelle, Paris. On a constricted urban site, the chapel has five bays of variegated, geometric, traceried windows, a high vault with bands of differently coloured masonry, and figured stained glass; it is polygonal-ended, with a heavily buttressed exterior crowned with a soaring flèche. Morris designed the sacristy curtains, made of woven wool with bird motifs, as well as making the tapestry of the Adoration of the Magi, designed by Edward Burne-Jones in 1890.

A third piece of Gothic revival was the virtual rebuilding of Balliol College. Here the intellectual dominance of Benjamin Jowett, Master of the College 1870–93, was given architectural expression. He was not lacking in self-confidence and is said to have told a friend: 'If we had a little more money we could absorb the University'. His laconic (and at times brutal) manner in dealing with undergraduate idleness was exemplified in the case of Walter Morrison who, as finals approached, was summoned by Jowett: 'You are a fool. You must be sick of idling. It is too late for you to do much. But the class matters nothing. What does matter is the sense of power which comes from steady working.' Such a man as Jowett confessed to 'a general prejudice against all persons who do not succeed in the world'. Balliol, in fact, produced a succession of notable politicians, churchmen and public servants in Jowett's time, including Matthew Arnold, Hilaire Belloc, Gerard Manley Hopkins, Archbishop Lang, Cardinal Manning, Archbishop Temple, Lord Asquith, Lord Curzon, Viscount Grey, the Marquess of Lansdowne and Alfred (afterwards Viscount) Milner. 'Effortless superiority' might well have been their watchword. Architecturally, Balliol College is an eclectic plum pudding of a building. It has a little bit of everything and a lot of the nineteenth century, namely Salvin (1852–3), Butterfield (1856–7) and Waterhouse (1867–77). From Broad Street, the longest façade of any college in Oxford is a curious mishmash of thirteenth-century French architecture, Scottish baronial and eighteenth-century neo-Classical.

The colleges need to be seen in their setting of gardens and parks. Oxford's gardens are not only profoundly beautiful in appearance but are rich in literary and academic associations. I will take four examples of my favourites. At Christ Church you can see (through a gateway) the garden where Dean Liddell's daughter Alice played, watched by Charles Dodgson (Lewis Carroll) who was a mathematics don here in the 1880s. The very bough on which the Cheshire cat appeared out of nowhere and disappeared in a smile is pointed out. A large mulberry tree, reputedly one of those planted at the command of James I, when he wished to encourage the breeding of silk worms to help England's textile industry, still flourishes. In one of the canons' gardens round the great quadrangle there is a wall with a number of niches. Here Dean Buckland, Professor of Geology, tested the old wives' tale by walling up toads and opening the holes after a year to see if they were still alive! A personal anecdote illustrates the constant need for vigilance. In the late 1970s one of the canons' wives wished to remove a tree in her garden because its roots were interfering with her getting the lawn mower in and out of the shed. The tree, a *Pseudacacia Robinia* had been there at least since 1800 (it was recorded on a lithograph of Christ Church after a fire in 1815) and its position in front of the majestic pile of the cardinal's college made it one of the most important trees in Oxford. Mavis Batey, wife of the Treasurer of Christ Church, and later to be the Chairman of the Garden History Society, called me out urgently from Woodstock, and strengthened by the presence of Ken Burras, the Curator of the Botanic Garden, we homed in on the hapless canon's wife. She needed little persuasion to relent and the tree still stands.

New College garden has to be seen from the top of its newly furbished prospect mound to be appreciated. It was laid out on the rectangular piece of land acquired by Bishop William of Wykeham, between the encircling and bastioned city wall and the churchyard of St Peters-in-the-East. Loggan's bird's-eye view in his *Oxonia Illustrata* shows the formal layout of the late seventeenth century, with a terraced and tree-lined walk on the earth rampart backing the wall, a faceted and pyramidal mount, with stepped walks up to its summit. This provided a viewpoint from which to survey the four parterres below, complex designs including the college and royal arms in (presumably) coloured earths, sand, crushed brick, bordered with box, lavender or plants with similar obedience. Shaven grass covers the rest. Much of this reverted in the drought summers like that of 1995 to dried-up lawns. The tree-lined terraces have been replaced with herbaceous borders, so in general a softening and romanticizing of the hard rectilinearity of the former formal layout has been engineered.

Worcester College has the most romantically designed garden in Oxford. The site is unpromising, flat and marshy, between the canal (backed by the railway) and the College. Largely because of a curvaceous lake lined with trees, their boughs gracefully dipping over the duck-frequented surface, Worcester offers the only college garden where water plays a major part.

Magdalen had the advantage of being built outside the wall of the city. It was ringed round with its own crenellated Long Wall of great blocks of Headington stone. Loggan again shows interesting Renaissance-type formal gardens to the north of Bishop Waynflete's college. There were a series of rectangular plots, no doubt kitchen gardens, with gravelled walks and walls to protect them from the deer (which are first mentioned c.1720). Also a bowling green, a slightly embanked and sunken area which can be traced on the ground in the park today. This was kept level by mower's scythes. The large park-like area was criss-crossed with avenues of elms and limes. The deer park is unique among the colleges of Oxford and Cambridge. The formal gardens were removed in the mid eighteenth century following the construction of the New Buildings in 1733. The venerable elms, a much loved feature of the grove until the 1940s, began to die off with Dutch elm disease and had to be felled. Aerial photographs taken in the 1995 drought summer showed clearly the positioning of the elm avenues and the earlier gardens.

Turning to a twentieth-century Oxford garden, that of Green College, I was recently conducted round by its creator, a philosophically-minded gardener, Michael Pirie. The Radcliffe Trustees had spent £10,000 in the 1770s when they employed two architects, Keene and Wyatt, to build the great octagon and the astronomer's house. They followed the example of the Physic (now Botanic) garden, enclosing their land with a limestone wall. The nineteenth-century astronomers had their kitchen garden on the north-east part of the site near St Giles. A tennis court now covers the area. Green College took over the site when it was realized that Oxford in the 1970s no longer had clear or dark skies suitable for astronomical observation. Within this setting, Pirie's garden does nothing to distract attention from the looming monumentality of the octagon. There are curving gravel walks, discreet greenhouses, trellised bowers, beds of aromatic and medicinal herbs, appropriate to a College frequented by 'medics'. Green College garden appeals to those who like the idea of 'toil unsever'd from tranquillity' as Matthew Arnold had it.

While the University was reordering itself or being reformed through the Royal Commissions by government, the town was similarly undergoing momentous changes. These turned it from an undistinguished provincial market centre off the beaten track into a medium-sized industrial city, one of the more important in the South Midlands. Four major developments took place: an increase in population; a growth in industry; the enlargement of the built environment; and the linkage of the city to the national communications network.

In 1801 the combined population of the city and the University was below 12,000. Between 1811 and 1831 it grew by fifty per cent. By 1901 it had increased, rather more slowly, to about 50,000 with the University on vacation when the census was taken. By 1971 it had again doubled to 108,805 persons living within the bounds of the County borough. This increase was not evenly distributed. As the centre declined the extramural parishes, St Ebbes's, St

Thomas's, St Clement's and St Giles's grew rapidly. The boundary had accordingly been extended in 1889 when the city was raised to the status of a county borough. This meant that the City Council assumed a full range of local government powers and to celebrate they built themselves a grandiose new town hall.

Oxford's late Victorian town hall is the successor of an eighteenth-century building which in turn replaced the seventeenth-century council house. It was designed by Henry T. Hare and is an ornate building 'partaking of the characteristics both of Elizabethan and Jacobean work'. Underneath it is a cellar with a quadripartite vault of the fifteenth century, within which is displayed a magnificent collection of civic plate. This is accessible to the public on application to the porter. To combine all the manifold purposes of a town hall into a compressed site, Hare's ingenuity was stretched to the utmost. He performed with panache, creating an impressive staircase, an exuberantly decorated great hall with seats for 2,000 people, a library now disused when the function was transferred to the Westgate centre, a council chamber, a committee room and the mayor's parlour. Added to this was a police station (used until 1930) and an underground police drill hall, a court, a couple of cells and a spacious public convenience. A quart in a pint pot! The basement has been used since 1975 for a lively museum display run by the County, providing an authentically flavoured history of Town and Gown and showing the public the latest results of the extensive archaeological work within the city. As I write, the Museum of Oxford is under threat from cuts in local government funding. Such a valuable interpretation point of Oxford's past should in my view be funded tripartitely by the City, the University and the County. Too long has the County borne the brunt – it now needs help.

This increase of population could not have been supported if there had not occurred a corresponding upsurge of industrial activity. The biggest employer during the eighteenth and early nineteenth century was the University, but the discontinuity of demand for goods and services from an institution that was on vacation for half the year caused chronic underemployment. Fortunately, there was a big expansion in the printing industry when in the 1830s the decision was taken to remove the Oxford University Press from Clarendon Building and build a new, imposing, neo-Classical works on Walton Street. It prospered mightily, and in the late nineteenth century the numbers of operatives rocketed from ninety to between 250 and 300 people, making the Press the largest single Oxford employer. This occurred for two reasons: the extraordinary expansion of the Bible trade as the empire painted large parts of the world's map red, and the phenomenal growth of the educational as well as the academic market. OUP provided school books for the newly educated working classes by the million. In the next century it would do the same for the world.

Another considerable employer in the same part of town was the Eagle Ironworks in Jericho. Here on the banks of the Oxford canal William Carter had begun an iron foundry in 1812. The works acquired the name Eagle under Carter's successor, Charles Grafton. The firm changed its name when William Lucy became manager in the 1860s and Lucy and Co. became well known for agricultural machinery, lamp-posts and ornamental ironwork. Cast iron does not wear out; their serviceable products are still met with in the streets of Oxford. At the end of the century Lucy and Co. went into the production of heavy-duty library shelving. Much of the underground shelving of the Bodleian Library was made here. More recently, electricity transformers have provided a lucrative mainstay. The still waters of the canal contrast with the shuddering jar of the great presses.

Oxford's industrial expansion on this scale would not have been possible before the advent of the railway. But as in other places, like Stamford and Warwick, its coming was strenuously opposed. At an enquiry into the extension of the Great Western Railway to Oxford in 1836 and 1837 the University professed its anxiety about how the discipline of its young men would suffer if they could escape within an hour or so up to London. When it arrived in 1842 the railway promptly proved fatal to river trade and, in the long run, to coaching and canal-borne traffic. A big opportunity for local employment was lost in 1865 when the University successfully opposed the establishment of the G.W.R. company workshops. These went to Swindon. A small colony of 150 railway workers was established at Oseney New Town but this never grew to the size of Swindon's railway suburb.

The railways have left a considerable mark on the city. They have helped to determine the strange shape of its growth. Lack of bridges meant there was relatively little spread in the Victorian period west of the barrier of the north–south railway. Borrow pits provided the Lake Street area with a long stretch of water. Oxford's inimitable skyline of towers and spires can be viewed with advantage as the trains slow to a stop outside the site of Oseney Abbey. The smoke, soot and steam generated by the engines had a disastrously damaging effect on the stone surface of many of Oxford's buildings. The city rapidly became soot-blackened and decaying. The old London and North Western railway opened a station as the terminus of the Buckingham line on the site of Rewley Abbey. It was constructed out of similar components of cast iron and glass to those used in the celebrated Crystal Palace. Recent research by Julian Murby of the Oxford Archaeological Unit has discovered a complex and efficient drainage system in which roof water is dispersed down the cast-iron columns into underground drainage channels. This makes it technically difficult and undesirable from a heritage point of view to move the structure. My feeling is that road requirements, which currently threaten the building's future, should give way here to railway interest. Speeding up by a second or two the traffic flow at the cost of such an important piece of railway architecture is unacceptable.

To accommodate its increase in population and industry, Oxford was enlarged between 1850 and 1950, changing its shape in four main directions. It expanded north towards Wolvercote along the flood-free gravel ridge between the Thames and Cherwell; south along the Abingdon road

towards the villages of Hinksey and Kennington; east covering the heights of Headington and ringing round Shotover
with housing; and south-east over Cowley Marsh towards
Iffley. Each area produced housing development of a distinctive kind. North Oxford developed as a result of the
investment of St John's College laying out the first garden
suburb to house professors, successful Oxford tradesmen,
and the professional classes. Their Italianate villas, spacious
Gothic mansions with ample accommodation for servants,
and planned leafy gardens have only partially survived
multiple occupation, while the scourge of the motor car has
all but destroyed the croquet lawns, tennis courts and
rosebeds. Even the trees are threatened by the insertion of
cable television.

Jericho, to the west, was developed as an artisan suburb
with rows of solid brick and slate terraces, the great variety of
designs reflecting the small-scale investors and jobbing builders who put them up. The locality was plentifully supplied
with pubs, but saved from damnation by St Paul's with its
classical façade and the Italianate tower and Byzantine
interior of St Barnabas (built by Arthur Blomfield at the
expense of Thomas Combe, superintendent of the Clarendon
Press, an early patron of the Pre-Raphaelites). To provide for
the religious needs of the north Oxford middle class, G.E.
Street was commissioned to build St Philip and St James
church, an austere and dignified thirteenth-century design
(1864–6) with polychrome stone banding and a broach spire
which would not be out of place in neighbouring Northamptonshire.

The spread of Oxford towards the east and south-east in
the twentieth century was largely driven by the need for
housing of the work force employed in the motor car
assembly industry. William Morris, Lord Nuffield, exerted a
greater influence on modern Oxford than any other individual. He began at the age of fifteen by assembling bicycles (he
used to cycle over to Birmingham for spare parts) and then
moved to producing motor cars. Oxford was convenient in

that it was centrally situated, near good road communications and had a large pool of underemployed non-militant labour. Morris applied the principles of mass production pioneered by Henry Ford and quickly outstripped all his competitors. He first encouraged other firms to specialize in the production of components; then he bought them up. Furthermore, he showed a willingness to plough a considerable part of the profits back into the company. His sturdy independence made him unwilling to tolerate union membership in his companies, let alone union interference. His concern for the welfare of his staff, which appeared to some to smack of managerial patronage, did in fact ensure a loyal and relatively strike-free work force. Finally, his moral altruism meant that he was easily the most munificent benefactor the University of Oxford had ever known, donating ten million pounds to build Nuffield College (a graduate institution mainly devoted to the social sciences) and founding medical institutions such as the Nuffield Orthopaedic Hospital.

I have three further reflections to add. In 1952 I spent a day in the Cowley works as an undergraduate visitor and experienced at first hand the Morris car assembly line. The impressions made on me by the noise, smells, flashing lights, moving machinery and the human effort directed towards the production of an unending stream of vehicles, turned me away from the manufacturing industry into schoolmastering – another assembly line with partially educated young men as the end product! Secondly, as County Archaeologist in 1980, I had to record Morris's office above 21 Longwall Street where he made Bullnose Morris cars in the 1920s, before it was turned into student accommodation. I recall the austerity of the room, the small plain table, the green shaded reading lamp. His lack of interest in the panoply of power is, I think, well born out in the furnishings and fittings of Nuffield Place, between Henley-on-Thames and Wallingford, donated like the bulk of his fortune to the University of Oxford. Finally, it is said that despite his elevation to the peerage his application for membership of the local village golf club was rejected. He may have been a millionaire but he was 'trade'. If this is true, it is a deplorable comment on the pervasiveness of the English disease, the class system thoughout our public life.

Perhaps the most bizarre episode in Oxford's recent housing history is the scandal of the Cutteslowe walls. Briefly, in 1934 an Urban Housing Company built an estate for white-collar workers in north Oxford. The City, three years before, had also built an estate for largely working-class tenants on an adjoining piece of land. The Company, to protect its owners from the infection of their slum clearance neighbours to the east, built two seven-foot high walls with revolving spikes across the two roads connecting the two estates. This considerably inconvenienced the Cutteslowe people who had to go for a long diversion round the impediment. It was also a flagrant episode in class warfare. Despite twenty years of ineffectual political action, recourse to the courts and changes in the Town Planning legislation, the walls remained until on 2 March 1959, watched by a small crowd, councillors and workmen demolished the 'insult to the working class'. The stumps of the walls remained until a few years ago and now the only sign of the Cutteslowe walls is the curious change of road names at the point where they used to stand. Aldrich Road becomes Wentworth Road; Carlton becomes Wolsey Road.

X

Religion and Ritual

Judging from the degree of public interest fostered by the current controversies about how to manage Stonehenge, there seems little doubt that ancient religious and ritual sites exert an enduring and magnetic attraction for large numbers of people. This is connected frequently with their location in lonely, comparatively inaccessible and high places. Scale is another lure. They are usually greater in size and therefore more impressive than ancient industrial or domestic remains. The feeling that large numbers of people in the remote past have co-operated in raising these mounds and circles (whether they are of stone, timber or earth) is a further draw. Finally, the visitor's imagination is fired and ranges free as he speculates about the rituals, processions, sacrifices and acts of worship which may have been performed around or in them. They enlarge our vision of the past.

Oxfordshire is fortunate in having three religious and ritual sites dating from the Prehistoric which have national significance. These are the Rollright Stones, the Devil's Quoits and the Uffington White Horse. Each has been the subject of recent and detailed archaeological survey and excavation so that myths fostered by them through the ages have been supplemented by much hard information about their dates, mode of construction, affinities, if not their purpose. These three sites also illustrate well how varying ownerships result in the differential treatment of the monuments ranging from the scandalously destructive to the virtually ideal.

The Rollright Stones straddle the Warwickshire/Oxfordshire boundary. They are a group of burial and ritual monuments standing high on the limestone ridge over 200 metres above sea level. In such a conspicuous position and on a much used trackway they have attracted visitors since the Middle Ages when they were regarded as one of the 'Wonders of Britain'. They have been studied intently by antiquaries since the seventeenth century who have produced a wonderful series of drawings and engravings from the study of which we can establish how the stones have been treated in the last 300 years. Not surprisingly they have accumulated a mass of folk lore and superstition.

Robert Plot in his *Natural History of Oxfordshire* (1676) summarizes the folklore current at his time:

> The common people call the Rollrich Stones and dream they were sometimes men by a miraculous metamorphosis turned into hard stones. The highest of them all, which without the circle looketh into the Earth, they call the King, because he should have been king of England (forsooth) if he had seen Long Compton, a little town lying beneath, and which one may see, if he go some few paces forward. Of the five standing on the other side [the Whispering Knights] touching as it were one another they imagine to have been knights mounted on horseback, and the rest the Army

They consist of four elements. The King Stone is a standing stone, just over the Warwickshire border. It can be reached by courtesy of the farmer by walking a few yards across a field from the road. Its function seems to have been that of a marker of the Bronze Age cemetery consisting of a cairn and a barrow found recently nearby. Its likely date is *c.* 1800–1500 BC. The King's Men circle is to the south of the road and lies in Oxfordshire (just). It is a ring of fantastically eroded and pitted stones, irregularly spaced in a thirty-metre diameter circle. There are now about seventy uprights (traditionally they are uncountable), but archaeologist George Lambrick of the Oxford Archaeological Unit has established that the original design was of about 105 stones forming a continuous wall with a narrow entrance to the south–south-east. Many of the stones disappeared, no doubt to make roads and farm buildings. Some simply fell over or were broken off at the base. About a third were re-erected *c.*1882. A study of the lichen growth has helped to establish the relative age of the various stones. The original ones were erected c.2500–2000 BC. It is difficult even to suggest what kind of rituals were enacted here but there do not seem to be any astronomical alignments. Clearly the enclosure was meant to exclude the worshippers and to create a sense of mystery. It certainly still does this. I remember approaching it from the south one November day, through a field of cabbages in the thick mist. The stones loomed eerily out of the fog, their contorted shapes suggesting immense age and a religious aura totally alien to the sceptical late twentieth century. The fourth component of the group is the Whispering Knights across a field about 150 metres from the road to the south-east of the King's Men. This is a 'Portal Dolmen', a type of megalithic burial chamber with portal stones flanking a closing slab; the capstone has slipped. This is somewhat older than the other two being dated c.3800–3000 BC.

This group of monuments has suffered badly from neglect, deliberate destruction and now visitor erosion. The ground surface around the stones has been worn by the pressure of human feet; fires are lit at the centre of the circle and occasionally against the stones. They have even been thrown onto the road and the soil round the Whispering Knights has been progressively ploughed away leaving a little island with the railings standing on visible concrete supports which are ludicrously ugly. It is to be hoped that current proposals for improving the management of this important site will improve access and reduce damage. However, too much manicuring like the building of an intrusive interpretation centre and coach lay-bys might destroy the numinous atmosphere of the place. The low profile approach followed by the present owner, one feels, is in the interest of both the stones and the visitor experience of them.

For thirty years sand and gravel lorries thundered through the shuddering village of Stanton Harcourt. A bypass has now been built, but the dust still drifts over the thatched cottages in a westerly wind. All round this flat river plain is a landscape of dereliction; the penalty for allowing the sand and gravel extraction industry to have its way is a string of lakes, unwanted by man but frequented by birds, and the waste of hundreds of acres of agricultural land. Perhaps the most notable loss has been the archaeology, for these Thames gravels were highly favoured by early man. Their farms, roads and fields traced in aerial photography form a close knit mesh across it. In the fields around Stanton Harcourt, too, are the remains of a great ritual complex, of similar size and importance in the Neolithic and Bronze Ages to that centering on Stonehenge. This ceremonial complex consists of a cluster of Neolithic mortuary enclosures, long barrows (c.3500–1800 BC), Late Neolithic and Beaker burials (c.2600–1800 BC), two rows of round barrows represented now by ring ditches since they have been flattened by the plough (c.2000–1200 BC) and the Devil's Quoits circle-henge. Much of this has been irretrievably lost to gravel digging, World War II aerodrome construction, and obliterating agriculture using pan busting heavy machinery.

I remember visiting the Devil's Quoits in 1974 when Margaret Gray was busy excavating, trying to retrieve information from the monument already shattered by runway damage and threatened again with total destruction by quarrying. The great internal ditch was visible in cross-section, bands of wind-blown soil showing it had backfilled during a dry period in the Bronze Age when the climate in Southern England reached an optimum. The stones, great irregular masses of conglomerate pebbles cemented together, lay on the ground where they had probably been overthrown by bigoted medieval churchmen, afraid of a local relapse to paganism. The Henge, attributed by medieval minds to a construction of the Devil, still had power to draw. Despite the fact that for the last forty years the latter-day owners, All Souls College, and A.R.C., the gravel operators, have known full well the importance of the site nationally, no management scheme protecting the monument (which is scheduled) has ever been implemented. The latest stage in this lamentable tale of indecision, compromise and philistinism is to replicate the monument, making an artificial island, putting the stones back and saving a fragment of the Bronze Age landscape which is still intact. It is too little, too late.

The Uffington White Horse, the third of these Oxfordshire prehistoric ritual sites, lies spreadeagled athwart the crown of a green turfed down 800 feet high overlooking the Vale of the White Horse. The elongated and loosely-linked shape of the animal is sprawled over the grass and apparently cut deeply into the chalk. The head is almost that of a dragon with staring eyes and a snout. The horse has figured in documents since the twelfth century when, like the Rollright Stones, it was one of the 'Wonders of Britain'. Theories about its origin and function are legion. Was it an Anglo-Saxon monument to Alfred's defeat of the Danes at Ashdown? Or a tribal emblem of the Iron Age Atrebates? Or was it a ceremonial horse-cult figure? The similarity between the figure's disarticulated outline and representations of horses on Iron-Age coinage has been noted since the 1930s. Now in 1995 David Miles of the Oxford Archaeological Unit has proposed a fresh interpretation in the light of excavations over a period of years on this very popular site, visited annually by thousands of visitors. It is now realized that instead of being etched into the chalk the outline of the horse is in fact deeply trenched into the brown soil wash on the side of the slope and filled with impacted pure chalk. Using a new technique developed at the Research Laboratory for Archaeology at Oxford University (known as Optical Stimulated Luminescence), samples from the lower parts of the back of the horse were dated to 1240+/-360 BC, 900+/-340 BC and 1030+/-360 BC. This means that the horse belongs to the late Bronze Age. If this sounds implausible I think we need to seek a context for the animal in a society heavily dependent on horses. A number of Iron Age sites in Wessex and the Thames Valley have yielded horse bones up to fifteen per cent of the total assemblages. At Blewburton hill fort, only ten miles to the east, a series of four ceremonial pony burials were found. Whether the horse was free-living or trained for traction, riding or chariots is more difficult to prove. The dip slope at the western end of the downs, divided by linear ditches, was certainly suitable for ranching and this could have been supervised by herdsmen on horseback. What seems undoubted is the deep respect accorded to the horse in Iron Age society and the subsequent and extraordinary tradition of scouring the figure shows that this admiration transcended time. It has yet to be demonstrated that the horse occupied a comparable place in Bronze Age society.

One other finding of Miles's diggers is that the horse sits in a ritual landscape peppered with barrows, graves, cremations. This bleak, high place must have reverberated with the cries of mourners, the crackling of sacrificial fires and the thud of earth piled over corpses. The horse figure, freshly cleaned at intervals, must in its heyday have been only one shining white feature among a group of chalk mounds, visible from afar.

The future of the Uffington White Horse is more hopeful than that of the other two ancient monuments. That it has survived to its present state is the result of local care over the centuries. The regular scouring with the ceremonies associated with it was recorded by Thomas Hughes, author of *Tom Brown's Schooldays*. The fair, games and cheese rolling still flourishing in Browne's day, were redolent of the ancient ceremonies. They reflected a degree of local care and commitment vital to encourage for a monument if it is to be saved from a future conserved in aspic. Secondly, the White Horse and its context, 200 acres of farmland around, is owned by the National Trust. They are determined to restore this portion of Downland to its unimproved state, that is to say to encourage its flowers and herbage to recover after decades of neglect and destruction by fertilizers. Lastly, they have laid out the main car park for visitors to this much loved site about 600 metres away downslope – so they will have to walk from afar, keeping the motor car, that powerful element of destruction, at a safe distance. With careful husbanding of the fragile turf covering, visitor erosion, one hopes, will be kept to within bounds.

A less desirable method of preserving these prehistoric ritual and burial monuments is to excavate them (thereby destroying them) even if it is followed by recording and publication. This means in effect to create a paper record of a three dimensional monument. A proposed road widening (which never happened) led to the excavation of Ascott-under-Wychwood long barrow, towards the southern edge of the Cotswolds, between 1966–71. A number of the finds and the major stones of the burial chamber were brought to the County Museum headquarters (as it then was) at Woodstock and erected in the form of dramatic displays. The long barrow at Ascott was aligned east–west and trapezoidal, 7–16 metres wide, about 50 metres long and 1.5 metres high. It had an impressive façade built of well laid limestone drystone walling. Its construction was in twenty-one bays, each defined by hurdling or stone partitions and is thought to have involved some 7,000 man hours in its building. The burials were in two pairs of opposed burial chambers made of local limestone slabs which lay transversely across the barrow two-thirds of the way down. Ascott was a communal grave with adults and children, both male and female, buried there. All shared in common the fact that the bones when buried were de-fleshed or at least represented only portions of the corpse. This implies that they had previously been exposed for a considerable time. Forty-seven individuals were represented and Humphrey Case, who has studied the evidence closely, concludes that 'the burials were thus as it were token deposits in a co-operative shrine.' Despite the lapse of twenty-four years no detailed report has ever appeared of this important excavation. Was this digging without a sense of responsibility? One difficulty is that excavations were undertaken at public expense without making provision for the considerable work involved in preparing the results for publication.

The Ascott barrow forms part of a much wider group of tombs in the west and south-west of England. A particularly well preserved one is at Wayland's Smithy, excavated by Pigott and Atkinson in 1963. Most visitors approach it by walking west along the Ridgeway from Uffington White Horse and Hill Fort, or east from Ashbury. It was surrounded in the eighteenth century by a plantation mound and a clump of beeches so it can be spotted miles away. Under the beeches is the façade of gigantic sarsen stones, derived from the broken crust of hard siliceous sandstone which overlay the chalk. Excavation has established that there were two periods of construction. The first barrow was aligned north –south, 54 feet long and 27 feet wide standing 6 feet high. At least fourteen individuals, mostly young adults, had been buried in a wooden chamber after their corpses had disintegrated by exposure to the outside. Three leaf-shaped arrowheads were found with the bones. Two posts, one at each end of the chambers, may have protruded above the surface of the barrow acting as markers. The monument was a few decades later enveloped in a more ambitious and architecturally more significant replacement. This was also trapezoidal in shape, 180 feet long and 20–48 feet wide. The earth and rubble were dug from flanking ditches and piled up. A kerb of sarsens bounded it all round and its façade was made, as we have noted, of sarsens. The three burial chambers opening off a short corridor behind the façade contained the interments of eight persons. It is calculated that erecting the façade stones would have required the efforts of thirty-five to fifty people.

Wayland's Smithy, like the Rollright Stones, attracted its fair share of folklore. There is an old tradition that if a groat (a small silver coin) were placed on the capstone of the burial chamber and a horse left to be shod, an invisible blacksmith, Wayland the Smith, would shoe the horse and take the groat. A mile north of Ashbury, the next village to the west is a spot called Snivelling Corner. Wayland is said to have been short of nails one day so he sent his imp Flibbertigibbet to the village to fetch some. The imp tarried, bird's-nesting, and Wayland flung a stone boulder at him. This can still be seen at Snivelling Corner; the imp, whose heel was hit with the stone, went away snivelling!

These communal graves of the Neolithic were succeeded in the Bronze Age in Oxfordshire by circular barrows and ring ditches which are the most frequently found prehistoric survival in the modern landscape. On the Cotswolds, in woodland such as Wychwood and on the chalk downlands in the south, the round burial mounds still stand. In the upper

Thames gravel region only the ditches remain, the mounds themselves have been ploughed flat. These ring ditches show up as dark green circles in fields of ripening corn and they cluster round the earlier large monuments of the Devil's Quoits and the Big Rings at Dorchester.

Sometimes their presence seems to have been respected by later farmers who, for a time at least, left them on the margins of their fields; many of them were re-used, secondary cremations in pots being inserted in their sides. The vast majority were plundered during the eighteenth and nineteenth centuries. Picnic parties of top-hatted gentlemen and crinolined ladies under parasols are known to have 'excavated' several in one day. Nowadays it takes weeks of advanced planning and meticulous investigation by professionals, soil scientists, environmental specialists and trained excavators, to disentangle the complex rituals associated with the construction of these three-thousand-year-old burial mounds. Scheduling them as Ancient Monuments delays their destruction but does not necessarily ultimately protect them from the pressure of development. The linear Bronze Age cemetery at Barrow Hills, Radley is a case in point. Despite valiant attempts to salvage the evidence of these round barrows by amateurs or university-based and professional units, the cemetery has been swallowed up in an orgy of house building of Greater Abingdon. With more forethought and a real will to save our heritage the line of tumuli could well have been integrated into the open spaces which are a necessary part of every housing estate.

The Pre-Roman Iron Age left little behind it in Oxfordshire in the way of visible burial practices. The Romano-British inhabitants were better organized in some ways in their disposal of the dead. They insisted, for instance, that townspeople should be buried outside urban boundaries, such as those of Alchester and Dorchester. Their rural cemeteries, however, were pretty haphazard affairs. Late Roman burials have been found dug into the foot of the outer rampart of the Iron Age hillfort at Castle Hill, Little Wittenham. This lack of cemetery organization is echoed at

Wroxton where the conversion of a barn to living accommodation revealed a collection of disarticulated human bones and three graves. Some strange rituals including decapitation burials were apparent here. It seems certain that the head of one woman was removed after death and placed between the knees.

Worship of the numerous gods in the Roman pantheon was focused round rural shrines and temples. Some of these were sited on hill tops near Iron Age sacred places. Over the last three hundred years farmers have been retrieving Iron Age and Roman artefacts from the fields on a slope overlooking the Anglo-Saxon settlement at Woodeaton, five miles north of Oxford. These bronze objects, to be seen in the Ashmolean Museum, include figurines, possible bits of priestly headdresses, model axes and spears, brooches, bracelets and pins. Some of the axes are engraved with solar signs. Three of the six spears are deliberately bent double. Plaques of bronze and stone and a part inscription all point to the worship of Mars, an agricultural deity as well as a war god. The brooches and the jewellery are small and even child-size, the rings being poor trumpery things. The fact that many of these votive objects are feminine ornaments makes it likely that some of the women were in childbirth. Scrap metal tells us that they were made on the spot rather as the medieval pilgrim badges were fashioned at the place of pilgrimage. This also accounts for the finds being interpreted as the debris of a market or fair. Woodeaton was all these things, temple, workshop and shopping place.

Another sacred complex in the region is known to have been built on the Roman road near the river Ock at Frilford. Here was a considerable rural settlement which actually sported an amphitheatre, perhaps used for drama and religious ceremonies. On the flat meadows near the Noah's Ark public house excavations in 1937–8 recovered the plans of a series of temples. A *cella* or central enclosure twenty-five feet square was surrounded by a portico fifty-five feet externally. Around the area were found large numbers of coins, suggesting votive gifts. The coins were given as a payment (*salutio*) for favour received from the gods after making your request (*nuncupatio*). Only eighty feet away to the south was a second ritual structure, this time a circular building on top of an Iron Age horseshoe-shaped, ditched, penannular enclosure. The Roman builders had evidently dismantled the Iron Age shrine and built directly on top of it. Both Woodeaton and Frilford were on Iron Age tribal boundaries, the former where the Catuvellauni met the Dobunni, and the latter near the junction of the Atrebates and the Belgae. We may also have examples here of the Romanized Celts passing on their new culture to their less Romanized brethren. The Celtic culture was absorbed into the province by integration.

Evidence for a third Romano-Celtic temple site has been recently (1994) strengthened at Lowbury Hill, just north of the Ridgeway, eight kilometres south of Didcot and two kilometres north of Compton village. Of the three, Lowbury is the most accessible to the public. Its surrounding rectangular earthwork with a barrow to the east also provides the visitor with something visible to reflect upon. Excavations by Atkinson in 1915 and by Fulford in 1992 have shown interesting structural features including the fact that the enclosure seems to have been marked out originally by ploughing, a characteristic of Roman temple sites. The bone assemblage supports this; oysters in particular were found in large numbers and this food debris may well have been the remains of ritual meals. But the clincher is the presence, as at Woodeaton, of large numbers of copper alloy artefacts including miniature weapons which again make it likely that among the powers worshipped here was Mars, the God of War, but here a protective agricultural deity. The fact that several tracks and roads met here also makes it possible that, as at Woodeaton there was a market or at least a seasonal or occasional fair at this high spot.

Lowbury is also noteworthy as an example of a place continuing its sacred function well into the next period. An Anglo-Saxon, high-status, tumulus burial stands only fifteen metres to the east of the rectangular temple enclosure. The place name itself refers to both barrow and enclosure. 'Low' is Old English 'hlaw', 'bury' is Old English 'burh' implying that both barrow and temple were visible when the hill was named. The deliberate placing of barrows of the élite (distinguished by rich grave goods including a bronze bowl and spearhead with enamel decorations) next to the visible remains of the Roman past has been claimed by the excavators as demonstrating the association of the descend-ants of the German immigrants with the local past, the 'Romanitas' of the place. This may have given their rule an 'historical legitimacy'. The very unusual finds including the hanging bowl and a spear with Celtic decoration make it just possible that the person buried was a 'British' chieftain. We therefore need to look both ways, into the past and into the future, in studying (and visiting) these temple sites. The Romans had found it advantageous to re-use the sacred sites of the Iron Age for their own purposes. Their successors, Romano-Britons or Anglo-Saxons, or a mixture of the two, similarly adapted Roman shrines and religion to further *their* political ends.

This predilection of the pagan Anglo-Saxon settlers in Oxfordshire for burying their dead in or near the visually prominent earthworks, whether they were hill forts, temples, or barrows of previous occupants of the land, is borne out in a number of examples. Shipton Barrow near Shipton-under-Wychwood, Barrow Hills, Radley, and Dyke Hills, Dorches-ter, less than one kilometre north of the Iron Age Hill Fort at Wittenham Clumps are cases in point. In other areas along the flat alluvial plain of the river Thames burials were placed on the edges of the fields attached to settlements. One is reminded of burials in mid-China stuck out in the country-side; the belief was that the ancestors were watching over the fields. At Eynsham and Cassington, for instance, the Anglo-Saxon cemeteries were on the (later) parish boundaries. Here, the fact that the land was not yet cultivated may have been the decider.

A similar desire to be associated with a previous centre of power may have decided Birinus, the apostle of Wessex in the seventh century, to choose Dorchester-on-Thames as the centre of his See. The Roman town was an excellent communications centre from which to missionarize this part of Wessex and Mercia. It was situated on the main Alchester/ Silchester Roman road at a crossing of the Thames and was the successor of two Early Iron Age foci, Dyke Hills and Wittenham Clumps. There is a distinct possibility that here there was continuity of occupation during the period of the breakdown of Roman administration and the coming of immigrant settlers. Here, Bede tells us, Birinus, a missionary from Italy, baptized Cynegils, king of the West Saxons in AD 635. There may have been more to it than that. Being on the northern edge of Wessex, the choice of Dorchester may have been in the nature of a political statement to the pagan kings of neighbouring Mercia, a statement of intent to convert and maybe to subdue. The current political power bases of the kings of Wessex in the locality were in any case at Benson and Cuddesdon. Nicholas Doggett has suggested interestingly that Dorchester may have been chosen for religious reasons. He hazards a guess that here was a succession of holy place (*locus sanctus*), a *capella memoriae* – commemorating perhaps some forgotten Romano-British martyr – and, finally, a church. The siting of this, the precursor of Dorchester Abbey, was outside the Roman defences. This conforms with canon law, which until Archbishop Cuthbert's time, forbad burial within towns.

The basic missionary work was done by Birinus and the next generation of priests who followed him. Without the ready co-operation and economic support of the kings and their thegnly aristocracy the missionaries would have got nowhere. Minsters began to be founded by kings and ealdormen. These were centrally placed churches near or in royal estates, constructed on a large scale, staffed by groups of clergy and richly endowed. From the eighth to the eleventh centuries they were the leading Christian centres in Oxfordshire and elsewhere in Midland England. Much recent research has been lavished on them and their complicated history is beginning to be unravelled. At Bampton in west

Oxfordshire there was a string of three churches all aligned east–west and within a few hundred metres of one another. The central one, the present parish church, has much Saxon masonry and was likely to have been cruciform in shape. It was surrounded by an oval-shaped earthwork within which was the graveyard and probably the houses of the officiating clergy. The church and its possessions were granted by the Crown to the cathedral of Exeter. Bampton is near the river Thames at Radcot. Other early minster churches such as Eynsham and Abingdon were actually sited on waterfronts which were useful for the movement of building materials and perhaps for taking part in trade. The valleys of the rivers Cherwell, Evenlode and Windrush were favoured sites for other minsters, but water communications do not seem very practical in their cases. A stone-bearing barge needs a draught of up to three feet if it is not to drag the bottom. These streams, even in their Dark Age state of flood, are most unlikely to have afforded leeway. However, Cropredy, Bloxham and Adderbury all became major manorial centres of the Bishops of Lincoln and the Earls of Mercia after the Norman Conquest, and despite our lack of knowledge of the date or circumstances of their foundations, they seem to have had significant minster churches in pre-Conquest Oxfordshire.

One important feature of these minsters is that they became deeply involved in burial practice. They contained the graves of what have been termed 'the very special dead'. These exercised a magnetic attraction, and the cemeteries containing clustering burials were often more extensive than the present churchyard. At Shipton-under-Wychwood, graves, carbon 14 dated to the ninth or tenth centuries, have been found underlying the prebendal house adjoining the church. It shows that the cemetery was much larger in the pre-Conquest period. As chapels and parish churches were founded, pressure inevitably grew to decentralize burial rights. This was resisted since mortuary dues were important sources of revenue to Anglo-Saxon clergy, but in the end churches succeeded in negotiating burial rights. In the meantime, there was much corpse portage along the 'coffin ways' between outlying settlements and the mother church. Such a coffin way is pointed out between Dry Sandford and Besselsleigh church. Others converge on the minster church of Faringdon in the Vale of the White Horse. The inhabitants of Chimney and Shifford petitioned as late as c.1485 John Arundel, Dean of Exeter, 'that they might have a separate burial ground at Shifford. They had been accustomed to carry their corpses to Bampton; the muddy road was frequently inundated'. The Jews in Oxford, incidentally, used 'Deadman's Walk' between their homes in St Aldate's along the south face of the city wall of Oxford to the Jews Burying Ground in what became four centuries later the Botanic Garden of the University.

The next stage in the evolution of Christianity was the spread of proprietary churches over the landscape. This seems to have taken the form of a great surge of building in the late tenth, eleventh and first part of the twelfth centuries. Some were manorial chapels built next door to the noble and thegnly houses; some were the result of groups of people getting together to raise a church near the centre of settlement; some were devotional deeds, the foundations of proselytizing bishops or reforming abbots ensuring pastoral provision for their rich and scattered estates.

What were these late Saxon and Norman churches like? There are very few surviving as built. Langford is perhaps the best, probably the result of the patronage of Aelfsige of Faringdon, an Englishman who had taken the opportunity of accumulating a substantial estate after the Norman Conquest. He was trusted by William I, and Langford church is an interesting example of the Saxo-Norman overlap built by English craftsmen who had begun to assimilate the new style of the conquerors with their own traditional building methods. Hence the design of the late eleventh-century tower which combines Anglo-Saxon pilaster strips and double-splayed windows with the semi-circular arches and roll mouldings of the Romanesque style from Normandy. A dignified stone-sculptured rood also decorated the church. Cumnor church is another interesting example. Here there was a three-cell Norman building with a massive west tower, which probably housed a tribune gallery and was attached to a smallish nave, and an apsidal end (apsidal means semi-circular in plan). Its graveyard originally extended west under the grange which the abbots of Abingdon built in the fourteenth century. For a virtually untouched Norman church of the first generation after the Conquest, we need to visit Swyncombe in the Oxfordshire Chilterns. The name is evocative. The short steep-sided 'cumb' or valley associated with swine, which pannaged the surrounding woodland. It is small, aisleless, apsidal ended, of flint with herring-bone masonry. A grander Chiltern church probably at least fifty years later in date is at Checkendon. This is a three-cell building again, with apsidal end and built of flint. The interior has two Norman arches leading from the aisleless nave into the rectangular quire and semi-circular sanctuary. Here, early thirteenth-century paintings in red ochre outline on a white ground portray a procession of apostles with Christ in Majesty above.

The finest Norman church in richness of decoration and quality of design is found at Iffley on the outskirts of Oxford. This was built c.1170–80 by the St Remy family who held the manor in the second half of the twelfth century. It is difficult to say where the building material came from, so devastatingly complete has been the re-casing of the walls in the twentieth century, but the font apparently hies from Tournai in Belgium as did some of the internal wall shafts, so no expense was spared. There is much sculpture in Iffley church; some has apparent links with Reading Abbey, a royal foundation of Henry I only twenty-five miles to the east. Iffley benefited by being the target of learned and ecclesiologically-minded architects in the nineteenth century who made a creditable attempt to restore the crumbling design of the west front. Robert Bliss, R.C. Hussey and J.C. Buckler were all involved. In sum, Iffley is probably one of the richest visual experiences to be gained in Oxfordshire outside the city. It demonstrates well the advantages England gained by being drawn by the Normans into the European orbit.

The Jews in Oxford were a small but important element in the town's life from the late eleventh to the end of the thirteenth centuries. They congregated in St Martin's and St Aldate's parishes on both sides of St Aldate's Street so, in effect, in the hub of the town's commercial quarter. They acquired a burial ground beyond the Eastgate on both sides of the high road leading out of the city. Much of it was granted away, including 'the garden of the Jews' by Henry III in 1231 to the Hospital of St John but the Jews retained their burial ground on the later site of the Botanic Garden until their general expulsion in Edward I's reign in 1291. Recent excavations at Magdalen College exposed structures at ground-floor level that related to the hospital which occupied the site before the college. A long, beautifully built, stone-arched culvert also came to light underneath with steps leading down. This was tentatively identified by Brian Durham as part of the hospital, providing a source of healing water for the infirm, but alternatively it may be suggested that it is twelfth century in date and belongs to the phase when the ground was used as the Jewish cemetery. It bears a number of resemblances to the *mikveh*, or ritual cleansing place for mourners, who would need to wash, preferably in running water, before and after consigning a corpse to the earth. Only one other such medieval Jewish ritual bath has been found in England at Jacob's Well, Bristol. This has steps, a source of running water, and is built with care, copying a prototype such as the *mikveh* in Cologne. A clinching message in Hebrew, inscribed above the well at Bristol, is missing at Oxford, but otherwise the similarities of the structures at Oxford and Bristol are sufficiently close to merit further examination.

We have seen how the minsters provided the first effective network of Christian communities from which a rash of parish churches and chapels developed in the period AD 1000–1200. By this date Oxfordshire had acquired over 300 parish churches and the parochial organization that went with them. Some parishes were subdivisions of the *parochiae* of the minsters. Their inhabitants still owed dues, such as a proportion of the tithes, soul scot (mortuary fees) and church scot, to the mother churches. In many parishes the boundaries were co-terminous with Anglo-Saxon lordly estates. Some respected the boundaries of pre-existing features such as roads, rivers and the limits of the shire itself. Much investigation of parish boundaries remains to be researched.

The parochial organization of Oxfordshire after William I's removal of the See of Dorchester-on-Thames to Lincoln was the responsibility of the Bishops of Lincoln. This huge diocese, consisting of nine and a half counties, meant that Oxfordshire was remote from the centre of the bishop's power. It may have favoured the growth of an independent university of Oxford. The bishop, however, was still a great feudal landowner in the county. Domesday Book records that he possessed the manors of Dorchester (ninety hides), Banbury and Cropredy (each fifty hides) and the manors of Thame and Milton (sixty and forty hides). He had a castle built at Banbury and a house called Bishop's Court at Dorchester. As a tenant-in-chief of the king, the eleventh-century bishops owned the heavy burden of finding sixty knights for the king's service. These duties as landowner and feudal lord were uneasily combined with being shepherd of his very scattered flock. Bishops were responsible for the building and dedication of churches, the appointment and scrutiny of the suitability of parochial clergy, their discipline and the elimination of clerical marriage through the operation of the episcopal courts. They had to combine this with incessant travelling round their diocese, service to the king (they had a residence in the Old Temple, London) and obedience to the Papacy. A final problem was exercising control over the various religious houses, many of which claimed exemption from their jurisdiction.

As influential as the lords and bishops of late Anglo-Saxon and early Norman Oxfordshire in founding and building of churches in the landscape were the houses of the various monastic orders. Monasticism had come to the area in the eighth century with St Frideswide's minster at Oxford. This was restarted twice, once as a college of secular priests and secondly as a house of Augustinian canons. The present church, now the cathedral of the diocese of Oxford, created by Henry VIII as a sop to ecclesiastical opinion after the unprecedented destruction and vandalism of the dissolution of the monasteries, contains the most substantial monastic remains in the county. It was his second choice. Henry's preferred site for a cathedral had been the Abbey of Oseney. Instead, he made the last Abbot of Oseney the first Bishop of Oxford and installed him at St Frideswide's. Much of the central portion of the church, including half the nave, dates from a rebuilding after a fire of *c.*1180. It was savagely damaged by Cardinal Wolsey who began to take down the nave to make way for his megalomaniac cloister quadrangle. This, with its vaulting shafts and buttress bases open to the sky, was never completed. Nor were his ambitions realized for an immense chapel planned to emulate King's College, Cambridge, on the north side of the quadrangle. The truncated cathedral became the chapel of Christ Church, known as 'Aedes Christi', or 'The House' (of God) to initiates.

Christ Church Cathedral has an uncommonly richly wrought interior. It is the smallest of the English cathedrals, but its stained glass and monuments of the thirteenth to sixteenth centuries are of excellent quality. The early four-teenth-century shrine of St Frideswide, now partly recon-structed (without the rich piece of medieval metalwork acting as a feretory for the body of the saint), was on the honorific north side, set in the middle of an aisle under painted and figured vaults. It was guarded from a lofty wooden watching chamber and pilgrims could perambulate it unencumbered and come near enough to the saintly relics to touch them. This no doubt brought a pleasing trickle of offerings to defray the expenses of the building programme. This pro-gramme included the thirteenth-century Chapter House. Here, under the groined vault and lit by lancet windows, I used to attend the aged Regius Professor of Ecclesiastical History, Canon Claude Jenkin's lectures on the papacy of Innocent III. Unfortunately, as the course proceeded and the number of undergraduates dwindled to two or so, the Canon reluctantly put away his notes and stumped off, not to return. He had an original method of storing the overflow of his books, stuffed between the balusters of the staircase in his house. I recall the profundity of his learning and his total absorption in the minutiae of his subject.

The site of Christ Church slopes quite steeply down to the Thames plain, a reminder that it originally bounded on the Trill Mill stream, one of the many braided courses of the river. The river was the main line of communication in tenth- and eleventh-century Oxfordshire. Along its bank sprang up two Benedictine abbeys, those of Eynsham (in 1094) and Abingdon (originally a seventh-century foundation and re-founded in 954). Abingdon was by far the most richly endowed monastery in the upper Thames Valley with extensive estates, mostly in the part of Oxfordshire which was attached to the county after 1974. Some impression of the magnificence of Abingdon Abbey can be gained from the embattled fifteenth-century gateway which stands next to the medieval church of St Nicholas. Such a fortification was necessary for security after the severe riots of 1327. The monks had asked the Crown for permission to crenellate (i.e. to put a wall round the monastery). Of the church, nothing remains above ground, although the plan was established by mapping the robber trenches left by the post-Dissolution demolition contractors. Excavation also produced a grid of walls to the north of the Abbey church which are best explained as representing the base of a bell tower, conceivably of timber, which may have been a victim of the riots of 1327. Abingdon Abbey is still worth a visit. The administrative buildings of the Abbey retain some fireplaces and a splendid chimney which dates to the fourteenth century, a rare survival. These remnants have been restored as a theatre and the monastic mill as a restaurant.

At the other end of the monastic scale was Godstow Nunnery, founded in 1133 by a widow, Lady Ediva, who spent a period in solitary retreat before being inspired in a vision to set up a nunnery for religious gentlewomen. She chose a tongue of higher land above the floodable Thames pastures separated by four miles of Port Meadow from the town of Oxford. The plan is unusual. Instead of the standard monastic cloister there were communal halls. The nunnery community in fact seems to have been fragmented into smaller households of women – the so called *familiae*. The sense of separation from the outside world was secured by a substantial enclosure wall which survives. In one corner of the inner court is a chapel, two-storeyed at the west end, which was probably the nuns' chapel. To the north was a doorway through the enclosure wall which may have admitted priests. Godstow was an upmarket nunnery, catering for high-ranking religious women. It attracted the interest of Henry II, who allowed the body of his beloved mistress, the Fair Rosamund, to be buried here in the church. Such was the unseemly interest of pilgrims that Bishop Hugh of Lincoln, whose See included Oxfordshire, insisted that the body be exhumed and buried outside 'for she was a harlot'. Godstow, like many nunneries, was not well endowed. The nuns had to rely on family support to eke out exiguous rents from the conventual estates.

The buildings stand by the banks of the Thames looking rather forlorn. The main enclosure is unfortunately used as a cattle yard and recently damage was done, with a coffin lid being fractured. As a noteworthy nunnery it needs loving care and attention if it is not to suffer further at the hands of vandals and other animals.

The biggest contrast with Godstow in terms of size and numbers of religious and wealth was Oseney, one kilometre to the west of Oxford. I am reminded of this great Abbey, the second richest in the county after Abingdon, every time I come to Oxford by train from Paddington. When we are a few hundred yards from our destination the train grinds to a halt. I glance up and sure enough it has stopped outside the municipal cemetery which now occupies the site of the monastic church of Oseney. A moment for reflection about the transitoriness of human aspirations. The tombs of Victorian Oxonians now stand in grassy seclusion where once the magnificent Augustinian abbey reared. When one penetrates the maze of derelict industrial buildings and brick terraces which now cover the site there are other clues: a portion of a barn with a fine fifteenth-century queen-post roof, several walls of Headington stone, a rebuilt four-centred arch, architectural fragments now green with moss, which turn out to be vaulting bosses, while the stone-lined revetments to the river frontage are also likely to date from the monastic phase. Our only concept of what Oseney looked like is a scene painted in the background of a portrait of the first bishop in Christ Church Cathedral, and a view drawn by John Aubrey. It is a sad end for a building which might have come down to us as one of the great post-medieval cathedrals.

Monasteries were among the prime promoters of churches on their estates. Whereas the older abbeys like Abingdon and Eynsham were the possessors of huge landed estates given to them by Anglo-Saxon kings and confirmed by Norman kings, other monasteries, newly founded in the eleventh and twelfth centuries were often endowed with pre-existing churches and the lands supporting their fabrics and priests. Lordly donors, penitentially disposed after a roistering and bloodstained life, handed over some of their proprietary churches with the glebe (church lands), the right to levy tithes and advowson (the right to appoint the priest) to monasteries. The monks thus 'appropriated' resources originally designed for the support of the parish church. Sometimes an Anglo-Norman lord would endow a monastery near his continental home with English church lands and rights. The Arsic family, Norman lords of Cogges, near Witney, in this way endowed Fécamp Abbey in Normandy with the church and glebe and Cogges thus became an 'alien' priory. But it was not as simple as this. Cogges church had begun as a chapel of Eynsham Abbey. In 1238 the Abbey took the crop of four acres of demesne land in return for allowing the right of burial in Cogges churchyard. Monasteries on both sides of the channel tenaciously held on to their rights.

Churches also grew up at the gates of monasteries to cater

for the parochial needs of the settlement servicing the community of monks. Eynsham parish church began in this way. It is first recorded in the twelfth century and is dedicated to St Leonard, a saint favoured by the Benedictines. From the mid thirteenth century the Abbey appointed vicars and went on doing so up to the Dissolution. Vicars performed the pastoral duties in place of (Latin *vicarius*) the Abbey. They were paid a small stipend. The church of St Nicholas was similarly created at the gateway to Abingdon Abbey. No doubt such sitings siphoned off would-be pilgrims as well as relieving the monks of the necessity of providing spiritual services for the parish in their more secluded venue.

At Cassington the monastic connection came after the church was built by a lay lord. It was founded by Geoffrey de Clinton in 1123 within the parish of Eynsham Abbey, which was keen to retain burial rights. The fine ashlar masonry, well designed doorways and effective groined vault of the chancel at Cassington betokens a builder who had a good grasp of the new Norman style. The lords of the manor in the fourteenth century, the Montagu family, are likely to have paid for the upper part of the tower and the spire. Eynsham Abbey again had the right of appointing vicars of Cassington up to the Reformation.

In other places in the county churches are associated with defensive sites. Oxford is a case in point. Here the Anglo-Saxon burh is ringed round with churches sited at the principal gates. St Michael at the Northgate retains its late Saxon tower. St Mary the Virgin is on the site of the former east gate before the late Saxon extension of the walled town eastwards. There was formerly a church at St Michael Southgate, while St Ebbes and St Peter le Bailey are both on the putative line of the former burh. They seem to originate in some form of dual function – defensive capability and pastoral activity. Churches, particularly their strong towers, doubled up as fortifications. They are, moreover, found closely connected with moated sites and motte and bailey castles. A classic example is the juxtaposition of the church and earthwork castle at Middleton Stoney. Here, in the early

1970s, Trevor Rowley of Oxford University carried out an excavation involving several hundred adult education students, making a major contribution in creating an archaeologically aware public. He found that the church was contemporary with the earthwork castle which had a tower whose base lay hidden under the bank. The two towers, church and castle were a visual reminder of the alliance of lay and ecclesiastical power. The parish church of Cogges, too, stands next to an eroded ringwork which enclosed the Arsic manor house. A quarter of the moated area has been gobbled up by the extended churchyard containing late nineteenth- and twentieth-century inhabitants of the enlarged village. Again, church and manor house stand together.

Churches, therefore, could be given away to continental religious communities or were built to serve as defensive outposts in the fight for survival against opposing lords or the Devil himself. A church like Barford St Michael has an interesting dedication and location. St Michael was the archangel who did battle with the Devil, represented as a dragon in the Book of Revelation (Rev. 12: 7–9). His cult in the Middle Ages is frequently associated with high places and as many as 686 churches were dedicated to him throughout England. He is shown as weighing souls in wall-paintings at Swalcliffe and South Leigh. The church at Barford is perched on a steep hillock. Such high locations are so popular (Garsington and Cumnor spring to mind) that they colour the immemorial pictures of the English countryside we all have in our mind's eye.

An example of a country chapel given to an Oxford monastery is Elsfield, on the heights only three miles to the west of the town. Here, in 1122, Henry I gave the chapel to St Frideswide's Priory. Hugh of Elsfield confirmed the grant and the canons reconstructed the church. The chancel arch dates from 1170–80 and was built by a man who was well aware of the work being currently done in the nave and crossing of the priory church. Elsfield has the same stumpy cylindrical responds and fleshy-leaved capitals as are found in the cathedral. The appearance of the church was changed to a striking Early English design in the thirteenth century; it was rededicated to St Thomas à Becket and reconsecrated in 1273 by Reynold Bishop of Cloyne. The consecration crosses are painted on the walls. I came here in 1952, met the aged vicar Walter Aste, and received a commission to write a guide-book of the church provided I could finance it! I visited Lady Tweedsmuir, who was still living in Elsfield Manor after the death of her husband John Buchan twelve years earlier, and was given £5 towards the publication fund as well as an invitation to tea. John Buchan's bones lie under a flat circular slab in the highest part of the churchyard. I was shown the manuscript of *Cromwell*, clearly written in pen and ink in a quick, flowing hand without emendations. Buchan used to travel daily between Elsfield and London by train; he managed the firm of Thomas Nelson, the publishers. A highly popular novelist in my father's generation, Buchan's clean-jawed officer-material Englishmen, such as his hero Richard Hannay, had less of an appeal to National Service conscripts such as myself.

Parish churches in Oxfordshire reflect in their evolving fabric changing liturgical fashions. Excavation has established elsewhere that small apsidal-ended chancels were much more frequently found in Norman churches than the present distribution suggests. There was in fact a remarkable chancel rebuilding programme lengthening, heightening and making rectilinear the eastern end component of parish churches. This was in response to a move towards greater liturgical complexity in the early thirteenth century and an increased tendency to separate the priest from the people. It is emphasized by the provision of piscinas (drains for washing the sacred vessels), aumbries (cupboards for locking them away) and sedilias (stone seating for the clergy), usually in the south wall of the chancel. These changes can all be studied in the little country church at Woodeaton in the Cherwell valley near Oxford. Here there has been a surprising succession of buildings not all of which were necessarily churches. The late Saxon church was succeeded by a small Norman building slightly to the north and more truly aligned east–west. This in turn was reconstructed in the thirteenth century to bring it up to date liturgically speaking. It has lancet windows throwing a more dramatic light on the altar than in Norman interiors. A late medieval wooden screen separates off the chancel (priest) from the nave (people). It is, however, pierced with viewing holes so the devout inhabitants of Woodeaton could spy the priest elevating the host (the sacred wafer, the body of Christ). If he did this with his back to the people (i.e. facing east) they would be dazzled by the sight of his cope. Medieval churches were so denuded of their fittings, images, stained glass and wall decorations by the Reformation that we only have a very partial understanding of their former richly wrought interiors. The disappearance and destruction of metalwork shrines and vestments is almost total. The Steeple Aston cope, dating from 1310–40, is the sole remaining piece of medieval English embroidery (the famous *Opus Anglicanum*) from Oxfordshire. It is worked with barbed quatrefoils composed of oak and ivy branches enclosing scenes of the martyrdom of saints. The most delectable feature is the little angels playing musical instruments on horseback. The cope, like most medieval ecclesiastical vestments, was sliced up to make an altar frontal for a Protestant communion table. It now spends its life in the Victoria and Albert Museum, London. An indication of what has been lost in terms of rich metalwork is the Thame hoard, medieval ecclesiastical rings belonging to the Cistercian abbots of Thame Abbey and now in the Ashmolean Museum.

Destruction of elaborate decorative schemes was less complete during the Protestant Reformation than is sometimes imagined. Some Nottingham alabaster retables were sold abroad and others buried to be recovered by a later antiquarian-minded age. Such are the three panels in Yarnton church presented by Alderman Fletcher in the nineteenth century and said to have come from St Edmund Hall. As the winds raised by the Reformation began to subside, collectors such as John Tradescant began to collect alabasters and other ecclesiastical objects as curiosities. There are panels in the Ashmolean Museum (see plate section) representing the martyrdom of St Erasmus by the peculiarly gruesome method of winding out his entrails using a windlass. The saint lies prone on a plank with his mitre firmly on his head. Also a crowded crucifixion scene with plenty of colour still adhering: red, blue, green and gold showing that the translucent beauty of the stone was largely hidden in the Middle Ages. Most interesting is a head of St John the Baptist carved on a charger, with Christ issuing from the sepulchre, wearing a crown of thorns beneath. The panel is in its original wooden housing but the doors are missing. Such figurative scenes would have been set in a heavy wooden framework and would have provided a lively backing for an altar. St John's Head, on the other hand, is more likely to have been part of the furnishing of a private chapel or oratory. The bright colours with which these alabaster panels were decked were also used to heighten the more usual earthen pigments used by rural artists to cover the walls of parish churches. Oxfordshire has two splendid examples of almost complete schemes of iconographic decoration, at South Newington and Chalgrove. They have survived virtually intact under the whitewash layers of the Protestant iconoclasts who carried out the royal injunctions in the reign of Edward VI to deface these images of Catholic and papistical religion.

Chalgrove's sequence is particularly interesting. The church itself is dedicated to the Assumption of the Blessed Virgin Mary and therefore is an instance of the growing popularity of the cult of the Virgin in the twelfth to fourteenth centuries. The human traits of Mary were emphasized at the time and an accretion of apocryphal stories was generated. Hence, in addition to the complete life cycle of Christ in fifteen scenes from the Nativity to the Ascension on the north wall, there is a series on the Death of the Virgin on the south wall. The east wall shows the conclusion of the life of Christ including the Harrowing of Hell, the Resurrection and the Ascension, while the south wall also shows the Last Judgement.

This last scene was more commonly displayed in the best didactic position, over the chancel arch, symbolically at the junction of the nave (the world) and the chancel (heaven). At North Leigh, Combe, Cropredy and Hornton are representations of the Last Judgement. Christ is usually shown enthroned on a rainbow displaying his wounds. His full-face, seated posture, reminds one of the images of kings seated on thrones on royal seals. On Christ's right, the blessed are led off by angels to heaven. At his feet, the dead rise from their graves. St Michael is there weighing souls (shown as small, shivering, half-naked praying figures) and St Mary intervenes on behalf of souls, touching the scales with her rosary to give them the benefit of the doubt. On Christ's left, the damned are led off in droves towards the mouth of hell, prodded by demons and exposed to tortures. At Beckley, on the nave wall, there is a picture of the Virgin (faceless) and some sadistic details of souls in torment, being trussed-up and spitted like chickens in the kitchen. Often the kitchen metaphor, with devils fishing for souls boiling in torment with meat hooks is seen in this crude but vigorous art.

Great strides have been made recently in the discovery, technique, iconography and understanding of the conservation of wall and panel paintings. In the 1930s the doyen of mural painting was Professor E.W. Tristram, whose spirited watercolour copies succeeded in capturing the fleeting and scaling images of medieval wall painting. Unfortunately this was not matched by an understanding of the chemistry of conservation. Too often wax was applied to the surface, which trapped water behind it and caused the painting to deteriorate as the plaster rotted. With powerful solvents it is now possible to remove the layer of painting from a wall completely and remount it on a firmer backing. This is where the plaster covering the wall surface is too badly decayed. William Morris inveighed against the vandalistic removal of medieval plastered wall surfaces in his 'anti scrape' campaign, but it came too late to save very many church interiors during the mid-Victorian period. Churches were scraped down and repointed, leaving the bare masonry which gathered dust and darkened the interiors. More damage was wreaked by the Victorian vicars and their compliant architects than by the

Reformers of the sixteenth and seventeenth centuries. E. Clive Rouse is an example of someone who treats medieval and Renaissance wall and wood decorations in a more feeling way. It is one of my clearest and dearest memories to have helped the portly frame of Clive, well into his eighties, up ladders to inspect the wall paintings of Thame, while he expatiated between gasps, about their origins, influences and the methods used by these rustic painters.

Science is called on to carry our understanding beyond dating and meaning. Much is learned by taking tiny flakes of the ancient tempera paint and enclosing them in a resin matrix. This is then thin-sectioned and the resultant sandwich of paint looked at under a microscope. We learn not only the nature of the pigments used, but also the medium employed to bind the colour together. When we discovered painted heraldic beams re-used in the roof of Ducklington Rectory, we submitted samples to the National Gallery, and Dr Ashok Roy informed us that the paint had apparently been applied without prior preparation of the surface except where blue paint had been laid over a white ground comprising a mixture of chalk and lead white (a manufactured lead carbonate). Black was a ground wood charcoal. Blue was a dyestuff such as indigo or woad – microscopically indistinguishable. The orange red was red lead. The medium had been wax of some sort. The date was fifteenth-century.

The pigments used most frequently in medieval wall paintings are the so called earth colours, red and yellow ochre. The source of this was on Shotover Hill. Dr Plot in 1677 described the ten kinds of earth enclosing these deposits. The poorer quality ochre was soaked, beaten into cakes and dried on trestles. It was then used in the seventeenth and eighteenth century to paint the waisted sides and wheels of Oxfordshire wagons.

The parish churches of Oxfordshire, as all over England, exhibit a tendency to enlargement or total rebuilding during the fourteenth and fifteenth centuries. Aisles are added to naves, chapels are tacked on to chancels and towers – particularly western towers – are reared, porches protect south doorways. The motivations, patronage and financing of this development are problematical. Certainly Oxfordshire was among the more prosperous shires in Midland England in the early fourteenth century, so the surplus wealth for building was there. Equally certain is the catastrophic fall of population at the time of the Black Death. So there were fewer people to be housed after 1349 and yet the churches in the main got bigger. Some churches, which exhibit total or near total rebuilding in one style, were in the hands of royal, lordly or ecclesiastical patrons who are likely to have defrayed the expense of rebuilding and who would be in touch with the latest stylistic developments. Paradoxically, those with a close connection to a manor house might survive and even enlarge by the addition of family chapels, despite the fact that there were few other houses nearby. Certain churches lost their aisles and a very few were totally ruined and even disappeared. This is likely to have been connected with rural depopulation, resulting in settlement shift and the abandonment of some sites altogether. A church in these circumstances would have no one to care for it.

To flesh out the bare bones of these generalizations some examples are needed. Very many Oxfordshire churches acquired aisles (Latin, *ala*, 'wing') for the first time in the thirteenth century. They were usually added on the north side in the first instance. The reasons for this can be guessed at. The north was considered unlucky and so burials clustered on the south side of the graveyard. A north aisle would disturb fewer graves. The north side was particularly associated with the commemoration of the dead. Here was likely to be the Easter Sepulchre, where parishioners enacted the elaborate Easter ceremonies. Aisles increased the available numbers of altars as well as providing overspill space for increased congregations. With the advent of pews more space would be taken up with furniture and so less was available for people. Witney, Bampton and Thame are among the most complete examples, all having cruciform plans with central towers and aisled naves.

Furthermore, elegant chancels in the Early English style

were added to many churches. They are the local response to the definition of eucharistic doctrine at the Fourth Lateran Council in 1215. The widespread lengthening of chancels placed the priest at a greater distance from his congregation. Among the more elaborate chancels are Stanton Harcourt (with an original screen, one of the earliest pieces of carpentry in the county), Langdon and Uffington. In the last named prototype, additional chapels were built on to the transept arms, all in the new style. Oxfordshire cannot match the profuseness of neighbouring Northamptonshire's broach spires, but Broadwell, Witney, Bampton and Shipton-under-Wychwood have notable examples. The two latter were churches in the hands of rich prebendaries of Exeter and Salisbury Cathedrals respectively.

Looked at generally in the Middle Ages, church building is an index of the surplus wealth of a region. Later, in the Tudor and Stuart periods, successful merchants, financiers and landowners channelled their profits into almshouses, schools and ever larger houses. The medieval economy of the Cotswolds was based on the twin pillars of wool production and clothmaking. Despite fluctuations imposed on the industry by royal taxation and war these upland communities engaged in building on an extravagant scale. Virtually complete remodelling took place at Church Hanborough (c.1399 when a Papal Indulgence was granted to contributors to the church fabric), Eynsham (1450) and Chipping Norton (c.1485). This last bears all the marks of a 'woolchurch' as found in Gloucestershire and East Anglia. Fine ashlar masonry, airily designed arcades, walls of glass and a lofty west tower. The prosperous merchants at Henley-on-Thames, enriched by the London grain trade, were able to indulge *their* burghal pretensions by adding a mighty flint tower and enveloped their prominent church at the bridge crossing with guild chapels.

All this building would not have been possible if there had not been a well organized industry to support it. Master masons need not have contributed great numbers. The Poll Tax of 1380 indicates only twenty-three resident masons out of a craft-working population in Oxford of 456. Their influence was out of all proportion to their numbers; they travelled extensively and their striking advances in structural design were accordingly disseminated widely. They were backed up by an army of quarrymen, carpenters (who were responsible for the scaffolding) and local builders willing to work doggedly and dutifully following another man's design. Many church alterations were simply achieved by the process of plagiarism, copying another church down the road. Often the patrons insisted on it. Make the tower at X similar to the one at Y. Most masons who worked in Oxford during the Middle Ages were local men and this accounts for the strongly vernacular feel to the county's parish churches.

The anonymity of medieval craftsmen is gradually receding as more and more names pop out from the rich records. Richard Winchcombe who served his apprenticeship in the construction of the great manorial barn of New College at Swalcliffe is subsequently thought to have been engaged in works at Broughton, Deddington, Bloxham and the Wilcote chapel at Northleigh, already mentioned. He was undoubtedly employed at Adderbury and was sacked for an over-rich design leading to what his patrons regarded as extravagance in the Divinity Schools at Oxford.

The close connection between the quarry providing the stone with the building process is illustrated by the person of Thomas Prat who figures prominently in the early rolls of Merton College. He was certainly a quarry owner at Wheatley and may have been the designer of the chapel with its intricate geometric tracery. Richard, the mason of Abingdon, acquired his experience building for the Abbey before being involved in the design of the rocketing tower and spire of St Mary the Virgin, Oxford. William Wynford, again an Abingdon Abbey master mason, was responsible for the design (with William of Wykeham) of New College Chapel. Another quarry owner (this time at Headington) was William Orchard who was master mason at Magdalen College in the 1480s. John Beckley, builder of the north transept of Thame, begun in 1442, is another example of someone related to a quarry master of the same name. There seems little reason to disagree with Dr John Harvey when he links areas of stone quarrying with the training of high grade masons.

A master mason would draw on a wide area for his materials. When Adderbury church was equipped with a new chapel in 1413–14 Richard Winchcombe, master mason, visited the quarries at Taynton, twenty miles away, near Burford, for high grade freestone for the quoins, buttresses, mullions and jambs. For the wall stone less choice material could be had by simply opening up a small quarry in the rectory garden. When the Rectorial barn was built at Swalcliffe (1407–9) slate stone was brought from Lower Slaughter, timber for the cruck trusses from Bewdley, Worcestershire and limestone ashlar for the gable ends and ridges from Winchcombe, Gloucestershire. The basic wallstone, beautifully worked blocks of iron-impregnated malmstone, was dug in a linear quarry on site.

The pattern of patronage diversified in the fourteenth and fifteenth centuries. Manorial lords, bishops and the abbots of monasteries who had dominated the church-building field earlier in the Middle Ages are now joined by colleges, prosperous townsfolk and the new and upcoming gentry families. Colleges, which became large landowners, took over the responsibility for building and maintaining churches on their estates. New College, for instance, expended more on the rebuilding of the chancel at Adderbury 1413–14 than its income from the manor. Wallingford, never a large town, acquired no less than twelve churches. The growth of new gentry families led to the construction of family chapels added to the chancel or occupying the aisles. Such building, housing the accumulating stock of ancestral tombs, would have served to validate claims to local power. Hence the Bardolf chapel at Mapledurham, described in a will of 1381–95 as 'new built', and intended for the tomb of Sir Robert Bardolf who died 1395. His brass remains. The Wilcote chapel attached to the north side of the chancel at North Leigh was begun c.1439 by Elizabeth Wilcote as a chantry for her two husbands and two sons. It is attributed by Dr John Harvey to Richard Winchcombe, master mason; it certainly has spectacular fan vaulting and an elaborate alabaster tomb with effigies of the knightly figure of Sir William Wilcote and his wife. A third example of a family monument which was housed in a newly furbished setting is the effigy and table tomb of Lady Elizabeth Montacute (d. 1354) in St Frideswide's Priory (the cathedral). This is noteworthy because of the extent of the survival of the polychrome decoration and the presence of little figures, weepers or mourners, in fashionable garments standing under arches on the sides of the tomb.

This flood of new building showed no sign of lessening during the last two generations before the Reformation. Wills proliferate, leaving legacies for lights, images, roods, glass. Religious fervour in Oxfordshire expressed itself in the multiplication of altars, the cult of the saints and the commemoration of the dead. An outstanding example illustrating a number of these themes is seen in the tomb of Alice Chaucer, Duchess of Suffolk, in Ewelme church. The context is the church, reconstructed using Suffolk masons in the middle years of the fifteenth century. The elegant Perpendicular arcades, lack of a chancel arch, use of flint flushwork and brick crenellation are all alien to the local county style, but would not be out of place in Suffolk. The tomb is shaped like an altar and is located next to the altar in the position of highest status, as befits the rank of the deceased. The alabaster effigy lies, an idealized image dressed magnificently, with the Order of the Garter on her left arm. Below, seen dimly between the tracery, is a ghastly *memento mori*, 'a wizened cadaver only partly covered by its shroud, a grim example of the late Gothic love of the macabre' (Pevsner). The adjoining chapel, divided from the church by a screen, is full of further tombs of the fifteenth century, brasses, and painted shields, emphasizing the genealogical connections and political affinities of this family. The Suffolks had come far in a century, from being fishmongers in Hull to obtaining the highest office in the land. The Duchess's husband had forfeited public support over his perceived responsibility for the loss of English possessions in France and was intercepted by pirates (or political opponents) and had his head hewed from his shoulders by a lewd fellow in mid channel. Alice had recovered his lands and retained her position. Now backed by the battery of ecclesiastical aids, she waits confidently for the resurrection.

The disposal of the dead with due ceremony, their commemoration and hoped for resurrection were all fundamental to Christian practice and all focused round the graveyard and the church. Graveyards often preceded the earliest timber churches and it is unsurprising that the accumulation of bodies over five hundred or a thousand years has resulted in the radical raising of the ground level. Paths converge on church doors overshadowed by the embanked remains of generations of parishioners. Medieval stone coffins with the outline of the body ending in a key-hole-shaped slot for head and shoulders are found carved out of single blocks. The earliest tombs are usually inside the church, where knightly and ecclesiastical effigies survive from the thirteenth century. Those at Dorchester Abbey and St Frideswide's cathedral are noteworthy. Purbeck marble brought coastwise and upriver from Dorset to Oxfordshire was a favoured material for setting incised sheets of latten (copper alloy hardened with zinc) known popularly as monumental brasses. Alabaster tombs ordered from contractors at Chellerton Derbyshire and Nottingham were brought into Oxfordshire and can be seen at Magdalen College, St Aldate's Church, Oxford, as well as at Wilcote and Ewelme, as already noted. The tomb of Richard Patten, the founder's father, at Magdalen College has had a chequered history. It was originally set up by Bishop William of Waynflete as an act of filial piety in the church of Wainfleet All Saints, Lincolnshire. When this church was taken down in the early years of the nineteenth century it was stored for a time at Wainfleet school, also founded by the Bishop. Magdalen College then transported it to Oxford and erected it in their chapel in a little chantry on the north side as their contribution to the Tractarian revival. In 1980 the tomb was removed from the choir and set up in the ante-chapel in a niche prepared by the early Victorian architect – Cottingham. Here it was cleaned and its details can now be seen clearly. Richard, dressed in the long robe of a merchant, with his purse and rosary, lies prone, fingers pressed together in prayer awaiting the last trump. His head is supported by miniature figures of his two sons, one Bishop William of Winchester, the other John, Dean of Chichester.

Tombs can be moved around. Bodies of saints, too, were frequently translated into places of greater honour within the church or where pilgrims could perambulate more easily. Until the mid nineteenth century the remains of the vast majority of the population lay outside the church, in rows, and subsequently in layers upon the rows beneath. The extension of churches to provide the latest fad, rooms for socializing, coffee shops and lavatories, inevitably disturb them. Such remains contain information vital for an under-standing of the health, pathology, stature, and mortality of past populations. They require scientific examination before reverent reburial. The scandalous disturbance of parts of the churchyard at Thame without proper archaeological excava-tion is a blot on Oxfordshire's past.

Occasionally cemeteries are discovered which have previ-ously been forgotten but which pour light on important events in the county's history. The revolutionary nature of the events in the Civil War was highlighted by the discovery of a cemetery at Abingdon. The north–south alignment of the 250 burials shows a departure from normal Anglican rite (east–west) because such cemeteries no longer needed a Bishop's licence during the period of the Commonwealth. The dating was arrived at because one corpse had a musket ball between its ribs. The burial register for 1644–5 contains an entry 'for the burial of nine prisoners from the town gaol'. The burials, in regular rows, were presumably marked above ground. Both sexes and every age were represented, most were buried in coffins (the nails survived) or shrouds (copper pins). One had two Scottish silver shillings of James VI or

Charles I. Burial in churchyards reverted to normal practice with the Restoration of the monarchy in 1660.

As towns grew rapidly larger in the nineteenth century the graveyards surrounding urban churches became overcrowded and overflowing. In 1843 it was reported that every church-yard in Oxford was full and that some, especially St Ebbe's, were offensive to passers by. In 1848 new parish cemeteries were marked out in Oseney, Holywell and Jericho (St Sepulchre's). Holywell lost a bowling green when it acquired this extension to their parish graveyard. The extension of parish graveyards only proved to be a temporary expedient. What was needed (before the ultimate solution, disposal by cremation) was the creation of large urban cemeteries on the fringes of towns. The newly formed Corporation of the City of Oxford bought Rose Hill from Christ Church in 1889 and thirteen acres at Cutteslowe from the Dean and Chapter of Westminster. Banbury did similarly. Its burial board con-ducted its affairs from 1858–97 and raised two chapels on the town side of the cemetery itself on the fringe of the late nineteenth-century built-up area. These chapels were delight-ful examples of late Victorian Gothic, with portes-cochères, gable-end bell turrets, receding buttresses and steep-pitched roofs with alternate bands of blue and red tiles capped with a spiky ridge. One was taken down in 1978.

This discussion of Religion and Ritual has taken us from the Neolithic of c.3800 BC to the late Victorian period. The Nonconformist contribution has been totally ignored, but that is not to say that it is uninteresting in its own way. A pair of adult students of mine, Mr and Mrs Eustace of Kirtling-ton, carried out a major recording job of the fast vanishing Nonconformist chapels of the county in the late 1970s. Their work can be studied in the County Sites and Monuments Record. Many of the buildings themselves have been con-verted into other uses, residential, commercial and commu-nal. The twenty-first century is going to have to find a solution for what to do with the crumbling fabric of Oxfordshire's churches and chapels in an age of faithlessness.

The City of London has shown the way with its flexible approach to alternative uses.

One regrettable but irrefutable conclusion emerges from this study of the present state of Oxfordshire's landscape. It is that the historical heritage is in mortal danger, due to neglect, ignorance and an insensate search for profit. Although the legal framework now insists that recording the past of a site or a building is a necessary precursor to development, there are no grounds for complacency. Each time an excavation takes place, each time a listed building is altered, there is a diminution of the total archaeological resource. The past cannot be re-run; it is a non-regenerating asset. The paradox is that at the very moment when the public is begining to understand the nature of the riches of the past that surrounds them these riches are being plundered and destroyed. In return, fragments of the past are packaged up and sold to us. Theme parks proliferate; old buildings in the way of 'progress' are taken down and moved into open air museums, as if they were endangered species in zoos. The natural environment is subect to a similar threat. Amidst prairies of monocultured grain we are offered small oases of nature reserves.

There are also grounds for optimism. Powerful lobbies such as the National Trust, English Heritage and the Ramblers Association are assembling. Underpinning their efforts is a conviction that knowledge about the past is a life enhancing source of power.

Bibliography

Chapter I

Ager D.V. *et alia Geologists' Association Guides No 36: The Cotswold Hills* 1973

Arkell W.J. *The Geology of Oxford* Oxford 1947

Bridgeland D.R. *Quaternary of the Thames* London 1994

Buckingham C.M. and Roe D.A. *A Preliminary Report on the Stanton Harcourt Channel Deposits (Oxfordshire England)* unpublished report 1995

Buckland W. *The Life and Correspondence Of* Ed. by Mrs Gordon, London 1894

Edmonds J.M., Sandford K.S. and Beckinsale R.P. 'Geology and Physiography' in Martin A.F. and Steel R.W. *The Oxford Region* Oxford 1954

Jarvis M.G. and Hazelden J. *Soils in Oxfordshire* Newton Abbot 1982

Jenkins P. *Geology and the Buildings of Oxford* Oxford Polytechnic 1988

Jones R.L. and Keen D.H. *Pleistocene Environments in the British Isles* London 1993

Macrae R.J. 'Palaeolithic Artifacts from Stanton Harcourt' *Oxoniensia* LII 1987 pp. 179–81

McKerrow W.S. and Kennedy W.J. *Geologists' Association Guides No. 3 The Oxford District* 1973 (2nd edition)

Oxfordshire County Council *Oxfordshire Minerals and Waste Local Plan Deposit Draft* Oxford 1993

Phillips J. *Geology of Oxford and the Valley of the Thames* Oxford 1871

Plot R. *The Natural History of Oxfordshire* Oxford 1676

Roe D.A. 'The Palaeolithic Archaeology of the Oxford Region' *Oxoniensia* LIX 1994 pp. 1–15

Woodward H.B. *Stanford's Geological Atlas of Great Britain and Ireland* London 1913

Young A. *General View of the Agriculture of Oxfordshire* Newton Abbot 1969

Chapter II

Alcock N.W. and Barley M.W. 'Medieval Roofs with Base-Crucks and Short Principals' *Antiquaries Journal* LII 1972 Part 1 pp. 132–69

Allen T.G. and Robinson M.A. *Mingies Ditch Hardwick-with-Yelford, Oxon* Oxford University Committee for Archaeology 1993

Allen T. 'Abingdon' in *Current Archaeology* No. 121, XI, 1, pp. 24–8

Allen T.G. 'A Medieval Grange of Abingdon Abbey at Dean Court Farm, Cumnor, Oxon' *Oxoniensia* LIX 1994 pp. 219–448

Allison K.J., Beresford M.W. and Hurst J.G. *The Deserted Villages of Oxfordshire* Leicester 1965

Barclay A., Gray M. and Lambrick G. *Excavations at the Devil's Quoits, Stanton Harcourt, Oxfordshire, 1972–3 and 1988* Oxford 1995

Biddle M. 'The Deserted Medieval Village of Seacourt' *Oxoniensia*, XXVI/XXVII 1961–2 pp. 70–201

Blair W.J. *Anglo Saxon Oxfordshire* Stroud 1994

Briggs G., Cook J. and Rowley T. *The Archaeology of the Oxford Region* Oxford 1986

Chambers R. 'Deserted Medieval Farmstead at Sadler's Wood, Lewknor' *Oxoniensia* XXXVIII 1973 pp. 146–67

Copeland T. 'The North Oxfordshire Grim's Ditch: a Fieldwork Survey' *Oxoniensia* LIII 1988 pp. 277–93

Council for British Archaeology, *Group 9 Newsletter* 1970 onwards

Cunliffe B. *Iron Age Communities in Britain* London 1974

Currie C.R.J. 'Larger Medieval Houses in the Vale of the White Horse' *Oxoniensia* LVII 1992 pp. 81–245

Gunther R.T. (Ed.) *The Architecture of Sir Roger Pratt* Oxford 1928

Harding D.W. *The Iron Age in Lowland Britain* London 1974

Holden B. 'The Deserted Medieval Village of Thomley, Oxfordshire' *Oxoniensia* L 1985 pp. 215–38

Keeley H.C.M. *Environmental Archaeology A Regional Review* Vol. II London 1987

Lambrick G. *Archaeology and Agriculture* Council for British Archaeology 1977

Medieval Settlement and Research Group *Annual Report* 5 1990 pp. 28–30

Medieval Settlement Research Group *Annual Reports* 1985 onwards

Miles D. *Archaeology at Barton Court Farm, Abingdon, Oxon* Council for British Archaeology Research Report 50 Oxford and London 1986

Miles D. and Rowley T. 'Tusmore, Deserted Medieval Village' *Oxoniensia*, XLI 1976 pp. 309–15

Page P.'Chalgrove, Hardings Field' in Council for British Archaeology, Group 9 *South Midlands Archaeology* 12 1982 13 1983

Paine C. and Rhodes J. *The Worker's Home* Oxfordshire Museums Service 10 1979

Rahtz S. and Rowley T. *Middleton Stoney, Excavation and Survey in a North Oxfordshire Parish* 1970–82 Oxford 1984

Roberts B.K. *The Making of the English Village* London 1987

Roberts B.K. *Village Plans* Princes Risborough 1982

Robinson M. 'Excavations at Copt Hey, Tetsworth, Oxon' *Oxoniensia* XXXVIII 1973 pp. 41–115

Rowley T. and Wood J. *Deserted Villages* Princes Risborough 1982

Russell J.C. *British Medieval Population* Albuquerque 1948

Salway P. *The Oxford Illustrated History of Roman Britain* Oxford 1993

South Midlands Archaeology Council for British Archaeology Group 9 Annual Journal

Tiller K. 'Charterville and the Chartist Land Company' *Oxoniensia* L 1985 pp. 251–67

Victoria County History *Oxfordshire* Vol. XII
Wilson J.W. 'Antiquities found at Woodperry, Oxon' *Archaeological Journal* III 1846 pp. 116–28

Chapter III

Applebaum S. 'Roman Britain' in Finberg H.P.R. (Ed) *The Agrarian History of England and Wales* vol II AD 43–1042 Cambridge 1972

Bond C.J. 'Otmoor' in Oxford University Department of External Studies *The Evolution of Marshland Landscapes* Oxford 1981

Bradley R. and Ellison A. *Rams Hill* British Archaeological Reports 19 1975

Chinnor Historical and Archaeological Society *The Fields of Emmington* Occasional Paper No 5

Gelling M. *The Place Names of Oxfordshire* Cambridge 1953

Hallam H.E. (Ed) *The Agrarian History of England and Wales vol II* 1042–1350

Havinden M.A. *Rural Economy of Oxfordshire 1580–1730* Unpublished B Litt thesis Oxford University 1961

Harvey P.D.A. *Manorial Records of Cuxham, Oxon c.1200–1359* Oxfordshire Record Society 50 1976

Hey G. 'Yanton' *Oxford Archaeological Unit Annual Report* 1991–2

Lambrick G. and Robinson M. *Iron Age and Roman Riverside Settlements at Farmoor Oxfordshire* Council for British Archaeology and Archaeological Unit 1979

Miller E. (Ed) *The Agrarian History of England and Wales vol III* 1348–1500 Cambridge 1991

Parrington M. *The Excavation of an Iron Age Settlement, Bronze Age ring ditches and Roman features at Ashville Trading Estate Abingdon, Oxfordshire 1974–6* Council for British Archaeology Research Report 28

Postles D. 'The Oseney Abbey Flock' *Oxoniensia*, XLIX, 1984, pp.141–153

Postles D. 'Some differences between Seignorial Demenses in

Medieval Oxfordshire' *Oxoniensia*, LVIII, 1993, pp.219–233

Rhodes P.P. The Celtic Field Systems on the Berkshire Downs *Oxoniensia*, XV, 1950, pp.1–29

Sutton J.E.G. 'Ridge and Furrow in Berkshire and Oxfordshire' *Oxoniensia*, 29–31, pp.99–115

Tate W.E. Oxfordshire Parliamentary Enclosures 1676–1833

Wordie J.R. 'The South: Oxfordshire, Buckinghamshire, Berkshire, Wiltshire and Hampshire' in Thirsk J. (Ed.) *The Agrarian History of England and Wales vol V 1 1640–1750* Cambridge 1984

Chapter IV

Bond J. 'Oxfordshire Field Names: A Progress Report on the County Survey' *Oxfordshire Local History* Vol. I, 4, Spring 1982 pp. 2–15

Calendar of Close Rolls Public Record Office *passim*

Calendar of Patent Rolls Public Record Office *passim*

Day S.P. *History and Palaeoecology of Woodlands in the Oxford Region* Unpublished Oxford University D.Phil. thesis 1990

Gelling M. *The Early Charters of the Thames Valley* Leicester 1979

Havinden M.A. *Estate Village A Study of Ardington and Lockinge* Reading 1966

Hyde P. *The Winchester Manors at Witney and Adderbury, Oxon, in the later Middle Ages* Unpublished Oxford University B.Litt. thesis 1954

Preece P.G. 'Medieval Woods in the Oxfordshire Chilterns' *Oxoniensia* LV 1990 pp. 55–73

Rackham O. *Trees and Woodland in the British Landscape* London Revised edn. 1993

Rackham O. *The History of the Countryside* London 1986

Rickard R.L. (Ed.) 'The Progress Notes of Warden Woodward round the Oxon Estates of New College Oxford 1659–75' *Oxfordshire Record Society* XXVII 1945

Schumer B. *The Evolution of Wychwood to 1400: Pioneers, Frontiers and Forests* Leicester 1984

Steane J. 'Bernwood Forest – Past, Present and Future' *Arboricultural Journal* 9 1985 pp. 39–55

Steane J, 'Medieval Forests, Woods and Parks of Berkshire' *Arboricultural Journal* 1981 pp. 189–200

Steane J. 'Stonor A Lost Park and a Garden Found' *Oxoniensia*, LIX 1994 pp. 449–70

Steel D. *Shotover: The Natural History of a Royal Forest* Oxford 1984

Watney V.J. *Cornbury and the Forest of Wychwood* London 1910

Woodell S.R.J. *The English Landscape Past, Present and Future* Oxford 1985

Woodward F. *Oxfordshire Parks* Oxfordshire County Museum 1982

Chapter V

Albert W. *The Turnpike Road System in England 1663–1840* Cambridge 1972

Blair W.J. *Anglo Saxon Oxfordshire* Stroud 1993

Chambers R.A. 'A Roman Timber Bridge at Ivy Farm, Fencott with Murcott, Oxon, 1979' *Oxoniensia* LI 1986 pp. 31–7

Chambers R.A. 'The Archaeology of the M40 Motorway through Buckinghamshire, Northamptonshire and Oxfordshire 1988–91' *Oxoniensia* LVII 1992 pp. 43–55

Gelling M. *Place Names of Oxfordshire* Cambridge 1953

Grundy G.B. 'Saxon Oxfordshire Charters and Ancient Highways' *Oxfordshire Record Society* XV 1933

Grundy G.B. 'The Evidence of Saxon Land Charters on the ancient Road System of Britain' *Archaeological Journal* LXXIV pp. 293–6 2nd ser XXIV Nos. 1–4, pp. 79–95

Houghton F.T.S. 'Saltways' *Birmingham Archaeological Society Transactions* 1929–30 LIV pp. 1–17

Jope E.M. 'Oxfordshire' in Darby H.C. and Campbell E.M.J. *Domesday Geography of South-East England* Cambridge

1962

Lambrick G. *The Rollright Stones* Oxford 1983

Lambrick G. 'Some Old Roads in North Berkshire' *Oxoniensia* XXXIV 1969 pp. 78–92

Lawrence K. *Milestones of Oxfordshire* Oxfordshire Museums (no date)

Lawrence K. *Drove Roads in Oxfordshire* Oxfordshire Museums 1977

Lawrence K. *Tollhouses of Oxfordshire* Oxfordshire Museums (no date)

Lawrence K. *Turnpike Roads of Oxfordshire* Oxfordshire Museums 1977

Margary I.D. *Roman Roads in Britain* 2nd edn. London 1967

Mawer A. and Stenton F.M. *The Place Names of Worcestershire* Cambridge 1927

Steane J.M. 'How Old is the Berkshire Ridgeway?' *Antiquity* LVII 1983 pp. 103–8

Steane J.M. *Medieval Bridges in Oxfordshire* Oxfordshire Museums 1981

Stenton F.M. 'The Road System of Medieval England' in Stenton D.M. (Ed.) *Preparatory to Anglo Saxon England*, being the collected papers of F.M. Stenton Oxford 1970

Victoria County History *Berkshire* Vol IV

Victoria County History *Oxfordshire* Vols IV, X, XII

Chapter VI

Banks L. and Stanley C. *The Thames: A History from the Air* Oxford 1990

Bloxham C. and Bond J. *The Oxford Canal* Oxfordshire Museums 1981

Davis R.H.C. 'The ford, the river and the city' *Oxoniensia* XXXVIII 1973 pp. 258–67

Day C.J. 'Communications' Victoria County History *Oxfordshire* Vol IV London 1979 p. 291

Dodd C. *Henley Royal Regatta* London 1989

Durham B. *et alia* 'The Thames Crossing at Oxford: Archaeological Studies 1979–82' *Oxoniensia* XLIX 1984 pp. 57–101

Graham M. *Images of Victorian Oxford* Stroud 1992

Hadfield C. *The Canals of the East Midlands* Newton Abbot 1970

Naruhito H.I.H. Prince *The Thames as Highway* Oxford 1989

Peberdy R. 'Navigation along the Thames between London and Oxford in the late Middle Ages', forthcoming in *Oxoniensia*

Peberdy R. *The Economy, Society and Government of a Small Town in Late Medieval England. A Study of Henley-on-Thames c.1300 to c.1540* Unpublished PhD thesis University of Leicester 1994

Prior M. *Fisher Row* Oxford 1982

Prior M. 'The Accounts of Thomas West of Wallingford, a Sixteenth Century Trader on the Thames' *Oxoniensia* XLVI 1981 pp. 73–94

Thacker F.S. *The Thames Highway, vol I: General History* Newton Abbot 1968

Wilson D. *The Thames: Record of a Working Waterway* London 1987

Chapter VII

Allen Brown R., Colvin H.M. and Taylor A.J. *The History of the King's Works: The Middle Ages* London 1963

Arkell W.J. *Oxford Stone* London 1947

Aston M. *Stonesfield Slate* Oxfordshire County Museum 1974

Beckinsdale R.P. 'The Plush Industry of Oxfordshire' *Oxoniensia* XXVIII 1963 pp. 58–67

Bolton J.L. and Maslen M.M. *Calendar of the Court Books of the Borough of Witney 1538–1610* Oxfordshire Record Society LIV 1981/2

Bond J., Gosling S. and Rhodes J. *Oxfordshire Brickmakers* Oxfordshire Museums 1980

Bond J. and Rhodes J. *The Oxfordshire Brewer* Oxfordshire Museums 1985

Cumnor History Society *Cumnor Wills and Inventories* (no date)

Hardy T. *Jude the Obscure* London 1895

Harvey J. *English Medieval Architects* Stroud 1984

Hodgkins V. and Bloxham C. *Banbury and Shutford Plush* Banbury Historical Society 1980

Leyland N.L. and Troughton J.E. *Glovemaking in West Oxfordshire* Oxford City and County Museum 1974

Mellor M. *et alia* 'A synthesis of Middle and Late Saxon, Medieval and Early Post-Medieval Pottery in the Oxford Region' *Oxoniensia* LIX 1994 pp. 17–219

Oakeshott W.F. (Ed.) *Oxford Stone Restored* Oxford 1975

Stebbing N., Rhodes J., Mellor M. *Oxfordshire Potters* Oxfordshire Museums no. 13 1980

Victoria County History *Oxfordshire* Vol. II London 1907

Chapter VIII

Ballard A. *Chronicles of Woodstock* Oxford 1896

Blair W.J. *Anglo Saxon Oxfordshire* Stroud 1994

Bradley R. *et alia* 'Rescue Excavation in Dorchester-on-Thames' *Oxoniensia* XLIII 1978 pp. 17–39

Briers P.M. Henley Borough Records Assembly Books 1395–1543 *Oxfordshire Record Society* XLI 1960

Colvin H.M. *A History of Deddington Oxfordshire* London 1963

Frere S.S. 'Excavations at Dorchester-on-Thames 1962' *Archaeological Journal* CXIX 1962

Gibson J.S.W. and Brinkworth E.R.C. Banbury Corporation Records Tudor and Stuart *Banbury Historical Society* Vol 15 1977

Graham M. (Ed.) 'Oxford City Apprentices 1697–1800' *Oxford Historical Society* NS XXXI 1987

Gretton R.H. *The Burford Records* Oxford 1920

Harman M., Lambrick G., Miles D. and Rowley T. 'Roman

Burials around Dorchester-on-Thames' *Oxoniensia* XLIII 1978 pp. 1–17

Hassall T. 'Archaeology of Oxford City' in Briggs G., Cook J. and Rowley T. *The Archaeology of the Oxford Region* Oxford 1985

Laithwaite M. 'The Buildings of Burford: a Cotswold Town in the Fourteenth to Nineteenth Centuries' in Everitt A. (Ed.) *Perspectives in English Urban History* London 1973

Rodwell K. (Ed.) *Historic Towns of Oxfordshire* Oxford 1975

Rodwell K.A. 'Excavations on the Site of Banbury Castle, 1973–4' *Oxoniensia* XLI 1976 pp. 90–148

Rowley T. *The Roman Towns of Oxfordshire* British Archaeological Reports 15 1975

Stacey M. *Tradition and Change: A Study of Banbury* Oxford 1960

Stone E. and Hyde P. 'Oxfordshire Hundred Rolls of 1279' *Oxfordshire Record Society* XLVI 1968

Trinder B. *Victorian Banbury* Chichester 1982

Victoria County History *Oxfordshire* Vol VI (for Bicester), Vol VII (Dorchester and Thame)

Young C.J. 'The Defences of Roman Alchester' *Oxoniensia* XL 1975, pp. 136–71

Chapter IX

Acland H. and Ruskin J. *The Oxford Museum* London 1859

Acland H.W. *Memoir of the Cholera at Oxford in the year 1854* London 1856

Andrews P.W.S. and Brunner E. *The Eagle Ironworks Oxford* London 1965

Arkell W.J. *Oxford Stone* London 1947

Aylmer U. *Oxford Food* Oxford 1995

Badcock J. *The Making of a Regency Village: Origin, History, and Description of Summertown in 1832* Oxford 1983

Barker N. *The Oxford University Press and the Spread of Learning* Oxford 1979

Briggs N, 'The Foundation of Wadham College Oxford' *Oxoniensia* XXI 1956 pp. 61–81

Buckler J.C. *Drawings of Oxford* Bodleian Library 1979

Catto J.I. (Ed.) *The History of the University of Oxford, I: The Early Oxford Schools* Oxford 1986

Catto J.I. and Evans T.A.R. *The History of the University of Oxford, II: Late Medieval Oxford* Oxford 1992

Clapinson M. *Victorian and Edwardian Oxfordshire* London 1978

Colvin H.M. *Unbuilt Oxford* Newhaven and London 1983

Colvin H.M. *The Canterbury Quadrangle, St John's College Oxford* Oxford 1988

Curl J.S. *The Erosion of Oxford* Oxford 1977

Durham B. *et alia* 'Oxford's Northern Defences: Archaeological Studies 1971–82' *Oxoniensia* XLVIII 1983 pp. 13–41

Durham B. *et alia* 'The Infirmary and Hall of the Medieval Hospital of St John the Baptist at Oxford' *Oxoniensia* LVI 1991 pp. 17–77

Eddershaw D.G.H. *The Civil War in Oxfordshire* Stroud 1995

Green V.H.H. *A History of Oxford University* London 1984

Green V.H.H. *Oxford Common Room* London 1957

Green V.H.H. *The Commonwealth of Lincoln College 1427–1977* Oxford 1979

Halpin C. 'Late Saxon Evidence and Excavation of Hinxey Hall, Queen St, Oxford' *Oxoniensia* XLVIII 1983 pp. 41–71

Harrison B. (Ed.) *The History of the University of Oxford, VIII: The Twentieth Century* Oxford 1994

Hassall T.G., Halpin C.E. and Mellor M. 'Excavations in St Ebbes' Oxford, 1967–1976, Part 1: Late Saxon and Medieval Domestic Occupation and Tenements and the Medieval Greyfriars' *Oxoniensia* LIV 1989 pp. 71–279

Highfield J.R.L. *The Early Rolls of Merton College, Oxford* Oxford 1964

Hinchcliffe T. *North Oxford* Newhaven and London 1992

Hutchins R. 'Charles Daubeny (1795–1867)' *Magdalen College Record* 1995 pp. 81–92

Ker I. *John Henry Newman* Oxford 1988

Kowaleski M. *Local Markets and Regional Trade in Medieval*

Exeter Cambridge 1995

Lambrick G. and Woods H. 'Dominican Priory, Oxford' *Oxoniensia* XLI 1976

MacCarthy F. *William Morris* London 1994

McConica J. (Ed.) *The History of the University of Oxford, III: The Collegiate University* Oxford 1986

Morris J. *The Oxford Book of Oxford* Oxford 1978

Mudd A. 'Excavations at Whitehouse Road, Oxford 1992' *Oxoniensia* LVIII 1993 pp. 33–87

Munby J. *et alia* 'Zacharias's: a 14th century Oxford New Inn and the Origins of the Medieval Urban Inn' *Oxoniensia* LVII 1992 pp. 245–311

Oakeshott W.F. *Oxford Stone Restored* Oxford 1975

Palmer N. 'A Beaker Burial and Medieval Tenements in the Hamel, Oxford' *Oxoniensia* XLV 1980 pp. 124–226

Prest J. (Ed.) *The Illustrated History of Oxford University* Oxford 1993

Royal Commission on Historical Monuments England *City of Oxford* 1939

Salter H.E. *A Cartulary of the Hospital of St John the Baptist* Oxford 1917

Salter H.E. *Medieval Archives of the University of Oxford* Oxford Historical Society LXX Vol. 1 1920

Salter H.E. *Medieval Oxford* Oxford Historical Society 1936

Salter H.E. 'Survey of Oxford' I–II in Pantin W.A. and Mitchell W.T. (Eds) *Oxfordshire Historical Society* NS XIV 1960 and XX 1969

Shadwell C.L. and Salter H.E. *Oriel College Records* Oxford 1926

Sharpe T. *Oxford Replanned* London 1948.

Stone L. (Ed.) *The University in Society, vol I, Oxford and Cambridge from 14th to Early 19th century* Princeton 1975

Sturdy D., Munby J. *et alia* 'Early Domestic Sites in Oxford Excavations in Cornmarket and Queen Street 1959–62' *Oxoniensia* L 1985, pp. 47–95

Sutcliffe P. *The Oxford University Press* Oxford 1978

Sutherland L.S. and Mitchell L.G. (Eds) *The History of the*

University of Oxford, V: The Eighteenth Century Oxford
1986
Turner H.L. 'The Mural Mansions of Oxford. Attempted
Identifications' *Oxoniensia* LV 1990 pp. 73–9
Victoria County History *Oxfordshire* Vol III: The University
of Oxford 1954
Victoria County History *Oxfordshire* Vol IV: The City of
Oxford 1979

Chapter X

Barclay A., Gray M. and Lambrick G. *Excavations at the
Devil's Quoits, Stanton Harcourt, Oxfordshire 1972–3 and
1988* Oxford 1995
Biddle M. and Myres J.N.L. 'The Early History of Abingdon
and its Abbey' *Medieval Archaeology* XII 1968 pp. 26–70
Blair W.J. and Steane J.M. 'Investigations at Cogges, Oxford-
shire 1978–81, The Priory and the Parish Church' *Oxo-
niensia* XLVII 1982 pp. 37–127
Blair W.J. 'Saint Beornwald of Bampton' *Oxoniensia* XLIX
1984 pp. 47–57
Blair W.J. *et alia* 'Investigations at Tackley Church, Oxford-
shire 1981–84, The Anglo-Saxon and Romanesque Phases'
Oxoniensia L 1985 pp. 25–47
Blair W.J. 'St Frideswide Reconsidered' *Oxoniensia* LII 1987
pp. 71–129
Blair W.J. (Ed.) 'Saint Frideswide's Monastery at Oxford:
Archaeological and Architectural Studies' *Oxoniensia* LIII
1988 pp. 1–277
Blair W.J. *et alia* 'The Early Church at Cumnor' *Oxoniensia*
LIV 1989 pp. 57–71
Blair W.J. *Anglo-Saxon Oxfordshire* Stroud 1994
Bowler D. and Robinson M. 'Three Round Barrows at King's
Weir, Wytham, Oxon' *Oxoniensia* XLV 1980 pp. 1–9
Bradley R. *The Social Foundations of Prehistoric Britain*
London 1984
Burgess F. *English Churchyard Memorials* London 1979

Cox M. *The Story of Abingdon* Abingdon 1986

Crawford S. 'The Anglo-Saxon Cemetery at Chimney Oxfordshire' *Oxoniensia* LIV 1989 pp. 45–57

Doggett N. 'The Anglo-Saxon See and Cathedral of Dorchester-on-Thames: The Evidence Reconsidered' *Oxoniensia* LI 1986 pp. 49–63

Duffy E. *The Stripping of the Altars* Newhaven and London 1992

Durham B. 'The Infirmary and Hall of the Medieval Hospital of St John the Baptist at Oxford' *Oxoniensia* LVI 1991 pp. 17–77

Esdaile K.A. *English Church Monuments 1510–1840* Oxford (no date)

Farmer D.H. *The Oxford Dictionary of Saints* Oxford 1992

Fletcher J.M. and Upton C.A. 'Destruction, Repair and Removal An Oxford College Chapel during the Reformation' *Oxoniensia* XLVIII 1983 pp. 119–31

Foster M.R. 'Durham Monks at Oxford *c.*1286–1381: A House of Studies and its Inmates' *Oxoniensia* LV 1990 pp. 99–115

Gilchrist R. *Gender and Material Culture* London 1994

Gray M. and Clayton N. 'Excavations on the Site of Eynsham Abbey 1971' *Oxoniensia* XLIII 1978 pp. 100–23

Haigh C. and Loades D. 'The Fortunes of the Shrine of St Mary of Caversham' *Oxoniensia* XLVI 1981 pp. 62–73

Harvey B. *Westminster Abbey and its Estates in the Middle Ages* Oxford 1977

Kirk K.E. *Church Dedications of the Oxford Diocese* Oxford 1946

Lamborn E.A. *The Armorial Glass of the Oxford Diocese 1250–1850* Oxford 1949

Lambrick G. 'Ritual and Burial in the Thames Valley' *Current Archaeology* 121 XI 1, pp. 6–13

Lankester P.J. 'A Military Effigy in Dorchester Abbey, Oxon' *Oxoniensia* LII 1987, pp. 145–73

Morris R. *Churches in the Landscape* London 1989

Newton P. and Kerr J. *The County of Oxford: a Catalogue of*

Medieval Stained Glass, Corpus Vitrearum Medii Aevii Great Britain London 1979

Palmer N. 'A Beaker Burial and Medieval Tenements in the Hamel, Oxford' *Oxoniensia* XLV 1980 pp. 124–226.

Plot R. *The Natural History of Oxfordshire* Oxford 1677

Power E. *Medieval English Nunneries* Cambridge 1922

Roth C. *The Jews of Medieval Oxford Oxfordshire Historical Society* NS IX 1951

Rubin M. *Charity and Community in Medieval Cambridge* Cambridge 1987

Sharpe J. 'Oseney Abbey Oxford: Archaeological Investigations 1975–83' *Oxoniensia* L 1985 pp. 95–131

Slade C.F. and Lambrick G. 'Two Cartularies of Abingdon Abbey' *Oxford Historical Society* NS XXXII and XXXIII Oxford 1992

Staniland K. *Medieval Craftsmen: Embroiderers* London 1991

Thomas R. 'Bronze Age Metalwork from the Thames at Wallingford' *Oxoniensia* XLIX 1984, pp. 9–19

Timmins T.C.B. (Ed.) The Register of John Chandler, Dean of Salisbury 1404–17 Wiltshire Record Society 1984

Index

Abingdon, causewayed
enclosure 19, vineyard 24,
Roman villa at Barton Court
27–8, Roman town 28, abbey
33, 40, 266, Abingdon Road
121, ford and bridge 123–4,
wooden bridge 126, Guild of
Holy Cross 128, Christ's
Hospital 128, road 133, cuts
140, lock 144, maltsters 145,
bricks 160, 163, proto-town
179–80, 181, riots in 1327
187, 266, barrows 255, 260,
grange 262, church of St
Nicholas 269, cemetery 282.
Abingdon, Earl of 134
Academic Halls 196–7, decline
213
Acland, Sir Henry 51, 234
Acts to improve navigation 144
Adam, glovemaker 176
Adderbury 66, 130, 208,
minster 260, church 279
Aerial photographs 27, 55, 61,
110, 113–4
Agas, Ralph 221
Agnellus, St 200
Aisles added to churches 276
Akeman Street 26, 114, 119,
129, 130
Alabaster retables 272–3
Alchester 26, 61, 113–4, 116,
180, 255

Alder 85–6
Aldrich, Dean 229
Alexander, Bishop of Lincoln
186
Alfred, King 123, 193, 195, 250
Alfred's Castle 22–3
Alice in Wonderland 77, 238
Allen, Major, 24
Allen, Tim 18, 40, 126
Alluviation 59, 74
Alma, Battle of 104
Althorp House 103
Ambrosden 69
Amphitheatre 118
Andrew, John 125
Angel Inn, Oxford 134
Anglers 138
Anglo-Saxons 26, 28, boundary
charters 58, roads 119–123,
huts 181
Anne, Queen of Bohemia 43
Antiquaries, Society of 52
'Appropriations' 268
Arabic, Chair of 218
Ardington 104–5
Ardley 119
Arnold, M. 237, 240
Arsic family 270
Ascot-under-Wychwood long
barrow 87, 253
Ash 102
Ash bark 119
Ashbury Manor 33, 198, village
254

Blackland 65
Blackstone, Sir William 134
Blackwell's bookshop 211
Bladon 90
Blair, J. 120, 193
Blanket Hall, Witney 167
Blankets 164–5
Blanket weavers, Company of 167
Blenheim Palace 44–5, servants 50–1, Park 97, 103–4, mill in park 139
Blewbury 173
Blewburton Hill 22, 58, 61, 251
Blomfield, Arthur, Architect 244
Blount, Sir Richard 43
Bloxham, J.R. 224
Bloxham, 78, 169, minister 260, church 278
Bloxham, Christine 168
Boars Hill 13
Bodleian Library 208–10, shelves 242
Bodley, Sir Thomas 209, monument 210
Bond, J 39, 138
Bookshops in Oxford 211
Boston 163
Botanic Garden 238
Botley 120, 134
Bottle Kiln 158–9
Boundaries 64
Bourton 169
Bowling Greens 239
Brackley 120
Bradford, Cynthia 121, 203
Bradley, R. 55, 57, 108, 112
Braksper of Henley, brewers 175
Breeches, making 177

Brewing equipment 171
Brick 14, Mapledurham 43, Grey's Court 42, Stonor Park 47, 157, 160–1
Bridges, Roman 117, Medieval, Folly Bridge 121, Burford and Culham bridges 124, 125, wooden at Abingdon 126, Wallingford 127, Bridge chapels 128, canal 147, Oxford 194
Brightwell 139
Brill, hunting lodge 90
Brindley, James 146
Bristol 166, Jewish ritual bath 263
Brize Norton 54
Broadwell Church 277
Bronze Age, farmers 20, riverside site 21, ploughmarks 59, barrows 74, 254, woodland 86, ridgeways 109, 110, clothmaking 161, climate 250
Broughton Castle 41–2
Broughton, Sir John 41
Brown David 213
Brunel 13
Buckingham Line 243
Buckinghamshire 129
Buckland 168
Buckland, William, geologist 7–9, 238
Buckler, J.C. 262
Bucks 138
Bullingdon Green 117
Burford 120, decline 133–4, White Hill and Witney Street 134, Bull Hotel 134, inns 134, quarries 150, 154, sheepmarket 163, Tolsey

188, houses 188
Burford Bridge, Abingdon
124–5, 126
Burford stone quarries 11
Burgage plots, threatened 184,
Burford 188
Burh, Saxon at Oxford 219
Burne-Jones, Edward 236–7
Burton, R 143
Buscot 143, lock 144
Butterfield, William 161, 202,
236

Cambridge, King's College
Chapel 265
Camoys, Lord 14
Campion, Edward 48
Canals 135, 146–9, Oxford
canal 160
Carroll, Lewis 238
Carterton 53–4
Carfax, Oxford 121, 151
Case, H 108, 253
Cassington Big Rings 24, Field
name 68, 108, smiths 142,
oppidum 180, barrows 158,
church 269
Castle Mills, Oxford 139, 148
Castles, Broughton 41–2,
Grey's Court 42–3, Oxford
121, 148, 157, Shirburn 159
Catte Street, Oxford
Cattle 122
Catuvellauni 24, 26, 257
Causewayed enclosures 19–20
Causeways 126
Cave, George 133
Caversham bridge 126, 142,
lock 144
Chalgrove, Harding's Field
38–9, church 39, Field name

70, brick works 161, wall
paintings 273
Chalk 13–4, 71, 112
Chambers, R.A. 39, 116
Chancellor of Oxford
University 196
Charcoal 92, 99
Charlbury 25, 78, 178, 187
Charles I, King 217, 219, 223,
283
Charles II, King, coin 49, 70,
224
Charney Bassett 33
Charters, Anglo Saxon 119
Chartism 53
Chastleton House 46–7,
servants 51, 172–3
Chastleton Hill fort 23
Chazey Wood 100
Chaucer, Alice, Duchess of
Suffolk 280
Checkendon 67, 68, church 262
Cheney Lane 122
Cherbury Hill fort 23
Cherwell river 62, 77, 115, 121,
125, 243, 260, 271
Chesterton 114
Chestnuts 102
Chichele, Henry, Archbishop
201
Children's toys 50
Chilterns 10, 13, barns in 36,
Stonor Park 47, 62, field
names 65, 69, 71, 78, 96–7,
98, 101–2, 141, 187
Chinnor Cement Works 14
Chipping Norton 129, 133, 190
Chiselhampton bridge 125,
sheep 163, 164
Cholera 51
Church Enstone barn 35

Havinden, M. 64
Hawks 69, hawking equipment 9
Hawksmoor, Nicholas 229
Hay, Iron Age evidence 60, 71, hay meadows 75–8, 80
Hazel 85–6, 97
Hazleton, long barrow 87
Headington hill 122, quarries 150, 151–2, 155, stone 231, 239
Heafod 61
Hedges 60, 63, 64, destruction of 82
Hendred 110
Henley-on-Thames 68, 70, 98, bridge at 99, 102, 125–6, 128, guild 128, roads 133, 141, maltsters 145, 158, 165, 190, 245, merchants 277
Henry Chichele 195
Henry de Blois 184
Henry I, King 89
Henry II, King 163, 186, 195, 267
Henry III, King 34, 94, 103, 200
Henry VI, King 195
Henry VIII, hawking equipment 91, 213, 215, 223, 265
Hensington Gate 104
Herefordshire 129
herepath 119
herestraet 119
Herrings 141
Hey, Gill 20, 29
Heyford 125–6
Higden, Dean 155
Highlands Farm, Henley-on-Thames 16, 17, 107
Highway, Act of 1555 130

Highwaymen 134
High Wycombe 102, 122
Hill Forts 22–4, 35
Hill, John of Banbury 170
Hinxey Hall 197
Historic Towns in Oxfordshire 179
History of the Rebellion 230
Holland, coal merchant 145
Hollow ways 31
Holly 68
Holywell cemetery 283
Hood, John 164
Hook Norton brewery 175–6
Hops 170
Hornbeam 97
Hornbrook, Ival 178
Hornton, stone quarries 11, 150
Horse racing 75
Horses 69, 93, Iron Age 251–2
Horton-cum-Studley, cruck cottage 36
Hoskins, W 64, 79
Hospital of St John the Baptist, Oxford 156, 204, 263
Houses, Iron Age 22, Anglo Saxon 29, medieval 31, 33, Cogges Manor Farm 48–9, Chastleton 50–1, Kelmscott 51–2, Charterville 53, Carterton 53–4, Saxon 181, Oxford medieval 197
Hughes, Thomas 252
Humphrey of Gloucester, Duke 208
Hunt, Holman 236
Hunt, Thomas, brewer 175
Hunting 88–9, 103, 107, 223
Huntingdon 187
Hussey, Revd Robert 116–7

224, 227, 233 gardens and deer park 239–40, 263, 278, 281
Merton College 32, 66, 78, 154, 156, 159, 201, 203, 205, 208, chapel and Reformation 215, 222, 278
New College 35, 66, 100–1, 154, 156, 200, 203, 204, 211, 215, 219, 220, 222, garden 238–9, 278, 279
Nuffield College 245
Oriel College 198, 223–4, 226
Oxford University Press 226, 242
Pembroke College 227
Research Laboratory for Archaeology 251
St Bernard's College 202, 216
St Edmund Hall 219, 228
St John's College 202, 216, 217, suburb 233, 244
St Peter's College 221
Sheldonian 225–6
The Queen's College 156, beer 173, buildings 229–30, 231
Trinity College 208, 216, 233
University College 195
University museum 6, 233–4, Science 6, Pitt Rivers Museum 17
Wadham College 203, 216, 224
Worcester College 198, 230, 239

Oxfordshire Building Trust 35, 37
Oxfordshire County Council 48, 201
Oxfordshire County Museum Service 18, 99, store 126, 133, 176, 186, 191, 253
Oxfordshire County Record Office 221
Oxonia Illustrata 222
Ozier beds 68

Pacey's bridge, Oxford 148
Pack horses 129
Page P. 39
Palaeolithic 107
Pantin, Dr W.A. 197
Paris, University of 195, Ste Chapelle 237
Parish boundaries 30, 79, 264
Parish churches, monastic promotion 268, defensive function 269, fight against devil 270, extension 271–2, rebuilding programme 275
Parish system 130, 263
Parks, deer 93
Parks Road, Oxford 193
Patten, Richard, tomb 281
Peas 67
Pebble Mill 117
Peberdy, R. 140
Peckham, John 195, 200
Peckwater quadrangle, Christ Church 229
Pembroke, Earl of 208
Peter des Roches, Bishop 163
Pettypont bridge 122
Pevsner, Sir Nicholas 41
Philips, brewers in Oxford 175
Philips, John, geologist 7, 9
Piddington 69
Pigs 68, 81, 99
Pigott, S 253
Pill boxes 25
Pinkhill lock 136, 144

Winchester, Dr Vanessa 185
Winchcombe, Richard 280
Winchcombe Abbey 35
Windrush river 25, 26, 163,
166, 183, 260
Windsor 99, 141, castle 150,
169, 220
Wine trade 141, 195
Wisdom's Copse 116
Witney 93, Mount House 94,
road to 122, 123, 131, fulling
mills 139, 145, textile
industry 163–8, tanning 177,
town of bishops of
Winchester 183–4, 268, 277
Wittenham Clumps hill fort 23,
258
Woad 67
Woden 26
Wolsey, Thomas, Cardinal 201,
230, 265
Wolvercote 16, 74, 107,
common 76, smiths 142, 146,
243
Women's Institutes 64
Women rowers 137
Wood, Anthony à 120, 224
Woodcote 99, 158
Woodeaton, Roman shrine
256–7, church 271
'Wonders of Britain' 248
Woodland clearance 59
Woodmen 98, 102

Woodperry 30
Woodstock 25, palace 44–5,
manor 78, 89, 92, park 90,
103, royal stud 94, road 133,
135, mill 139, gloving 177,
188
Woodward, B. architect 234
Woodward, Warden 100–1
Wool trade 277
Wootton 25, 79
Worcestershire 129
Wordington 169
World War I 234
World War II 25, 82, 234
Wren, Sir Christopher 225, 228
Wrench of Shutford 170
Wretchwick 69
Wroxton 11, 130
Wychwood, Forest of 27, 62,
77, 78, 89, 90–1, 93, 105,
116, 176–7, 254
Wyke, Cistercian grange 34, 39
Wykes, Thomas 157
Wytham 72, hill 122, 134

Yarnton, Neolithic settlement
20, medieval village 20,
Rectory Farm 21, Anglo
Saxon settlement 29, meads
72–3, 78
Young, Arthur 10–11, 131, 177